SHAKESPEARE
AND HIS COMEDIES

edited by John Russell Brown

★

THE MERCHANT OF VENICE
(Arden Shakespeare)

John Webster, THE WHITE DEVIL
(Revels Plays)

Shakespeare
and his Comedies

by

JOHN RUSSELL BROWN

METHUEN & CO LTD

11 NEW FETTER LANE · EC4

First Published September 19, 1957
Second edition, with a new chapter on the last comedies, 1962
Reprinted 1964 and 1968
2.3
416   59690   8

First published as a University Paperback 1968
1.1
416   29530   4

Printed in Great Britain by litho-offset
by William Clowes and Sons Ltd, London and Beccles

Distributed in the U.S.A.
by Barnes & Noble Inc.

TO
ALLARDYCE
NICOLL

Contents

Preface to the Original Edition

While writing this book I have held successively a Fellowship at the Shakespeare Institute, Stratford-upon-Avon, and a Lectureship in English at the University of Birmingham. I am greatly indebted to my colleagues and students, and to my other friends in both Stratford and Birmingham, for discussions, encouragement, and advice. To Professor Allardyce Nicoll and to Mr Roy Walker I am particularly indebted for reading and commenting upon my book in typescript.

I also gratefully and with pleasure acknowledge the debt which any writer on Shakespeare must have to earlier scholars and critics; the nature and scope of my present enquiry preclude any attempt to describe this debt in detail and I have therefore tried to do this in an article in *Shakespeare Survey*, viii (1955). I would, however, like to make particular mention here of my general debt to the criticism of Professor H. B. Charlton, Miss M. C. Bradbrook, Mr Nevill Coghill, Professor W. Empson, and the late Charles Williams; I have learnt most from these among all those who have written on the comedies. In the course of this book I have tried to note all debts to other writers for particular points which are not yet common knowledge among those especially interested in Shakespeare's comedies; if in any instance I have failed to do this, I tender my sincere apologies.

I have used the Globe Shakespeare (ed. 1911) for quotations and references, noting any exceptional quotations from other texts.

JOHN RUSSELL BROWN

STRATFORD-UPON-AVON
August, 1956

Preface to the Second Edition

I have added an entirely new chapter on the last comedies or romances. So this book is extended in range to consider Shakespeare's treatment of love and personal relationships in comedies throughout his career.

The present time is fit for this addition. In the four years since my book was published critical attitudes to the earlier comedies have changed significantly: my attempt to analyse the judgements informing them could now be presented without a reasoned apology and I could quote further responsible opinion on its behalf. This does not mean that I wish to alter my main exposition—its form allows me both to introduce and develop my subject—but rather that I believe I can now use my previous explorations to bring new attention to the last comedies which had seemed to be among the best understood of Shakespeare's plays. The new chapter speaks with confidence of the early and mature comedies and is speculative and, I hope, challenging about the later ones.

JOHN RUSSELL BROWN

Birmingham
April, 1962

9

CHAPTER I

The Implicit Judgement

Shakespeare's early comedies up to and including *Twelfth Night* have been described as 'natural', 'true to nature', 'good-natured'; they have been called joyful, golden, wise; they have been praised for their gaiety, variety, and healthful sanity, and praised above all for their humanity—a characteristic at once enigmatical and profound. But these encomiums are often lip service only, and those who pay them are loath to go further, to analyse and ask why they were made thus and not otherwise.

Encomiums have been lavished upon Shakespeare's other plays, but for them critics have proceeded to hard-working service, dissecting their variety, searching for unifying themes, and trying to discover why Shakespeare fashioned them as he did. A continual critical argument has developed around these plays. Within the last thirty or forty years, a group of Shakespeare's later comedies—*All's Well, Measure for Measure* and *Troilus and Cressida*—has assumed an entirely new importance among his works; previously ignored as ill-humoured conundrums, they are now readily accepted as 'dark' comedies, 'problem' plays, or 'comical satires', plays in which Shakespeare has grappled with serious intellectual issues. The history-plays have been newly considered as treatises in political theory and sociology. The last romances, instead of being judged as light-hearted fantasies or wistful improvisations of a master musician, are now widely regarded as symbolic treatments of regeneration or of nature and culture. Even the great tragedies are being revalued as studies in honour, justice, ambition, nature, grace, or politics.

But the early comedies have been largely untouched by these revaluations. Even while they are being praised as true to nature, golden, or wise, they have shown another aspect which seems to quell all precise inquiry. From one point of view, they reveal merely—

> Endless tiresome jokes about horns, obscure topical allusions, a far-fetched plot, incredibly credulous characters, [and] careless finishing off.[1]

Indeed, the early comedies can appear so light-hearted and capricious, so inconsequential, so beautiful and bawdy, so obviously pleasing courtier and groundling by turns, that the probing questions of the critic seem ludicrously inapposite. The critic is afraid of taking them too seriously. Professor Parrott in his recent book on *Shakespearean Comedy* says that *As You Like It* is the 'work of a playwright fully master of his art, yet . . . recklessly careless of construction', that Shakespeare is 'happy and carefree' in Arden, using 'little intellectual effort' to create a 'comedy of escape', and that all that is required of us is to 'fleet the time carelessly'.[2] For *Much Ado About Nothing*, Professor Parrott presumes that Shakespeare found 'little of interest' in the Claudio of his source and was therefore 'not reluctant to lower him in order to attain an effective scene.'[3]

Critics who are reluctant to follow Professor Parrott and lower Shakespeare's intentions to feckless escapism or sensationalism are in a difficult position; they are apt to disregard the impression of wilfulness and take refuge in the platitudes of praise, making large claims which define little and explain nothing. Neither party is eager to analyse or descend to particulars. So while a discussion of *Hamlet*, *The Tempest*, or *Measure for Measure* may be tendentious, provocative, or even absurd, a discussion of *As You Like It* or

[1] *The Observer*, 24 July 1955.
[2] *Shakespearean Comedy* (1949), pp. 176-7.   [3] ibid., p. 157.

Twelfth Night is often merely dull. This attitude is found in the theatre as well as in the study ; a playgoer visits a new performance of one of the early comedies without any expectation of being surprised or stimulated by a new interpretation. Recent revaluations of the other plays may over-simplify Shakespeare's intentions or be false to the impact of the plays in the theatre, but the critical inquiry from which they spring has certainly refined and extended our appreciation ; without such inquiry—and so far there have been only a few isolated studies[1]—our appreciation of the comedies must lag far behind.

The probing questions of a critic cannot be wholly inappropriate to dramas which have continued to hold the stage in popular esteem for over three hundred and fifty years. However carefree they may seem, there must be some elixir which distinguishes them from the majority of comedies and which bestows longevity upon Shakespeare's jests and fancies ; the pleasure that they give whenever they are performed proves that the elixir must be there and, however inappropriate the attempt may seem, the critic must try to isolate and describe it.

*   *   *

Critics who try to explain the lasting success of Shakespeare's early comedies, like *Much Ado*, *As You Like It*, and *Twelfth Night*, and those who merely exhort us to enjoy them, are all agreed that they have little satiric purpose. Shakespeare did not often write, as Ben Jonson would say, to 'reprove' mankind, nor did he invent characters for the sole purpose of showing

> . . . *the time's deformity*
> *Anatomiz'd in every nerve, and sinew.*[2]

His plots do not seem to be articulated around any satirical

[1] cf. my retrospective article, 'The Interpretation of Shakespeare's Comedies: 1900-1953', *Shakespeare Survey*, viii (1955), 1-13.

[2] *Every Man Out of His Humour*, Ind., 120-1.

viewpoint; they seem merely to exploit the sentiment of a romantic narrative, give opportunity for *divertissements* of fooling, and lead to a general reconciliation. They never culminate in a severe division of sheep from goats. Even at the close of *The Merry Wives of Windsor*, which, of the main group of comedies, is the one most nearly satirical in plan, Falstaff goes off, wheezing and contrite, to 'eat a posset' at Page's house and to laugh at Page's wife who just before had been laughing at him. We are invited to laugh at the good and the bad, heroine and clown. A few characters are clearly founded upon some human vice or failing—Shylock is greedy for money, Jaques seems to 'disable all the benefits' of his own country, and Malvolio wears his 'vice' of self-love so conspicuously that even daws may peck at it—but as these characters leave the stage alone, by their own choice rejecting the joyful conclusion of the comedy, the audience is somehow restrained from biting or barking at their heels; our impulse is rather to send after them and entreat them 'to a peace'. The most unmitigated villains, Don John of *Much Ado* and Duke Frederick of *As You Like It*, are not anatomized but only lightly sketched, and they slip out of the action unperceived by the audience; their defection is noticed later, only to be dismissed as unimportant:

Think not on him till to-morrow: I'll devise thee brave punishments for him,

and then the dance begins with 'Strike up, pipers'. Having created characters which are clearly actuated by vice and destructiveness, Shakespeare was not interested in evoking our serious reproof at the end of his comedy; he refused the clear cut of satire.

Hazlitt may represent this view for many later critics. For him Shakespeare's comic Muse is 'good-natured and magnanimous, it mounts above its quarry . . ., it does not take the highest pleasure in making human nature look as mean, as ridiculous, and contemptible as possible'; instead, Shakespeare presented certain characters which were a kind of *grotesques*, or solitary excrescences growing up out of their native soil without affectation, and which he undertook kindly to pamper for public entertainment.[1]

Having satisfied themselves that the early comedies have no clear satiric meaning, some critics have relaxed their vigilance, but others, more curious about their enduring appeal, have thereupon deduced that Shakespeare's serious intention was the creation of life-like characters and a plot which would allow the good-natured acceptance of both folly and virtue. The 'vital centre' of Shakespeare's comedies, wrote Edward Dowden, is 'not an idea, an abstraction, a doctrine, a moral thesis, but something concrete—persons involved in an action.'[2] This opinion has been echoed by G. P. Baker, H. B. Charlton, and, more recently, by John Palmer: according to Palmer, 'almost the whole secret' of Shakespeare's power is 'the facility with which he identifies himself imaginatively with all sorts and conditions of men and women'; being 'almost incapable of the judicial approach', Shakespeare 'enters into' the minds and hearts of his characters.[3] To Hazlitt Shakespeare's good-nature made his comedies 'deficient',[4] but to later critics the same good-nature suggested their *raison d'etre*. They were seen as vehicles for expressing a tolerance and love of human idiosyncrasies. In line with this view, the characterization of Shylock has suggested that Shakespeare was willing to give even the devil his due if he came in the guise of a man.

*   *   *

This explanation of the success of the comedies is based, in the first instance, on their manifestation of Shakespeare's interest in character and the oddities of human nature. But

[1] *English Comic Writers; Works*, ed. P. P. Howe, vi (1931), 36.
[2] 'Shakespeare as a Comic Dramatist', *Representative English Comedies*, ed. C. M. Gayley, i (1903), 638.
[3] *Comic Characters of Shakespeare* (1946), p. ix.
[4] op. cit., p. 38.

when one has recognized the throng of lively characters who make their way through the world of comedy, happily oblivious of the fact that they might have been food for powder, sitting targets for a satirist; when one has acknow-ledged Shakespeare's ability to turn such stock characters as servants, country clowns, or allowed fools into animated human beings; and when one has marvelled at the increas-ingly lively or poignant portrayal of his fairy-tale-perfect heroines, it may yet be questioned whether one has truly expressed either the content of the comedies as a whole, or the direction in which Shakespeare's ever-vigilant artistic conscience was developing his comic vision. If this were all, *A Midsummer Night's Dream* would be almost exclusively a play about Bottom and his fellow mechanicals, and *The Merchant of Venice* a play about Shylock. Hermia and Helena would succeed only for a brief moment each, and, since it is difficult to remember who wins Helena and who wins Hermia, Demetrius and Lysander might be held to fail completely. In *The Merchant*, Portia might perhaps rival Shylock as a lively character, but the conceits of her verse dialogue and the situations of the plot do not allow an immediacy of impact to compare with Shylock's passionate outbursts—she might succeed as a lively, but not as a life-like character. If the centre of a comedy is the impression of character, the Belmont scenes, including the whole fifth act, will seem merely peripheral to the five scenes in which Shylock holds the stage.

The notion that Shakespeare put the creation of life-like character first does not make sense of the sequence in which he wrote the early comedies. As these plays become more mature, more controlled in atmosphere, and more certain in style and dramatic technique, they do not show an equally general advance in characterization. Benedick may be more lively than Biron, or Viola more human than Julia, but this is certainly not true of the less courtly characters; Dogberry is neither more lively nor more human than Christopher Sly, Nick Bottom, Sir Nathaniel, or Holofernes. If Shakespeare

wished above all to portray human character in all the richness of spirit, folly, and individuality, it is almost inconceivable that he could have been content with either Sir Toby
Belch or the Falstaff of *The Merry Wives* after he had created
the Jack Falstaff of *Henry IV*.

Judged by their provision of life-like characters, none of
the comedies is flawless, and the flaws are frequently most
noticeable towards the end of the play, in the last scene which
should send the audience home well satisfied. The conclusion
of *The Two Gentlemen of Verona* is a glaring example : here
Valentine, who has loved Silvia steadfastly since Act II
Scene i, renounces all claim to her in a slick couplet ; she
makes no comment, and Julia, who sees her own hopes of
happiness dashed, quickly swoons—to recover before two and
a half lines have been spoken. On the grounds of characterization this conclusion is precipitous, heartless, and, possibly,
cynical. But Shakespeare does not seem to have worried
about this, for the later comedies are little better in this
respect than the majority of the early ones. In *Much Ado*,
Hero and Claudio are lightly sketched as characters—
according to some critics Shakespeare was plainly bored with
them—but whatever degree of life-like characterization
might have been established earlier, it could scarcely survive
the precipitous way in which Claudio is ready to accept
another Hero at the end of the play, or the readiness with
which Hero is prepared to forgive and forget ; if these two
lovers exist dramatically by virtue of what we know of the
workings of their hearts, or if Shakespeare is to be judged by
the way in which he demonstrates his insight into individual
human beings, then the end of *Much Ado* is at least one
half failure. If these be the virtues of his comedy, Shakespeare has failed again in matching Celia and Oliver in *As You
Like It*, and perhaps admits his defeat by introducing Hymen
to underline the inhuman neatness of the final arrangement
of *dramatis personae*. At the end of *Twelfth Night*, Olivia
and Orsino change the objects of their affections, and yet
Shakespeare refuses to exploit the situation he has created

for the full expression of thought and sentiment; it is over in a trice and we are left little the wiser about the individual characters involved.

Of course there are many occasions when (to quote Dowden again) Shakespeare *is* concerned with 'persons involved in action' and when (to quote Palmer) he 'identifies himself imaginatively' with his characters, but to claim that these are the chief purposes of his comedy is to admit major errors in his masterpieces and to suggest that his comic vision made only small advances as his technique leaped ahead. The humanity of his characters, particularly when they are compared with the type characters of satirical comedy, is indeed an important part of Shakespeare's comic vision, but clearly he was not limited to the creation of a gallery of amiable portraits; there must have been some overriding artistic purpose which, on occasion, led him to neglect the representation of individual character.

*　　　　*　　　　*

Perhaps Shakespeare neglected characterization on occasion in order to pack tight the action of his comedies with a great variety of fancy, realism, courtliness, bawdry, sentiment, and poetry. This almost amounts to saying that nothing came amiss if amusement came with it; but to some critics such variety is an expression of Shakespeare's good nature, of his indulgent love of all kinds and conditions of men. George Gordon claimed that the width of his vision was the secret of Shakespeare's comedy:

> Some of our modern analysts think that Shakespeare, in his comedies, might have gone deeper. The direction of his comedies, . . . is rather to width than depth: but what is wrong with width? 'The world *is* wide and its width supplies a kind of profundity in another dimension.'[1]

Shakespeare's comedies do indeed present a wide range of human characters and situations. For example, they are not

[1] *Shakespearian Comedy and Other Studies* (1944), p. 34.

restricted, as are some comedies, to light-hearted incidents. There is not one in which death or destruction is not imminent: in *The Comedy of Errors* there is the threatened death of Ægeon, in *Love's Labour's Lost* the death of the King of France, in *The Two Gentlemen* savage outlawry, and in *A Midsummer Night's Dream* dearth and disorder in nature, and the threatened death of Hermia; *The Merchant of Venice* presents murderous hatred, *Much Ado* a destructive, inbred malice, *As You Like It* envy and tyranny; in *Twelfth Night*, Olivia is left unprotected by the death of her brother and the happiness of all is threatened by a shipwreck and by an old and rancorous feud. We have already noticed that Shakespeare does not strive to provoke our reproof for evildoers; it must also be acknowledged that he does not seem to draw any moral from the evils themselves; destruction is averted by some fortunate chance and the final emphasis is upon the joy of those who are made happy.

In contrast with his practice in the history plays and early tragedies, Shakespeare has not provided explicit judgement upon the action. Those who do comment, like Biron or Katharina, are so much a part of the action that their opinions cannot be easily identified with the author's more Olympian view. There is no chorus as in *Romeo and Juliet* and nothing to compare with the dialogue of the gardeners in *Richard II* who seem to be introduced merely to make generalizations about the actions of others; there is nothing like the direct moralizing of the dying Gaunt or the Bishop of Carlisle, or like the ghosts at Bosworth Field in *Richard III*, or the hortatory conclusion to *King John*. In the early comedies Shakespeare presents a great variety of life but he does not preach as he does elsewhere; he seems only to invite us to look.

This suggests an analogy. When Bernard Berenson wished to describe the effect of some Florentine paintings, he used the phrase 'life-enhancing'.[1] The all-important,

---

[1] *The Florentine Painters of the Renaissance* (1890); ed. 1909, pp. 3-19, *et passim*.

distinguishing quality in these pictures seemed to have little connexion with earlier iconography or pictorial illustration ; it was a delight in the visual experience of the world as known to man. The enjoyment of these pictures extends the range of the viewer's visual experience ; they are not distinguished from earlier pictures because they exhort, or preach, or teach ; they do not appear to make any new claim on the viewer's moral response ; they are 'life-enhancing'. This phrase would express much of what we have already said about the early comedies of Shakespeare ; it would embrace the delight in human character, the absence of any desire to anatomize its faults, the lighthearted manner in which characterization is sometimes neglected for the sake of surprising or piquant situations, and, above all, the richness and variety of incident, character, diction, and verse. Like the Italian Renaissance pictures, Shakespeare's comedies do not seem to succeed by re-organizing our responses to life, but by helping us to a richer experience.

This agrees with our immediate sensations after seeing a successful performance of one of the comedies ; the experience seems to have been rich and lively, and yet, in an unexpected way, familiar. The richness may derive from the width of Shakespeare's vision, the liveliness and familiarity from his power to represent human nature ; the whole seems to enhance our experience of life. Confident in these recognitions, we do not wish to search further for explanations of enduring values. We are inclined to assert with J. W. Mackail that :

> to read a philosophy into Shakespeare, or to invent some 'obsession' in him and hunt for traces of it throughout his work, is not only idle but hurtful ; because this stands between us and Shakespeare and vitiates our view of him. . . . Shakespeare does not teach ; he illuminates.[1]

*   *   *

But it is shirking the critic's task to leave the matter here.

[1] *Shakespeare after Three Hundred Years* (1916), pp. 6 and 20.

If life-enhancement is the secret of the comedies, it does not follow that Shakespeare could see nothing wrong with the world, nothing to condemn, nothing to regret, nothing to construct. If the early comedies present the richness and variety of life, Shakespeare must still have exercised his judgement on life in order to select, order, and shape his material; one does not make a cake rich merely by adding a lot of whatever one fancies—if the finished cake is to be digestible, the ingredients have to be in just proportion and added in correct order. Like the Italian Renaissance pictures, the early comedies only *seem* to make no new claim on the viewer's moral response. They do not announce that they are going to persuade us into any new moral attitude, but nevertheless, in so far as we appreciate and respond to them, our attitudes must become those of their makers. To look at the richness and variety of the world as it is pictured in a work of art is to look with the artist's eyes, and this means that we must accept his selection of incident and share his perspective and emphasis of detail. To describe such selection and ordering will sound very much like 'reading a philosophy into Shakespeare', but more truly it is *inferring* a philosophy from him. Certainly Shakespeare does not preach in his comedies, but his philosophy and judgement on life must necessarily inform every detail of selection and presentation. It is one of the tasks of criticism to describe that implicit judgement, to say precisely how it was possible to achieve such life-enhancement.

By contrasting the early comedies with biting satires, critics have presented Shakespeare as a serene observer of good and evil, making no judgement and proposing no reform. But, once we believe that these plays are informed by his philosophy and judgement on life, this view is untenable in the light of his other early works; these manifest a very different attitude, an acute awareness of good and evil in human action. In the high Roman manner, he could show Brutus brought to disaster through his ideals, and Titus vindicating his honour by using the same cruelty that others had inflicted upon him. Enthused with national and political fervour, he could show what was wrong and what was beneficial in Bolingbroke's usurpation and how Prince Hal became king through the cold-lipped victory of his brother John and the sacrifice of Falstaff's heart. In *Romeo and Juliet*, in a mood and setting closer to those of his comedies, he could show a love which was at once ennobling and rash and unadvised. Nor did he avoid judgement : indeed one of the dominant themes of the history-plays is the way in which the sins of the fathers are visited upon their children, while in *Titus Andronicus*, he showed that hatred can only breed hatred, destruction only more destruction. This moral concern is too deeply felt to be put off easily or lightly ; it is inconceivable that in writing his comedies, at precisely the same stage in his career, he could simply ignore the duty of judgement and observe the capers of mankind with an amused tolerance. He is gay instead of grave, but his philosophy is the same. Shakespeare's philosophy was felt in the heart as well as in the mind, and such philosophy will be with a man always. The eyes which saw the world of the comedies were the same eyes that unflinchingly saw the world of the histories and early tragedies ; only the perspective has changed.

Our understanding of Shakespeare's early comedies has been seriously impaired by contrasting them with satirical comedies. It is true that Shakespeare does not make the explicit judgement of satire, but moral judgement is not the prerogative of the satirist. Shakespeare's comedies have happy endings, but it does not follow that he suddenly believed that all was right with the world. Clearly Duke Frederick and Don John have to be defeated : the fact that they do not trouble the happiness of true lovers at the close of the play does not imply that in Shakespeare's opinion their destructiveness is of no importance ; it only implies that in some situations such destructiveness appears irrelevant. The fact that we are invited to sympathize with Malvolio, Jaques, and Shylock does not mean that we must also

condone them; as with Falstaff in *Henry IV*, we wish that
they suffered less by their rejection, but we may also realize
that their rejection is necessary. Deeply felt judgements can
be stated explicitly in formulae, choric comment, or the
dénouement of satirical comedy, but they can also be stated
implicitly in the precise ordering of a romantic story. Indeed
they must be implicit in every detail of its presentation and, in
the absence of explicit statement, it is at this level and with this
particularity that we must look for Shakespeare's comic vision.

In choosing any single word—be it merely the choice
between dog, hound or cur, or between ask, beg, beseech
or implore—a writer must make a judgement, a choice which
depends on his attitude towards the object described.
Indeed, as the most trivial action, like the tying of a shoe-
lace, can express a whole personality to someone who knows
and loves the person who is doing the action, so the choice of
a single word can express the personality, the philosophy
and attitude to life, of the one who uses it. In this manner
every detail of the early comedies—their dialogue, stage
movement, and action, their proportion, structure, and
emphasis of detail—expresses Shakespeare's attitude to life.
If at times he wrote carelessly or confusedly, there is significance in the exact occasion and exact mode of those
lapses. These plays do not formulate a judgement in the
manner of the history-plays and early tragedies, nor in the
manner of satirical comedy, but a judgement is implicit
nevertheless.

Shakespeare may possibly have known this, and he may
have written purposefully to express his moral judgements
and ideals. A year or so after writing *Twelfth Night*, he
defined the purpose of stage performance:

> [*its*] end, both at the first and now, was and is, to hold, as
> 'twere, the mirror up to nature; to show virtue her own feature,
> scorn her own image, and the very age and body of the time his
> form and pressure.[1]

[1] *Hamlet*, III. ii. 24-9.

Such a statement is conventional enough and can be paralleled many times in Renaissance criticism,[1] but Hamlet speaks of the universality of this ideal with a considered emphasis—'both at the first and now, was and is, . . .'. At the lowest estimate, Shakespeare must have been aware that responsible critics thought that drama should help the world truly to see itself, and should therefore clarify its virtues and vices; it is just possible that this was Shakespeare's own justification for his life's work. Possibly, despite appearances, the comedies were written for the avowed purpose of expressing Shakespeare's attitude to life and his moral judgements upon it, to 'show virtue her own feature, scorn her own image. . . .'

*　　　*　　　*

In the absence of explicit statement, there are few immediately obvious clues to the judgements underlying and informing the early comedies up to and including *Twelfth Night*. The judgements are hidden, having been assimilated into a strangely glittering, humane, and lighthearted whole. One might have expected that Shakespeare would use his jests and fancies as stalking-horses so that under their presentation he might shoot his wisdom, but any attempt to detach and remove a trivial surface from one of the comedies will only destroy the whole, or at least greatly damage it. Shakespeare has not sugared a pill; romance and humour are the very substance, and it is with these recalcitrant subjects that criticism must concern itself. There is no retreat; a critic must take this lightheartedness seriously.

There are three main kinds of clues which help the search for the implicit judgement. First is the manner in which Shakespeare ordered his plots, the structure, proportion, and shape of his plays—and this must include his creation of characters and the interplay which he has arranged between

[1] cf. Madeleine Doran, *Endeavors of Art: a Study of Form in Elizabethan Drama* (1954), pp. 72 and 93. It is, perhaps, significant that Hamlet's defence of drama was the conventional defence of *comic* drama.

them. The second is his choice of situations, actions, and words—and this must include the colour, tone, and texture of the words, and the metre, rhythm, and syntax of the dialogue. The third is the judgement explicit in his other plays and poems, especially those written about the same time in his career. The search requires minute analysis and the relation of each detail to the rest of the play in which it occurs and to Shakespeare's work as a whole.

The ways of searching for the implicit judgement of the early comedies are obvious enough, but so far the work has only been done intermittently, generally for single comedies or for isolated aspects of a group of comedies. This book is an attempt to further the task. It briefly discusses the varieties of comic structure and then, by following a few themes, or ideas, through all the early comedies, it tries to discover the judgements which inform the individual plays. The themes which are chosen for discussion are explicitly treated in tragedies, history-plays, or poems composed at about the same time; this, together with their recurrence in many of the comedies, suggests that they were fundamental to Shakespeare's creative mind at this stage in his career. A separate chapter discusses the development of these themes in later comedies, *All's Well that Ends Well*, *Measure for Measure*, and *Troilus and Cressida*.

The extent to which Shakespeare was governed by the ideas which we shall discuss may be judged by certain obvious tests. Our analysis must, of course, help us to appreciate the virtues that we have already noticed in the comedies; in particular, they must find expression in the great 'human' characters and in the richness and variety of incident. Our analysis must also help to explain the incongruous elements; it must show why the conclusions are so often lacking in fully developed characterization and why life-like characters, like Bottom and Shylock, are given subordinate positions in plays which are mainly in another, less life-like, idiom. It must also help us to understand the sequence in which Shakespeare wrote the early comedies. If the recognition of certain ideas or themes can clarify these matters, then it may be assumed that they were at least a part of Shakespeare's concern while writing these plays. The recognition will then help us to see more clearly the world of the early and mature comedies, and to share more fully in the life-enhancement which this vision brings.

*   *   *

- At the close of the book there is a chapter on Shakespeare's last comedies, *Pericles*, *Cymbeline*, *Winter's Tale* and *The Tempest*. These are usually considered apart from the earlier comedies: they are labelled 'romances' and most critics believe that they clearly evince symbolic, mythopaeic or thematic intentions. But when we have deduced themes from the more immediately baffling early comedies and turn again to these later ones we become dissatisfied with customary opinions about them. All the earlier themes kindle these plays into life, as well as the obvious ones of regeneration, patience, nature and culture; and recognizing the contribution of the old interests we are led to a re-assessment of the new comic mode and of the reflection of our world that the last comedies present in performance.

CHAPTER II

Experiments in Comedy

study of the structure of the early comedies up to and including *Twelfth Night* establishes at once their astonishing variety and the energy of Shakespeare's creative mind. Shakespeare did not simply choose one of the several patterns in common use, but modified and supplemented whatever he borrowed. And having once pleased his audience, he was not content to repeat a single pattern but continued to modify his basic structure, adding or rejecting certain elements, and sometimes rejecting one for a time only to return to it later. This does not suggest a writer at ease with a formula which works to his own satisfaction and the pleasure of his audience, nor an artist indulging some trifling fancies for his own amusement ; the impression is of an artist seeking to express a vision which was always eluding a completely satisfactory presentation.

The nature of such an artist's vision will necessarily determine the kind of structure which he develops for its expression, and therefore the present search for the implicit judgement or the 'idea' which underlies Shakespeare's early comedies may begin with an examination of the various kinds of structure which he employed and the experiments by which he tried to adapt existing forms for his own purposes. By such investigations, we may begin to define the *kind* of vision or judgement on life which the comedies present.

An awareness of Shakespeare's restless experimentation in comic structure may also help in another way, for as recurring themes are identified the question of how conscious

27

these repetitions were, of how consciously Shakespeare was presenting a developing judgement on life, is almost bound to arise. Of course the boundary between conscious and unconscious intentions is neither constant nor precise, and, therefore, assurance in such matters can hardly be expected. To satisfy our doubts it is only necessary to establish the integrity of the comedies as works of art, for once we are convinced of Shakespeare's desire to create something which answered to his artistic conscience, the extent to which he was conscious of his workmanship ceases to be of more than incidental interest; as the imagination 'dissolves, diffuses, dissipates, in order to recreate',[1] the poet himself may fail to recognize every detail of the process. To establish the comedies as works of imagination, or of artistic integrity, one may refer to the brilliance and variety of their language; but on a wider view, to vindicate the overall planning of the comedies, one may refer to the skill, energy, and inventiveness of Shakespeare's continual experiments with comic structure. So we may speak of Shakespeare's 'intention', 'theme' or 'judgement' in an artistic sense which cuts across any facile distinction between the conscious and unconscious mind.

*   *   *

A dramatist in Elizabethan England could choose between two basic comic forms, intrigue comedy and narrative comedy. In the broadest terms, the former may be said to have aimed at making a certain number of characters look ridiculous, the latter to have aimed at telling a story. Some Elizabethan comedies elude this simple classification but the distinction seemed clear enough to critics like Sidney and Jonson. Intrigue comedy was the purer form, deriving principally from classical or neo-classical models; narrative comedy was both the more pervasive and, being of very mixed origin, the more fluid form.

Three of Shakespeare's comedies represent the intrigue form. The plots of such plays are usually woven around some

---

[1] S. T. Coleridge, *Biographia Literaria*, ed. J. Shawcross (1907), i. 202.

obstacle to happiness such as an old miserly father or jealous unloving husband, or around a separation of lovers or of parents and children. Their action usually springs from some crafty trouble-maker or intriguer, while their dramatic interest is maintained by misunderstandings and developed towards a dénouement which is at once precipitous and surprising. But while relying on this type of structure, each of Shakespeare's intrigue comedies contains some additional elements.

The Comedy of Errors, for example, is based directly on the *Menaechmi*, an intrigue comedy by Plautus, but Shakespeare discarded its soliloquizing prologue in favour of a fully dramatized exposition which is more in the manner of narrative comedy. In the course of the play he further modified his model by introducing sentimental and lyrical scenes which the quick farcical movement of the original could scarcely support. And his new introduction had to be matched by a new conclusion; this is not so slick as in the original, for the new opening scene is here remembered in the persons of the Duke and Ægeon, and the threat of death and the sympathy which has been evoked for the father have to be resolved in answering assurances. Yet in spite of these changes, there is no suggestion that Shakespeare was dissatisfied with the contrivance of his source; on the contrary, he doubled the intrigue elements by providing twin servants to attend the twin heroes.

For *The Taming of the Shrew* Shakespeare used the structure and much of the detail of Ariosto's intrigue comedy *I Suppositi*, and for its Pantaloon and Pedant he used the long established character types of the *Commedia dell'Arte*. Here again the beginning of the play has been altered, this time by the addition of an Induction in which Christopher Sly, the drunken tinker, is set to watch the exposition of the main plot. Upon the main structure derived from Ariosto is grafted the story of the taming of Kate by Petruchio which is, perhaps, in the tradition of unsophisticated farcical interludes. A new conclusion diffuses the effect of Ariosto's dénouement, for here the shrew story closes the play with Katharina's long and spirited speech on the duty of wives; this provides a more specific relation between the various strands of the plot and a more subtle impact of character than any moment of the preceding action. It is just possible that Shakespeare followed an earlier play or collaborated with some other author in modifying Ariosto in these ways, but since all scholars are agreed that the liveliest portions are from his hand alone, he must be largely responsible for the overall effect of *The Shrew* as we know it.

No definite source for *The Merry Wives of Windsor* is known but the structural similarity of the Falstaff scenes to a number of intrigue comedies about jealous husbands is so clear that it has been confidently asserted that Shakespeare worked upon a lost play of this type—one scholar has even gone to the lengths of describing the action and characterization of this hypothetical '*Jealous Comedy*'.[1] Shakespeare augmented this basic plan with incidents relating to Anne Page (which are themselves dependent on an intrigue formula of the hood-winking of mercenary parents) and with a final scene in Windsor Great Park. This latter addition is the more significant in that it breaks the unity of place and tone which the rest of the comedy inherits from its models, and turns the final condemnation of Falstaff into something at once more fantastic, more directly moralizing, and more good-humouredly self-accusing than any incident provided by the basic intrigue structure. It also allows for the resolution of the Anne Page story, and involves all the *dramatis personae* in a final action which puts some of them into unaccustomed roles and then sends them all home together to a banquet.

Shakespeare can never have been completely satisfied with the basic intrigue formula, for none of these plays is a pure example of the type. The lack of opportunities for pure lyricism and romance which are such important elements in his other comedies does not seem to have been his chief

[1] cf. S. A. Small, *Modern Language Review*, xxvi (1931), 281-7.

concern ; these elements are introduced only in *The Comedy of Errors*, probably the first of the three. The story of Anne Page might have provided an opportunity for lyricism in *The Merry Wives* but the parts of Anne and her lover are curtailed to a minimum. Shakespeare seems to have been more concerned about the mood in which the plays were received, for he twice provided contrasted introductions to prepare for the main action. From the unusually solemn, slow, and pathetic opening of *The Comedy of Errors*, the main plot starts into animated life ; the new high-spirited mood is sprung upon us and is accepted as a natural, opposite relief from the earlier strain. The Induction of *The Shrew* is a kind of stepladder towards the illusion of the main plot ; Christopher Sly, who is known to every one at the ale house, is first accepted and then, with him, we 'let the world slip' and more readily receive the fantastic contrivances which follow as 'a kind of history'. *The Merry Wives* has no contrasting introduction but the whole is set more firmly in the contemporary English scene than any other Shakespeare play ; in a sense, this extends the device of the Induction of *The Shrew* to the whole italianate plot of this later play.

In all three plays Shakespeare seems to be resisting the tendency of an intrigue comedy to narrow its interest. For example, plays of this type are often dominated by a single character who initiates all the action, but Shakespeare always avoided this by diffusing the interest of the audience over a wide range of characters. This development is clearest in *The Merry Wives* where even Mrs Page is gulled as well as gulling. In each play Shakespeare modified the conclusion, which in the normal form narrows the action towards a single dénouement. At this point he was always less concerned with providing a culminating *coup de théâtre* than with bringing the *dramatis personae* of his several plots into relation with each other. There is an accompanying *rallentando* effect giving scope for sentiment or characterization ; the plots run helter-skelter over the obstacles of intrigue yet finish their course in slow motion so that the final apprisal is then both detailed and sensitive. The slower tempo does not slacken interest, for the emergence of the new mood is a development of an interest which has been incipient throughout the play.

Although an intrigue plot could never provide Shakespeare with a ready-made model, he did not reject the form completely after his early experiments in *The Comedy of Errors* and *The Shrew*. It must have had some inherent virtue which, at the time of writing *As You Like It* and *Twelfth Night*, made him return to it for *The Merry Wives*.[1] By this time Shakespeare was relying mainly on non-dramatic narrative sources, and in structure his comedies more nearly resembled those of Lyly, Greene, and Peele. But even in these he still used some elements adapted from the intrigue model. The eavesdropping in *Love's Labour's Lost*, the misunderstandings in *A Midsummer Night's Dream*, the exchange of rings in *The Merchant*, the gulling of Benedick and Beatrice, and the discomfiture of Phoebe in *As You Like It*, all employ the technique of twin vision associated with an intrigue plot—the audience knows of the intrigue and knows that some of the characters do not. This invites the audience to observe with a kind of detachment, and, without resort to soliloquies or long, explanatory speeches, centres their interest upon a misunderstanding and its resolution. In these predominantly narrative plays the elements from intrigue comedy are often subtly modified. The merely sportive interest which Puck takes in the mortals places the intriguer and his victims in a new relationship, the victims never being able to understand how they have been misled. In *The Merchant of Venice* the gulling of Shylock as an old and miserly father repeats situations and techniques of presentation from intrigue comedies, but the way in which his frustration is voiced must silence the conventional delight and amusement which his dilemma would otherwise provoke.

---

[1] If Shakespeare was commanded by Queen Elizabeth I to write a play about Falstaff in love, he still exercised his own artistic judgement in choosing the form which that comedy should follow.

Twelfth Night is exceptional in that its mainly narrative form derives from the comparatively minor narrative element of an intrigue comedy, *Gl'Ingannati*. Here Shakespeare started with descriptive dialogue and soliloquy in order to establish his main characters and their sentiments, but for the conclusion he relied on a double dénouement, more swift than those in *The Shrew* and *The Merry Wives* and with little more direct expression of sentiment than is found at the end of the intrigue plot of *The Comedy of Errors*. At the very moment when misunderstandings are resolved and characters are placed in a final and stable relationship, the audience is told far less about their sentiments than at any other moment in the play. It is as if Shakespeare had removed happiness from our view either because he knew that it must always be a bitter thing to 'look into happiness through another man's eyes', or because he wished to express the ultimate privacy of lovers' contentment. The technique is equivocal, for it has also been suggested that Shakespeare lost interest in his theme as the complications were removed or that he felt so deeply for Malvolio that the expression of joy was stifled. The point is debatable and must await a discussion of the play as a whole. Here it is sufficient to note that *Twelfth Night* represents new and surprising modifications of some elements of intrigue comedy and that once more Shakespeare has experimented with the conclusion to his comedy. The first point suggests that any discussion of Shakespeare's early comedies up to and including *Twelfth Night* must give full weight to the three intrigue comedies and not ignore them as examples of a comedy foreign to Shakespeare's developed comic vision. The second point still further emphasizes Shakespeare's concern to provide a comprehensive final scene which is able to relate many characters to each other, rather than one which would express the sentiments of any one character or group of characters.

*   *   *

The majority of Shakespeare's early comedies are narrative

in structure, presenting a story of true love and using a variety of the devices associated with this form. But here again Shakespeare was always experimenting, modifying what he borrowed in accordance with his own purposes. In common with other writers, he used a double or multiple plot. In *The Two Gentlemen* the device is used in a structurally simple form, in the incidental dialogue of Launce and Speed, but in *Love's Labour's Lost* the main plot is less complex, and the sub-plot of Armado, Jaquenetta, and Costard is developed with greater freedom. Here the relationship is somewhat similar to that of the two plots in Lyly's *Endymion*, but by adding Sir Nathaniel, Holofernes, and Dull, and the pageant of the Worthies, Shakespeare went beyond Lyly's example ; this third story has a different pattern and serves to relate the characters from all three stories in the concluding scene. In some early comedies with multiple plots, such as Lyly's *Love's Metamorphoses* or *Midas*, or Dekker's *Shoe-Makers' Holiday*, the last scene was reserved for the main plot only, the sub-plots being concluded in earlier scenes. Clearly this did not satisfy Shakespeare ; as in his intrigue comedies, he devised final scenes which would hold all elements together. In *A Midsummer Night's Dream* he used a device very like that of *Love's Labour's Lost*, arranging that the performance of *Pyramus and Thisbe* in celebration of the nuptials brings the mechanicals to court, to be observed and commented upon by Theseus, Hippolyta, and the young lovers. But here the relation of the various plots is more complex, for the nuptials also bring the fairies to court, in their own way to honour the lovers.

Although the general tendency towards comprehensive final scenes is marked, Shakespeare was continually experimenting even here. In *The Merchant of Venice*, Shylock leaves the stage before the end of Act IV, and so does Don John in *Much Ado;* they are referred to in the dialogue of Act V, but they are not actually present. While it is true that Dogberry makes his last appearance in Act V Scene i, three scenes before the end, the conclusions of these two comedies are in other respects as comprehensive as those of preceding ones. It would seem that down-right villainy and hatred have no place in the resolution which Shakespeare wished to present; he preferred to show the relationship of the other characters *after* the defeat of villainy. This preference must have been modified when he came to write *As You Like It* and *Twelfth Night;* here Jaques and Malvolio, while they are not down-right villains, are discordant characters who cannot join in the final dance and celebrations, and yet they are kept on the stage until the very last moment; and, since theirs are the only stories which remain unconcluded, they retain our interest to the end.

Shakespeare also continued to experiment with the relationship of the various plots during the course of the comedy. In *A Midsummer Night's Dream*, the mechanicals and the lovers do not meet until the final scene, but they can be effectively contrasted with each other during the action because they are both in contact with the fairies and are thereby separate yet related. In *The Merchant of Venice* the story of the wooing of Portia and that of the bond for Antonio's flesh are kept separate by stressing the distinct locations of Belmont and Venice; Bassanio, Portia, and others journey between these places and the two threads of the plot are thereby related, but the conclusion waits until all the characters who share in the final resolution meet together at Belmont. There is a somewhat similar device in the first half of *As You Like It* where the location alternates between Arden and the world outside; in the second half the action is confined to Arden but the play concludes with the abrupt arrival of a messenger from outside. In *Much Ado* the same location is used throughout and the two pairs of lovers are constantly meeting each other, but here the plots are kept distinct by their contrasted tones of sentiment; there is a sense in which it is impossible for Benedick to communicate fully with Claudio, or Claudio with Benedick, until the concluding scene of the comedy.

Shakespeare seems to have developed towards a multiplicity

of plots and a greater subtlety in their inter-relation. The inter-relations are most complex in the Arden scenes of *As You Like It:* lovers, courtiers, shepherds, clowns, fools, philosophers, princes, young men, old men, children, villains, a god, and the deer of the forest are all linked together, not so much by the action, of which there is little, as by the observation of each other. The same tendency is apparent in the two main plots of *Twelfth Night.* These might have run independently, but Shakespeare has been at pains to relate them to each other : Viola, for instance, who has no part in the Malvolio plot, meets Malvolio, the clown, Sir Toby, Sir Andrew, and Antonio in incidents that are by no means essential to her story. Again all strands of the plot are only brought together in the last scene—and there is a sense in which they are not truly united until Feste sings on the deserted stage.

Shakespeare used the freedom of narrative form to pro-vide a great variety of plot interest, but he went beyond example in the subtle inter-relations which he contrived between the various elements and in the comprehensiveness of his final scenes.

*   *   *

In England, the narrative form of drama had many roots in the Middle Ages. Medieval poems, for example, may be the ultimate source of debates between characters represent-ing contrasted opinions in *The Two Gentlemen* and *Love's Labour's Lost*, and it has been suggested that woodland scenes, references to winter and summer, and the 'rebirth' of Hero in *Much Ado* may be in the tradition of folk ritual and drama.[1] But if so, in Shakespeare's hands, the traditions have been overlaid by a new and more comprehensive dramatic purpose ; his characters are seldom limited to type representation and his plays have a more complex structure than that dictated by the basic rhythm of life and death.

[1] N. Frye, 'The Argument of Comedy', *English Institute Essays* 1948 (1949), pp. 67-8.

The structure of Shakespeare's comedy is never simple. When, for instance, it is suggested that in choosing the narrative type Shakespeare conformed to the medieval conception of comedy as 'a poem changing a sad beginning into a happy ending', and that his comedies are capable of a medieval allegorical interpretation,[1] it is found that such an interpretation must ignore much of the detail of the individual comedies. So *The Merchant of Venice* has been considered as an allegory of Justice and Mercy or of the Old Law and the New, but the interchange of rings, the malignity of Shylock, and the wooing of Morocco, Arragon, Bassanio, and Gratiano are all irrelevant to this theme; even the trial scene, which centres on the single issue of Justice and Mercy, cannot be fully interpreted as an allegory, for the verbal quibble and the manner in which it is applied can offer no 'intendment'. Shakespeare's comedies do not have the necessary simplicity of characterization, narrative, or structure for allegorical terms to be appropriate for more than a few isolated moments. And those moments must be judged as part of a complex whole which draws on many traditions.

Besides narrative allegory and folk plays, the traditions lying behind Shakespeare's comedy include miracle plays with their broadly comic interpolations, morality plays, medieval farcical interludes, juggling turns, the jesting of professional fools, civic and courtly pageants and entertainments, impromptu masques, Italian tragi-comedy, pastoral eclogues and dramas, and the prose and verse novels which were the sources for Shakespeare's plots. All these traditions have their place, but not one of them solely governs the structure of any one comedy.

*   *   *

In structure Shakespeare's comedies are more like his

[1] cf. I. Gollancz, *Allegory and Mysticism in Shakespeare*, ed. A. W. Pollard (1931), and N. Coghill, 'The Basis of Shakespearian Comedy', *Essays and Studies*, new series, iii (1950), 1-28.

history-plays than any other one kind of entertainment or drama. But the histories can hardly be called a source of the structure of the comedies, for Shakespeare developed their pattern during the same years as he developed his comic pattern. The similarity is interesting not for traditional attitudes underlying the comedies, but because it suggests that his intentions were similar in both kinds of drama.[1]

We have already noted that the histories have more overt moralizing than the comedies, but in fact there are some signs that Shakespeare tried various experiments to introduce direct exposition in the comedies as well. At the close of Katharina's story in *The Shrew* she speaks out on how to win a losing match, and in *Love's Labour's Lost* Biron speaks of the power of love; but these are only approximations to the expositions of the histories, because in each case the dramatic context, or, to put it another way, the individual viewpoint, may well be felt to rob the exposition of general application. Mistress Quickly's unlikely disquisition on chastity when she is dressed as the Queen of Fairies, being wholly out of her own character, is more like the generalized comment of the histories; but here there is no suggestion that we are hearing the whole truth about love. The nearest attempt at direct, generalized comment by the lovers themselves is the chorus led by the simple Silvius in *As You Like It*, but here it seems that we can only marvel at their unanimity; we can hardly expect to gather the finer points from such a pack of Irish wolves howling against the moon.

But the absence of direct explication may be less significant than at first appears. The interest of an audience lies more in the sequence of events and dramatic contrast and conflict than in direct exposition. Hal's 'I do, I will' to Falstaff in the tavern and his 'I know thee not old man . . .' after the coronation are far more powerful in the theatre than the longer, more direct treatment of the same theme in his dialogue with the Chief Justice. Direct statement often

[1] This point was made by W. P. Ker, 'Note on the Form of Shakespeare's Comedies', *Edda*, vi (1916), 156-63.

points the moral in the histories but it never expresses their full meaning; it provides signposts only. The manner in which the Falstaff narrative has been developed alongside that of the state—every contrast in style, tempo, and tone, every contrast in the means of characterization, in the quantity and nature of discursive incident and dialogue, and in all the *minutiae* of stage-craft—is a most important part of the total meaning of *Henry IV*. If the comedies, lacking direct exposition, have many parallels with the histories in details of technique and structure, they too may be contrived not for delight alone, but also the expression of meanings as urgent and as complex as those of the histories.

In both forms Shakespeare developed a narrative structure which divided the audience's interest between a number of characters—a structure in contrast with that of the great tragedies which are dominated by single heroes, Hamlet, Othello, Macbeth, Lear. As in *Much Ado* interest is divided between Benedick and Beatrice, and Claudio and Hero, and in *Twelfth Night* between Viola, Olivia, Orsino, Malvolio, Sir Toby, and Feste, so in *King John* it is divided between the king and Falconbridge, and in *Henry IV* parts I and II, between Prince Hal, Hotspur, Falstaff, and Henry the Fourth. It is true that Richard the Third, and, to a lesser extent, Richard the Second and Henry the Fifth seem to be outstanding figures in the plays named after them, but this is only comparatively.[1] In *Richard II*, the king is offset by Bolingbroke, so that Richard's death-scene (which might have concluded the play with interest centred wholly in him, as Richard the Third's soliloquy before Bosworth tends to do) is counterpoised by two scenes dealing with Aumerle's plot against Bolingbroke; the final interest is at least two-fold, in Richard as a king who finds he must become a man, responsible for good and ill, and in Bolingbroke as a man who becomes a king and finds sorrow and guiltiness there.

[1] The balance of interest between several characters is clear in the three parts of *Henry VI*, though here the interests often succeed one another rather than develop together.

In *Henry V* the king's more dominant position may be a structural device to hold and link together the greater variety of characters with which the play is crowded, the ne'er-do-wells, home-loving soldiers, professional soldiers, the nobles, traitors, citizens, the clergy, and the French.

Shakespeare's handling of the ensuing structural problems is somewhat similar in both histories and comedies. In the first place, both kinds conclude in scenes which bring many characters together in a final resolution. The resolution in the histories cannot always be fully comprehensive since many of the characters are killed in the course of the narrative; the most complete are in the two parts of *Henry IV*, at the battle of Shrewsbury and at the coronation of Henry the Fifth—the former brings Henry the Fourth, Hotspur, Falstaff, and Prince Hal together for the first and only time, the latter brings Prince Hal and Falstaff together as prince and subject. In other histories the final relationships are suggested rather than presented dramatically; in *Henry V* Burgundy's speech on discord in France relates royal diplomacy to the lot of the common people who have figured so much in the preceding action, and in *Richard II*, the dead king's body is brought before the victorious Bolingbroke, and the fate of Mowbray who died

> *Streaming the ensign of the Christian cross*
> *Against black pagans, Turks, and Saracens,*

is recalled in Bolingbroke's own desire to expiate his guilt by a voyage to the holy land. In *Richard III* all the 'souls, whose bodies Richard murder'd', return as ghosts before the final battle and, by their prayers and imprecations, join in its action.

Another similarity between histories and comedies is the manner in which some strands of their plots are kept separate until the close of the play: as Hotspur and Harry only meet at Shrewsbury and the Gloucestershire gentlemen only come to town for the coronation, so the fairies and mechanicals come to court only at the close of their play, Rosalind meets her father only at her own marriage, and, in *Twelfth Night*, Olivia, Sebastian, Viola, and Orsino are together only in the last scene of all. The dialogue constantly relates these strands to each other during the course of the play, but the action does not bring them together ; this tends to emphasize the final scenes where relationship is actual.

Again, in both forms, minor characters are frequently emphasized during the course of the play in scenes where the major characters are not ; the minor characters are usually related to major ones, but only when they themselves are dominant. For example, Dogberry, Sir Nathaniel, Holofernes, Constable Dull, Jack Cade, Iden, the gardeners in *Richard II*, Launcelot Gobbo, Silvius, Corin, Shallow, Silence, and Gadshill, the carriers and the chamberlain, all exist in their own right before they are directly related to the major characters. Neither histories nor comedies give the impression that their minor characters are introduced solely to help forward the action which is necessary for our interest in the main characters. In short, minor characters are seldom supernumeraries only.

There are less tangible similarities. For both histories and comedies Shakespeare used different styles of verse and prose to contrast the various groups of characters within a single play. He also used several modes of characterization. The presentation of Falconbridge in *King John* is as different from that of the other characters in the play as Shylock's is from the others in *The Merchant of Venice;* in neither play is any other character so presented in soliloquy or dialogue that the audience can share his thoughts and feelings for the greater part of the action—these two characters are seen from the inside, the others almost wholly from the outside. The variation is complex in *Twelfth Night* in which the characters of Orsino, Sebastian, Antonio, Sir Toby, Malvolio, and Feste are shown in quite different ways, and in *Henry V* in which the clergy, Katharine, Bates, Pistol, Burgundy, and the king are not only different in status and character but also in mode of characterization : some of these characters are revealed in soliloquy, some described in set speeches, some revealed in dialogue which gives the impression of naturalistic interchange; some are type or 'humour' characters; some seem to have fully realistic backgrounds so that we can readily imagine their life outside the play, and some could only exist in the play itself.

The several features which link Shakespeare's histories and comedies may be found in other groups of Elizabethan dramas, but not so abundantly nor so subtly used. And certainly it would be hard to find two other series of plays which developed so much in step with each other. We may therefore conclude that Shakespeare's intentions in writing the individual plays and in developing the two kinds of drama must have had much in common. Clearly both kinds demand a varied and complex reaction, and, with their common emphasis on contrast, relationship, and resolution, they must both be equally thought-provoking.

This impression may be supported by some recent scholarly discoveries. For a considerable time it has been recognized that in writing history plays Shakespeare read more than one source, drawing attitudes and details from Hall's *Chronicles* as well as from Holinshed's, and from *The Mirror for Magistrates* and works by Sir Thomas More, Froissart, Daniel, and others as occasion suggested. We are now beginning to think that something of the same eclecticism may lie behind the comedies. Professor C. T. Prouty has given an authoritative account of Shakespeare's dependence and independence in writing *Much Ado;* here, as in the histories, he seems to have created his own narrative plot over against many other treatments of the same story.[1] More recently Professor Kenneth Muir has investigated the sources of the Pyramus and Thisbe story in *A Midsummer Night's Dream* and has found good reason for believing that 'Shakespeare consulted six or seven versions . . . before

[1] *The Sources of Much Ado About Nothing* (1950). In my Arden edition of *The Merchant of Venice* (1955) I suggested a similar growth for the narrative of that play.

writing his tedious brief scene.'[1] It therefore seems possible that, as in structure, so in their dependence on sources, the comedies were fashioned in the same way as the histories.

As it is obviously incomplete to regard the histories as narratives, portrait galleries, or simple moral *exempla*, so it may well be equally incomplete to take the comedies only on their most obvious levels of narrative, character, fancy, humour, or intrigue. Shakespeare's creative task in the comedies was not limited to dramatizing a given story and adding amusing decoration. Between the diverse elements we should look for such exquisite inter-relations as those between the youthful charade of kingship in the Eastcheap tavern, Falstaff lording it in an autumnal Gloucestershire, and the last commands of Henry the Fourth as he is moved into the Jerusalem chamber. Apparently the same kind of reading prepared Shakespeare for his work, and certainly he developed the same sort of original and subtle dramatic structure in order to present it.

*   *   *

An examination of the structural qualities of these plays reveals that they are neither simple intrigue comedies nor simple narrative comedies. Shakespeare was constantly experimenting in order to find a comic form which would present several characters or groups of characters in relation and contrast with each other and which would conclude in a scene which brought these various elements into some stable relationship.

Such contrasts and relationships were clearly more important to Shakespeare than the presentation of a story—*Love's Labour's Lost* and *As You Like It*, in which action is a small element, show this most clearly, but the subtle intertwining of the multiple plots in each comedy suggests that this is universally true. They were also more important than raising the wind of laughter ; not even the intrigue comedies

---

[1] 'Pyramus and Thisbe: a Study in Shakespeare's Method', *Shakespeare Quarterly*, v (1954), 152.

were allowed to culminate in a surpassingly ridiculous dénouement; no comedy is without its sober moment and the dominant note at the conclusion of each narrative comedy is one of romantic sentiment. Contrast and relation were also more important than the creation of any one lively and life-like character—the large number of major characters in each comedy is evidence for this and so is the manner in which *The Merchant of Venice* continues for a whole act after the disappearance of Shylock. The same overriding purpose occasionally led Shakespeare to dispense with life-like characterization, to put a story of action over against one of inaction or situation as in *Much Ado*, or to put a 'human' character over against type characters or those which are merely sketched in outline.

Characterization, humour, narrative, and intrigue seem to have been servants and not masters, and so Shakespeare's ultimate purpose in comedy must be described, not only in these terms, but also in terms of comparison and judgement. They are in fact—against all immediate appearances— comedies designed around some theme or judgement, a weighing of this against that, and against those others. This does not mean that the comedies are coldly intellectual, for Shakespeare's heart and mind can seldom be dissociated; it means that they present Shakespeare's vision of human life, and particularly, since they present tales of wooing and wedding, of love and personal relationships.

The skill, energy, and inventiveness with which Shakespeare developed his own varieties of comic structure demonstrate the artistic integrity of these plays and may encourage the attempt to define the implicit judgement which informs them. We may begin by trying to determine Shakespeare's ideals of romantic love, the motive of the main action in the majority of his comedies. And having defined those ideals we may look for the ways in which they inform the detail of the comedies up to and including *Twelfth Night*, and how they are represented in the contrasts and relationships suggested by their individual structural forms.

CHAPTER III

Love's Wealth and the Judgement of
The Merchant of Venice

Shakespeare thought of love, as many men have done, in terms of the sun, the moon and stars, night skies and vast seas, of spring and summer, the burning rose and the sweet dawn, of rich jewels, a phoenix riddle and everything of beauty; he saw engagement in love as a game, a quest, a war, a sickness, a willing servitude, and the understanding, meeting, and fulfilment of two human beings. But if we wish to discover what Shakespeare thought and felt about love, what implicit judgements shaped the romantic tales that are presented in the early comedies, it will be helpful to follow a single image through the plays, the image of love as a kind of wealth.

Again and again Shakespeare wrote of love in terms of merchandise. So Juliet, happy in new-wakened love, yearns for the night:

> *O, I have* bought *the mansion of a love,*
> *But not* possess'd *it, and, though I am* sold,
> *Not yet enjoy'd.*
>
> (III. ii. 26-8)

Romeo has pledged his troth in similarly commercial terms:

> *. . . wert thou as far*
> *As that vast shore wash'd with the farthest sea,*
> *I would* adventure *for such* merchandise.
>
> (II. ii. 82-4)

They both see love as a commercial enterprise; when they

first met they exchanged kisses and now, confident in each other's love, they begin to realize the riches that are at stake.

Such commercial imagery came readily to Shakespeare's mind for important climaxes of his romantic comedies. So Valentine glories in his hope of Silvia's love:

> *. . . why, man, she is mine own,*
> *And I as* rich *in having such a jewel*
> *As twenty seas, if all their sand were pearl. . . .*
>
> (II. iv. 168-70)

and, in *Love's Labour's Lost*, the Princess refuses to grant her love immediately, the time being—

> *. . . too short*
> *To make a world-without-end* bargain *in.*
>
> (V. ii. 798-9)

Troilus tries to find poetry to describe his love for Cressida:

> *Tell me, Apollo, for thy Daphne's love,*
> *What Cressid is, what Pandar, and what we?*
> *Her bed is India; there she lies, a pearl:*
> *Between our Ilium and where she resides,*
> *Let it be call'd the wild and wandering flood,*
> Ourself the merchant, *and this sailing Pandar*
> *Our doubtful hope, our convoy and our bark.*
>
> (I. i. 101-7)

It may seem *malapropos* to talk about such romantic love in terms of buying and selling, leaseholds, merchandise, and bargains, but in each of the early comedies, and in many other plays and poems, Shakespeare wrote of love as of a kind of wealth in which men and women traffic. By defining this idea and then tracing its influence upon the writing of the comedies and the inter-relation of their various narrative strands, we may more fully appreciate Shakespeare's implicit judgement on life.

*　　*　　*

The first seventeen sonnets, taking them in the order in which they were first printed, are Shakespeare's most sustained and straightforward account of an ideal love. In the comedies he always wrote within a dramatic context, expressing not his own thoughts but those of his *dramatis personae;* in the poems he was the professional story-teller, aware of his audience; and in the other sonnets he was either speaking for a character in a fiction or else was so involved personally that he could only record the fits, despairs, and joys of love in friendship and lust. But in the first seventeen sonnets Shakespeare wrote not so much as if he were in love himself, but as if he were trying to persuade a friend to love and marry; they describe, as it were from the outside, the fruits of love. Here we may look for love's lineaments.

The wealth of love is a dominant and unifying image in these sonnets. It is introduced in the first of them, allied to the idea of nature's abundance in harvest:

> *From fairest creatures we desire increase,*
> *That thereby beauty's rose might never die,* . . .

The word 'increase' alludes to nature's increase through generation but also to commercial gain; it prepares for another more obviously commercial word:

> *But thou,* contracted *to thine own bright eyes,*
> *Feed'st thy light's flame with self-substantial fuel,*
> *Making a famine where abundance lies,* . . .

There is, of course, a quibble on 'contracted', for besides alluding to a business contract, it also implies that the youth's eyes have not been *drawn* by love towards another person. The sonnet concludes by calling the youth a 'glutton'; he is told that instead of fulfilling a contract with another person and so giving the world its 'due', he makes 'waste in niggarding'.

This idea is repeated in the second sonnet, but instead of speaking of love's 'increase', the act of love is called 'use'—

a word which very commonly meant 'usury'.[1] The poet imagines the day when the youth has become a man of forty years :

> *Then being ask'd where all thy beauty lies,*
> *Where all the treasure of thy lusty days,*
> *To say, within thine own deep-sunken eyes,*
> *Were an all-eating shame and thriftless praise.*

The word 'thrift' was widely used among citizens and merchants ; its range of meanings included 'careful garnering of resources', 'profit', 'increase, or that which derives from thriving or breeding', and so 'usury'.[2] This last sense leads to the next lines :

> *How much more praise deserved thy beauty's use,*
> *If thou couldst answer 'This fair child of mine*
> *Shall sum my count and make my old excuse,* . . .

So beauty is seen as a treasure which decays unless, through love, its natural increase is taken. The theme is fully developed in sonnet iv :

> Unthrifty *loveliness, why dost thou* spend
> *Upon thyself thy beauty's* legacy?
> *Nature's* bequest *gives nothing but doth* lend,
> *And being frank she lends to those are* free.

One sense of 'free' in this passage seems to be 'generous' or 'liberal'[3]—so Nature's generosity should be answered :

> *Then, beauteous* niggard, *why dost thou abuse*
> *The* bounteous largess *given thee to* give?
> Profitless usurer, *why dost thou* use
> *So great a* sum *of sums, yet canst not live?*
> *For having* traffic *with thyself alone,*
> *Thou of thyself thy sweet self dost deceive.*

[1] cf. *N.E.D.*, s.v. 5.   [2] cf. *Mer. V.*, I. iii. 51-2 and 90-1.
[3] cf. *Oth.*, III. iii. 199-200: 'I would not have your free and noble nature, Out of self-bounty, be abused.'

> *Then how, when nature calls thee to be gone,*
> *What acceptable* audit *canst thou leave?*
> *Thy* unused *beauty must be tomb'd with thee,*
> *Which,* used, *lives th'* executor *to be.*

The next sonnet returns to the image of the rose, its final couplet claiming that:

> *. . . flowers distill'd, though they with winter meet,*
> *Leese but their show; their* substance *still lives sweet.*

This idea is made more explicit in sonnet vi, by a repetition of the earlier image of love's usury:

> *Then let not winter's ragged hand* deface
> *In thee thy summer, ere thou be distill'd:*
> *Make sweet some vial;* treasure *thou some place*
> *With beauty's* treasure, *ere it be self-kill'd.*
> *That* use *is not forbidden* usury
> *Which happies those that* pay *the willing* loan ;
> *That's for thyself to breed another thee,*
> *Or ten times happier, be it* ten for one ;
> *Ten times thyself were happier than thou art,*
> *If ten of thine ten times* refigured *thee:*
> *Then what could death do, if thou shouldst depart,*
> *Leaving thee living in posterity?*
> > *Be not self-*will'd, *for thou art much too fair*
> > *To be death's conquest and make worms thine* heir.

The sonnet is ingenious with its multiplying conceits and its final pun on a legal will, but this all serves to tie together several themes from earlier sonnets. In particular the idea of the 'willing loan' still further defines the contract of love: there is no obligation or claiming of rights, for Nature's 'largess' can only come to those who are 'free'—we see now that this meant 'unbound, unrestricted', as well as 'liberal'— and once the wealth of beauty has been recognized through love for another person, it grows by being 'used', it 'happies those that pay the willing loan'. While likening love to commerce, Shakespeare has also emphasized important contrasts; the wealth of commerce is controlled by gain and rights of possession, the wealth of love by giving, generously and of a free will.

The idea of love's wealth is not yet fully differentiated from commercial wealth, for in sonnet ix Shakespeare relates the traffickers in love to the world at large. When an 'unthrift' misuses the wealth he has inherited, the people among whom he squanders it may benefit:

> Look, what an unthrift in the world doth spend
> Shifts but his place, for still the world enjoys it . . .

In contrast love's wealth is squandered only by hoarding it for oneself:

> . . . beauty's waste hath in the world an end,
> But kept unused, the user so destroys it.

Such waste must be felt by all:

> No love towards others in that bosom sits
> That on himself such murderous shame commits.

But the theme which Shakespeare seems most anxious to develop is the loss that the youth himself will suffer if he does not spend his wealth. He has already likened love's wealth, or beauty, to a rose that must be 'defaced' by winter unless its sweetness is distilled, and he now suggests that it is like a house which will 'ruinate' (x. 7) if only its owner lives in it. Moreover this house is merely held in 'lease' (xiii. 5) and therefore the youth must provide an heir to inherit it. It is unthrifty and 'unprovident' (x. 2) to neglect such a possession when every man 'among the *wastes* of time must go', where 'sweets and beauties do themselves forsake' (xii. 10-11). The youth is told of only one remedy; love's wealth, the 'fresh blood' of youth which can bring 'wisdom, beauty, and increase', is a 'bounteous gift thou shouldst in *bounty* cherish' (xi. 12).

* * *

Clearly these judgements upon love's wealth, its likeness to and difference from commercial wealth, were in Shakespeare's mind when he wrote *Romeo and Juliet*. This early tragedy, like the comedies written about the same time, dramatizes a tale of romantic love and so we may look for such judgements implicit in its dialogue and action. But, unlike the comedies, *Romeo* contains direct moralizing as well, both in the two choruses and the concluding speech of the Prince; by these explicit judgements we may check deductions about the implicit ones.

The implicit judgements may be traced by listening for echoes of the sonnets. So Rosaline's resolution to avoid the encounter of love is rebuked as Shakespeare had rebuked the youth's:

> Benvolio. *Then she hath sworn that she will still live chaste?*
> Romeo. *She hath, and in that* sparing *makes huge* waste
>   *For beauty starved with her severity*
>   Cuts *beauty* off *from all posterity.*
>
>   (I. i. 223-6)

Compared with this, the Nurse's jovial and irresponsible chatter about how 'women *grow* by men' (I. iii. 95) is nearer to Shakespeare's glorification of love's 'use' or 'increase'. When the two lovers have, in the terminology of the sonnets, made the contract of their love, they know the happiness which comes to those who 'pay the willing loan': the 'measure' of Romeo's joy is heaped to overflowing (II. vi. 24-5), and Juliet protests that:

> *They are but beggars that can* count *their* worth,
> *But my true love is* grown *to such* excess,
> *I cannot* sum up *sum of half my* wealth.
>
>   (II. vi. 32-4)

The thought is close to the conceit of love's 'usury' for 'excess' was a synonym for 'interest', as in Antonio's assurance:

Shylock, although I neither lend nor borrow
By taking nor by giving of excess, . . .[1]

Both Romeo and Juliet know instinctively that Nature's
'bounteous gift' must be 'in bounty' cherished : so Juliet
proclaims,

My bounty *is as boundless as the sea,*
My love as deep; the more I give to thee,
The more I have, *for both are infinite.*

(II. ii. 133-5)

In the sonnets Shakespeare described the wealth of love ; in
Romeo and Juliet he presented dramatically the realization of
that wealth.

In the sonnets he saw only time and death as the enemies
of such a love but in this tragedy he opposes it with the love
for Rosaline, for Tybalt and for Mercutio, and, more
important, with the hatred between the families of the two
lovers, and with 'inauspicious stars'. This opposition and
their own precipitous action bring the lovers to desperation ;
their wealth seems to exist only in 'shadows' (V. i. 11), and
in such apparent poverty they each die reaffirming their
'dateless *bargain*' (V. iii. 115) with a kiss.

If the play ended here, one might complain that it does
not seem to be informed by the ideas of the sonnets ; there is
no discernible wealth when Capulet greets Romeo's father
in the tomb :

O *brother Montague, give me thy hand:*
This is my daughter's jointure, *for no more*
Can I demand.

(V. iii. 296-8)

Romeo and Juliet may be imperfect in the rashness of their
love, but their generosity, their willingness to give away the
'bounteous largess' given them to give, would seem to

[1] *Mer. V.*, I. iii. 62-3. See also *N.E.D.*, s.v. 6c, and P. Caesar, *Discourse*
(tr. 1578), DI^v: 'Usury, or as the word of God doth call it, excess . . .'

entitle them to some 'acceptable audit' in this world, some
heir other than 'worms'. And Shakespeare proceeds to show
just this : as Capulet and Montague recognize that in their
poverty they can 'demand' nothing, their memory of Romeo
and Juliet enables them to give, to give willingly in love to
each other for the first time :

> Capulet.   . . . *no more*
> *Can I* demand.
> Montague.   *But I can* give *thee more:*
> *For I will raise her statue in pure gold;*
> *For while Verona by that name is known,*
> *There shall no* figure *at such* rate *be set*
> *As that of true and faithful Juliet.*

Love responds to love :

> Capulet. *As* rich *shall Romeo's by his lady's lie;*
> *Poor sacrifices of our enmity!*
>   (V. iii. 297-304)

So it would seem that the tragedy, in its hard way, is
informed by the belief that if nature's largess is cherished in
bounty, more bounty must result, to the world as well as to
the lovers. Hatred has prevented its natural increase in the
world, but nevertheless the Prince can claim :

> *A glooming peace this morning with it brings . . .*
>   (V. iii. 305)

This, indeed, is the explicit judgement of the chorus :

> . . . . [*their*] *misadventured piteous overthrows*
> *Do with their death bury their parents' strife.*
>   (Prol., 7-8)

The generosity of Romeo and Juliet's love is answered by
the golden symbols of a new peace in the town of Verona;
the wealth of love is not cut off 'from all posterity'.

Romeo and Juliet is a more complex play than can be

indicated here—the manner in which lives can be 'star-crossed', the 'fearful passage' of a death-marked love, and contrasts of purity and impurity, carelessness and carefulness, were all in Shakespeare's mind when he was writing it —but by following through the ideal of love's wealth in dialogue and action we are brought close to the centre of the play, a centre which is identified by Shakespeare's explicit moralizing.

*   *   *

Following the clues of the sonnets and *Romeo and Juliet,* the ideal of love's wealth may be seen to inform the very earliest comedies. *The Comedy of Errors* is, in the main, an intrigue comedy which aims at making a certain number of characters look ridiculous; it deals therefore, not with the joys of giving in love, but with the follies and evils of possessiveness. Adriana's idea of love is to try to maintain a hold over her husband; the liberty of his actions galls her and she demands her rights. As part of this plan, she obtains the promise of a gold chain. Instead of the 'willing loan' of 'free' agents, Adriana sees love as a system of promises, duties and bonds. Even at her most submissive, when she cajoles her husband's twin, Antipholus of Syracuse, to come home as her husband, she harps upon rights and possessions:

> *Come, I will fasten on this sleeve of thine:*
> *Thou art an elm, my husband, I a vine,*
> *Whose weakness married to thy stronger state*
> *Makes me with thy strength to communicate:*
> *If aught possess thee from me, it is dross,*
> *Usurping ivy, brier, or idle moss.*

(II. ii. 175-80)

Her sister, Luciana, proclaims herself ready to submit to the man she should marry, but, not being in love herself, she only uses the same kind of arguments on Adriana's behalf, urging rights and duties:

> *If you did wed my sister for her* wealth,
>   *Then for her* wealth's *sake use her with more kindness.*
> (III. ii. 5-6)

This kind of love is further defined by contrasted loves, that of Antipholus of Syracuse who offers himself to Luciana unasked, and for whom giving is its own reward:

> *Sing, siren, for thyself and I will dote:*
>   *Spread o'er the silver waves thy golden hairs,*
> *And as a bed I'll take them and there lie,*
>   *And in that glorious supposition think*
> *He* gains *by death that hath such means to die* . . .
> (III. ii. 47-51)

or that of Luce who deals only in claims and possessions:

> Dromio of Syracuse. . . . *I am* due *to a woman; one that* claims *me, one that haunts me, one that will have me.*
> Antipholus of Syracuse. *What* claim lays *she to thee?*
> Dromio. *Marry, sir, such* claim *as you would lay to your horse; and she would have me as a beast: not that, I being a beast, she would have me; but that she, being a very beastly creature,* lays claim *to me.*
> (III. ii. 81-9)

This is the level of merely possessive love; and the fact is driven home by bringing these three loves together in one brief scene.

There are further contrasts in the juxtaposition of misunderstandings about love and misunderstandings about the possession of servants, a gold chain, and a bag of ducats. For the like of Adriana there is little difference between them; so when the Goldsmith asks for his money on the strength of a bond, Antipholus of Ephesus in his refusal likens the confusion to Adriana's sort of marriage:

> *Good Lord! you use this* dalliance *to excuse Your breach of promise to the Porpentine.*

I should have chid you for not bringing it,
But, like a shrew, *you first begin to brawl.*

(IV. i. 48-51)

But there is one difference between the two kinds of mis-understandings : those between masters and men, and merchant and purchaser are occasioned solely by confused identities—even after he has lost his money, the Goldsmith acknowledges that Antipholus of Ephesus is of 'credit infinite, highly beloved' (V. i. 6)—but Adriana's misunder-standings, her claims of rights and wrongs, ante-date any mistaken identity. The merchants treat their possessions naturally as best they may, Adriana treats hers unnaturally— her merchandise requires the use of love's wealth in which giving is more important than taking or keeping.

The misunderstandings of this comedy are set within the romantic narrative of old Ægeon's separation from his family : having forfeited his life, he is unable to pay the large fine incurred by visiting Ephesus in search of his son ; he is not worth a hundred marks and alone his position is desperate. But at the general recognition at the end of the play he finds a willing surety in his son, and the joy of the reunited family so turns poverty to wealth that, as soon as surety is offered, the Duke spares both life and fine, a deed which he had previously declared to be impossible.[1] This spirit of love, affection, and generosity sets the tone against which the misunderstandings are cleared away. When the facts are made clear, the Goldsmith is readily satisfied, and so are masters and men. Adriana's reconciliation with her husband is not presented in dialogue ; their misunderstanding in-volved more than mistaken identities, and cannot be cleared by such simple means. Yet the spirit of generosity is con-tagious and there is a hint that Adriana is now ready to give rather than demand : she has clamoured to the Abbess for possession of her husband, but to the Duke she uses a milder tone, basing her claim not on her rights but on the

[1] cf. I. i. 143-9.

plea that Antipholus of Ephesus is the one 'Whom I made lord of me and all I had' (V. i. 137); instead of demanding, as of right, to be 'his nurse' (V. i. 98), she simply begs that he may be 'brought forth and borne hence for help' (V. i. 160).

The last lines of the play suggest that generosity rules the day; the two Dromios, twin servants of the twin Antipholi, are talking:

–Will you walk in to see their gossiping?
–Not I, sir; you are my elder.
–That's a question: how shall we try it?
–We'll draw cuts for the senior: till then lead thou first.
–Nay, then, thus:
  We came into the world like brother and brother;
  And now let's go hand in hand, not one before another.

(V. i. 419-25)

Instead of arguing about the rights of seniority, they give in to each other. So in the last scene we are shown contrasts of give and take, in love and commerce, and something of the joy that comes with giving.

No one would argue that *The Comedy of Errors* is a very profound play, but reference to Shakespeare's ideas about love's wealth and its difference from commercial wealth, does suggest that its action is not merely that of a merry-go-round. Its elements were not chosen at random, but serve to present, in lively dramatic form, some of Shakespeare's judgements on personal relationships. It is a play of greater promise than the mere dexterity of its plotting suggests; its contrasts of love, commerce, and justice are simple enough but they foreshadow the more complex treatment of *The Merchant of Venice*. Adriana's dilemma is perhaps the most subtle element in the play, but its resolution, the manner in which husband and wife can willingly agree, is not fully expressed; this theme was taken up in another early comedy, *The Taming of the Shrew*.

In this play love and commerce are brought closer

together. Petrucnio, as he determines to woo Baptista's elder daughter Katharina, blatantly identifies the two:

> *I come to wive it* wealthily *in Padua;*
> *If* wealthily, *then happily in Padua.*
>
> (I. ii. 75-6)

Hortensio, more serious-sounding, picks up the idea:

> *Tarry, Petruchio, I must go with thee,*
> *For in Baptista's keep my* treasure *is:*
> *He hath the jewel of my life* in hold,
> *His youngest daughter, beautiful Bianca,* . . .
>
> (I. ii. 117-20)

Immediately afterwards, Gremio, another suitor for Bianca who has only wealth to recommend him, goes to work by commercial means, offering to pay Lucentio a 'largess' for forwarding his suit (I. ii. 151). Despite Kate's evident unwillingness, Baptista agrees to Petruchio's suit, seeing the whole affair in commercial terms:

> Baptista. *Faith, gentlemen, now I play a* merchant's *part,*
> *And* venture *madly on a desperate* mart.
> Tranio. *'Twas a* commodity *lay fretting by you:*
> *'Twill bring you* gain, *or perish on the seas.*
> Baptista. *The* gain *I seek is, quiet in the* match.[1]
>
> (II. i. 328-32)

He then proceeds to offer his younger daughter to the highest bidder:

> . . . *he of both*
> *That can assure my daughter greatest dower*
> *Shall have my Bianca's love.*
>
> (II. i. 344-6)

Judging from the sonnets, *Romeo and Juliet,* and *The Comedy of Errors,* we might expect this beginning to be

---

[1] 'Match' meant 'bargain, contract' as well as the pairing of two persons or things; cf. *N.E.D.*, s.v. 11.

followed by an intrigue plot which will make all the suitors
look ridiculous because of their commercial attitude to love's
wealth, their desire to gain rather than give. But the comedy
is more complex than that ; as we shall see later,[1] one of its
main themes is the disparity between appearance and
reality, and Petruchio's demand for a 'wealthy' wife may
bear a fuller, more generous, meaning than Grumio sup-
poses when he explains :

> *Nay, look you, sir, he tells you flatly what his mind is:*
> *why, give him gold enough and marry him to a puppet or*
> *an aglet-baby; or an old trot with ne'er a tooth in her*
> *head, . . . why, nothing comes amiss, so money comes withal.*
>
> (I. ii. 77-83)

Indeed in the long run, although Gremio and Baptista are
made to look foolish enough, it is on Hortensio, who doted
on his 'treasure', and on Lucentio, who could only exclaim
on Bianca's beauty, that the brunt of the ridicule falls, the
one for marrying a 'wealthy' widow, the other for marrying
Bianca who costs him a hundred crowns by her forward-
ness.

However this change comes about, its effectiveness is
manifested in new attitudes to love's wealth at the end of the
play. From the beginning Petruchio shows more generosity
than he brags of : having been assured of Katharina's dowry,
he immediately, with no prompting, is ready with his side of
the bargain, assuring her, in case of widowhood, all his 'lands
and leases whatsoever' (II. i. 124-6). And in marrying a
shrew whom no one else will look at, he may truly say that
his honest friends 'have beheld me *give away* myself'
(III. ii. 196). If he orders Kate about and bullies her, there
is never any doubt of his wish to tame her and to '*seal*' his
'*title* with a lovely kiss' (III. ii. 125)—the kiss which, as in
Romeo, can be a symbol of the mutual giving of two persons
in love. If Petruchio's intentions are capable of a generous
interpretation, Kate's for the greater part of the play, are

[1] See below, pp. 94-9.

not : she wants only her own will, she will have no teacher
who is not of her choosing, she must keep her own times, she
will not be polite to anyone, she will not even give thanks.
But, at the end of the play, all this is changed and she seems
as 'conformable' as any household Kate ; at her husband's
command she speaks of the duty of wives :

> *Thy husband is thy lord, thy life, thy keeper, . . .*
> *And for thy maintenance commits his body*
> *To painful labour both by sea and land,*
> *To watch the night in storms, the day in cold,*
> *Whilst thou liest warm at home, secure and safe. . . .*

It should be noted that she has no proof of all this, but is
taking it all on trust. To the other wives who are listening
this must seem to be going too far ; certainly Adriana from
The Comedy of Errors would protest at every line, for Kate is
not only obedient but takes no steps to make sure her husband fulfils his side of the bargain. Kate continues, and,
using the image of love's wealth, recognizes no ideal but
that of generosity on both sides :

> *And craves no other* tribute *at thy hands*
> *But love, fair looks and true obedience;*
> *Too little* payment *for so great a* debt.
> *Such duty as the subject* owes *the prince*
> *Even such a woman* oweth. . . .

This fine, spirited speech ends in a token of complete submission :

> *Then vail your stomachs, for it is no boot,*
> *And place your hands below your husband's foot:*
> *In token of which duty, if he please,*
> *My hand is ready; may it do him ease.*

She is willing to do the humblest service for Petruchio 'if he
please', and to such generosity there is only one answer :

> *Why, there's a wench! Come on, and kiss me, Kate.*

Great payment only results in great payment—Nature's bounteous largess is cherished only 'in *bounty*'—and Petruchio does not merely receive; he and Kate exchange kisses, and find contentment in mutual generosity. Adriana saw only one side of the contract of love and it seemed monstrous and unfair; Katharina's speech on the duty of wives and the paying of 'tribute' is joyful and elated because, in some mysterious way, she has confidence in Petruchio's love and in his willingness to give away his loan of Nature's bounty. There is no doubt at the end of *The Shrew* that he or she who gives most, not in the terms of commercial wealth but in terms of the contract of love, must inevitably get most. To present the happiness of this contract in lively dramatic terms is the great achievement of *The Shrew*. It is sometimes called a brutal and degrading play, but this could only be true if Katharina's submission had been abject, or if Petruchio, in triumph, had put his foot upon her hand; what happens, in fact, is that Petruchio and Katharina exchange kisses and her speech is confident and joyful, the most sustained and spirited speech in the whole play. Viewed against Shakespeare's ideal of love's wealth, this comedy presents, in its own gay, hilarious way, a profound mystery—how in love 'Property was thus appalled', how 'Either was the other's mine'.[1]

* * *

Of all the comedies, *The Merchant of Venice* is the most completely informed by Shakespeare's ideal of love's wealth.[2] Each of Portia's suitors has to choose one of three caskets and he who chooses the one which contains a portrait of Portia, wins her as his bride. Each casket is of a different metal and each bears a motto: one of gold reads 'Who chooseth me shall gain what many men desire', one of silver reads 'Who chooseth me shall get as much as he

[1] *The Phoenix and the Turtle*, ll. 37 and 36.
[2] The following section uses and develops some ideas which I first published in my Arden edition of *The Merchant of Venice* (1955).

deserves', and one of lead reads 'Who chooseth me must give and hazard all he hath'. Morocco, the type of those who make their choice in love for the sake of what they will 'gain', chooses gold and finds inside a skull—a reminder that death must cancel all such gain; Arragon, who presumes to take what 'he deserves', finds a fool's head; Bassanio who is willing to 'give and hazard', who does not mind the quality of the casket if he finds Portia within it, chooses lead and wins the bride of his choice. It could not be otherwise if love's true wealth, unlike commercial wealth, should be 'in bounty' cherished, if 'giving', not 'gaining' or 'getting', is essential to love. And so by these contrasts, clearly and formally, the wooing of Portia is related to Shakespeare's ideal.

As in *The Comedy of Errors* and *The Shrew*, this ideal is contrasted with a frankly commercial wealth, but here Shakespeare has broadened his theme. Previously commerce has been presented, in contrast to love, as concerned solely with possession and gain; now Shakespeare shows that it can involve personal relationships as well. Both Shylock and Antonio get their livelihood by commerce, but Antonio is ready to submit the rights of commerce to the claims of love; he lends freely to his friend Bassanio without security, although he has squandered previous loans and although it involves risking his own life by giving a bond to Shylock for a pound of his flesh. This is to 'give and hazard'. In contrast, Shylock, the Jew, demands his rights; repeatedly he claims his due according to the bond,[1] and sees no reason to relent:

What judgement shall I dread, doing no wrong? . . .
The pound of flesh, which I demand of him,
Is dearly bought; 'tis mine and I will have it.
If you deny me, fie upon your law!
There is no force in the decrees of Venice.
I stand for judgement: answer; shall I have it?
(IV. i. 89-103)

---

[1] cf. IV. i. 37, 87, 139, 242, 253, and 259, etc.

Shylock stands 'for law' (IV. i. 142): he disregards the plea for mercy because it has no 'compulsion' and he will not provide a surgeon to stop Antonio's wounds because there is no stipulation to that effect in the bond. He is content to cry:

> *My deeds upon my head! I crave the law,*
> *The penalty and forfeit of my bond.*
>
> (IV. i. 206-7)

In Shylock's eyes, this is to 'get what he deserves'. Both he and Antonio may be judged by the mottoes on the caskets.

The contrast between these two is emphasized much earlier in the play in a discussion about usury. As Antonio enters to negotiate the bond, Shylock discovers his hatred in an aside:

> *I hate him for he is a Christian,*
> *But more for that in low simplicity*
> *He lends out money gratis and brings down*
> *The rate of usance here with us in Venice. . . .*
>
> (I. iii. 43-6)

Shylock lends only for what he can gain, Antonio for the sake of friendship; he makes this clear to Shylock:

> *If thou wilt lend this money, lend it not*
> *As to thy friends; for when did friendship take*
> *A breed for barren metal of his friend?*
> *But lend it rather to thine enemy,*
> *Who, if he break, thou mayst with better face*
> *Exact the penalty.*
>
> (I. iii. 133-8)

This issue is maintained throughout the play. When Antonio is in prison because he cannot repay the loan, Shylock taunts him with 'This is the fool that lent out money gratis' (III. iii. 2).[1] Such generosity restricts the exercise of Shylock's rights and, as Antonio recognizes, is the main cause of his malice:

[1] See also III. i. 50-2.

I oft deliver'd from his forfeitures
Many that have at times made moan to me;
Therefore he hates.

(III. iii. 22-4)

It is sometimes argued that Shylock's affairs are so far
removed in kind from the affairs of the lovers at Belmont,
that the play falls into two parts. But, in one way the play
is very closely knit, for, besides contrasting Shylock with
Antonio, the discussion about usury is yet another contrast
between him and Portia and Bassanio. As we have seen from
the sonnets and *Romeo and Juliet*, Shakespeare saw love as a
kind of usury, and so in their marriage Bassanio and Portia
put Nature's bounty to its proper 'use'. Shylock practises a
usury for the sake of gain and is prepared to enforce his
rights; the lovers practice their usury without compulsion,
for the joy of giving:

> *That use is not forbidden usury*
> *Which happies those that pay the willing loan.*[1]

As soon as Bassanio has chosen the right casket, being ready
to 'give and hazard all', Portia knows love's 'increase':

> *O love,*
> *Be moderate; allay thy ecstasy;*
> *In measure rein thy joy; scant this* excess.
> *I feel too much thy blessing: make it less,*
> *For fear I surfeit.*

(III. ii. 111-5)

Antonio has already used the word 'excess' meaning
'usury',[2] and remembering Juliet's:

> *. . . my true love is* grown *to such* excess
> *I cannot* sum up *sum of half my* wealth *. . .*[3]

the same sense seems to be required here. Bassanio's first
reaction is to wonder at the beauty of the portrait[4] which he

[1] *Sonn.*, vi.   [2] I. iii. 62-3.   [3] *Rom.*, II. vi. 33-4.
[4] See below, pp. 105–9

finds inside the casket, then he finds a scroll ('The continent
and summary of my *fortune*') which tells him to '*claim*' his
lady 'with a loving kiss'; at this point he uses yet another
commercial image:

> *A gentle scroll. Fair lady, by your leave;*
> *I* come by note, *to* give *and to* receive.
> (III. ii. 140-1)

To 'come by note' meant to present one's bill or I.O.U.;[1]
Bassanio has 'ventured' all and can now claim his 'fortune'.
But as every bill in the commerce of love implies both giving
and receiving, he is ready 'to give *and* to receive'; these are
the conditions of love's usury and so it is fitting that their
'bargain' (III. ii. 195) should be 'confirm'd, sign'd, ratified'
(III. ii. 149) with an interchange of kisses.

The comparison of the two usuries is part of a more
general comparison of commerce and love which is likewise
maintained throughout the play. From the beginning
Bassanio's quest has been described in commercial terms;
indeed, he might have equal claim with Antonio and Shylock for the title of 'The Merchant of Venice'. To Antonio
he outlines his plans as a means of getting 'clear of all the
debts' he owes (I. i. 134), trying, with little success, to present his intention of paying court to Portia as a good business
proposition. Antonio tells him that all this is unnecessary,
that such values are inappropriate to friendship, and thereupon Bassanio changes his tone, praising Portia in the
'innocence' (I. i. 145) of his love: she is indeed rich,
and—

> . . . *she is fair* and, *fairer than that word,*
> *Of wondrous virtues.* . . .
> (I. i. 162-3)

He '*values*' her as Cato's daughter, renowned for constancy
and virtue, and her 'sunny locks' are as the '*golden* fleece' for
which Jason ventured. The comparison with the golden

[1] Halliwell pointed this out in his edition of 1856.

fleece is particularly significant, for the phrase was used of
the fortunes for which merchants ventured; Drake, for
example, was said to have returned from his voyage round
the world bringing 'his golden fleece'.[1] In Bassanio's
description of Portia there is a curious, but, to those who
trade in love, a natural, confusion of her wealth, beauty, and
virtue; all these comprise her wealth in love. In Bassanio's
eyes she has all perfections, and, amazed by them, he sees
no obstacle to his fortune:

> *I have a mind presages me such* thrift,
> *That I should questionless be* fortunate!
> (I. i. 175-6)

When Bassanio has chosen the right casket, and comes
'by note, to give and to receive', Portia responds in similarly
commercial terms:

> *You see me, Lord Bassanio, where I stand,*
> *Such as I am: though for myself alone*
> *I would not be ambitious in my wish,*
> *To wish myself much better; yet, for you*
> *I would be trebled twenty times myself;*
> *A thousand times more fair, ten thousand times*
> *More rich . . .*
> (III. ii. 150-6)

Portia desires greater wealth only for Bassanio's sake:

> *That only to stand high in your* account,
> *I might in virtues, beauties, livings, friends,*
> Exceed account . . .
> (III. ii. 157-9)

She cannot possess enough of this kind of wealth to enable
her to give as generously as she would wish:

---

[1] G. Whitney, *Emblems* (1586), C2. See *Mer. V.*, III. ii. 242-4 and
Arden ed. *Mer. V.* (1955), p. lv, for further examples.

> *. . . but the* full sum *of me*
> *Is sum of something, which, to* term in gross,
> *Is an unlesson'd girl . . .*
>
> (III. ii. 159-61)

Bassanio's willingness to give and hazard is answered by Portia's giving, and the contract of love is complete. So the willing, generous, and prosperous transactions of love's wealth are compared and contrasted with Shylock's wholly commercial transactions in which gain is the object, enforcement the method, and even human beings are merely things to be possessed.

Normally in Shakespeare's early narrative comedies, hero and heroine are betrothed at the end of the very last scene of the play where there is little time for the expression of sentiment ; *The Merchant of Venice* is the major exception to this, presenting Portia's modest, eager, rich-hearted committal to Bassanio in the third act. In consequence, Shakespeare is not only able to show how love's wealth is risked, given, and multiplied, but also how it is possessed. At the end of Portia's speech of self-giving, she 'commits' herself to Bassanio :

> *. . . to be directed,*
> *As from her lord, her governor, her king.*
>
> (III. ii. 166-7)

All her wealth is made over as if it were a commercial possession :

> *Myself and what is mine to you and yours*
> *Is now* converted : *but now I was the lord*
> *Of this fair mansion, master of my servants,*
> *Queen o'er myself; and even now, but now,*
> *This house, these servants and this same myself*
> Are yours, *my lord: I give them with this ring. . . .*
>
> (III. ii. 168-73)

Bassanio is told never to part with the ring, and in his confused joy, he can only swear that he will keep it for life. The story of Portia and Bassanio is by no means complete at this point; love is not like merchandise, it is not simply a question of possessor and possessed.

This is at once apparent: when news comes that Shylock is about to enforce the penalty to which his bond entitles him, Portia finds she has yet more to give; she is ready to forgo wealth and delay her marriage rights, and she urges Bassanio to leave for Venice before nightfall. A line sums up her response:

> Since you are dear bought, *I will love you* dear.
>   (III. ii. 316)

Pope relegated this to the foot of the page in his edition on the grounds that its commercial attitude was unworthy of Shakespeare, but 'dear' is used in the double sense of 'expensively' and 'with great affection'; the line, in fact, expresses Portia's willingness to continue to give joyfully in love. In the commerce of love, giving is the secret of keeping as well as of gaining.

Under this impulse, Portia herself goes to Venice and, disguised as a lawyer, defeats Shylock's claims. For this service she refuses payment:

> *He is well paid that is well satisfied;*
> *And I, delivering you, am satisfied*
> *And therein do* account *myself well* paid:
> *My mind was never yet more* mercenary.
>   (IV. i. 415-8)

Not recognizing Portia in the young lawyer, Antonio and Bassanio cannot know how deeply he is satisfied, how 'dearly' he has given; they do not know that he has acted with love's bounty. Portia chooses to bring this to their knowledge by the trick of asking Bassanio for the ring she gave him at their betrothal. At first he refuses because of his vow, but when he is left alone with Antonio, his love for this friend persuades him to send the ring to the young lawyer. This twist in the plot is resolved in the last act, and still further illustrates the kind of possession which is appropriate for love's wealth.

The act begins with music, and talk of ancient loves and of the harmony of the spheres, but when Portia, Bassanio, and Antonio enter, all harmony seems threatened by a quarrel over the ring of gold, the symbol of possession. They now talk about unfaithfulness, adultery, and cuckoldry. Bassanio's story is most unplausible and he is in a difficult position; as Portia protests with mock seriousness:

> *What man is there so much unreasonable,*
> *If you had pleased to have defended it*
> *With any terms of zeal, wanted the modesty*
> *To urge the thing held as a ceremony? . . .*
> *I'll die for't but some woman had the ring.*
>
> (V. i. 203-8)

Bassanio can only say that he was unable to refuse the one

> *. . . that did uphold the very life*
> *Of my dear friend. . . .*
> *I was beset with shame and courtesy;*
> *My honour would not let ingratitude*
> *So much besmear it.*
>
> (V. i. 214-9)

But when Antonio interjects that he is willing to 'be bound again', with his 'soul upon the forfeit', that Bassanio will 'never more break faith advisedly' (V. i. 251-3), Portia returns the ring, and perplexity is soon resolved. And Bassanio is soon pardoned, for he has erred only through generosity to his friend. The whole episode is a light-hearted reminder that Portia has saved Antonio's life, and that the claim of generosity must always rank as high as that of possession.

The bawdy talk, which the misunderstandings provoke, also serves an important purpose; hitherto Bassanio and Portia have conducted their courtship and love in unsensual terms, almost as if the body was always a quietly acquiesing follower of the mind and spirit, but the manner in which they weather the disagreement about the ring shows that their love is appropriate to the world as well as to Belmont, the 'beautiful mountain' of a fairy-tale. The wealth of love, although it exists in the free giving of both parties to the contract and is possessed by neither one of them, has yet to be kept safe and guarded: so the blunt, unromantic Gratiano who has been as merrily fooled by Nerissa as Bassanio has been by Portia, finishes the play:

> *Well, while I live I'll fear no other thing*
> *So sore as keeping safe Nerissa's ring.*
>
> (V. i. 306-7)

After the ring episode, we know that Bassanio and Portia will be equally wise. If *The Merchant of Venice* is seen as a play about Shakespeare's ideal of love's wealth, this last act is a fitting sequel to the discord of the trial scene where love and generosity confront hatred and possessiveness; it suggests the way in which love's wealth may be enjoyed continually.

The central theme of love's wealth is amplified in many other details which may seem irrelevant on casual inquiry. So Jessica's story has its contribution; she escapes with Lorenzo from behind the locked doors of Shylock's house, squanders the Venetian wealth she has stolen in joyful celebration, and then finds peace and happiness with her *'unthrift* love' (V. i. 16) in the garden of Belmont. If her reckless prodigality is a fault, it is a generous one and an understandable excess after the restriction of her father's precept of

> *Fast bind, fast find;*
> *A proverb never stale in* thrifty *mind.*
>
> (II. v. 54-5)

She has her due place at Belmont. And Launcelot Gobbo earns his place there by joining Bassanio's household; Shylock may have good reason for calling him an *'unthrifty*

knave' (I. iii. 177) but we also recognize Launcelot's good
sense in counting it a fine fortune

> *To leave a rich Jew's service, to become*
> *The follower of so poor a gentleman.*
>
> (II. ii. 156-7)

The ideal of love's wealth which relates and contrasts Shylock and Antonio, and Shylock and Portia and Bassanio, also
informs the contrasts and relationships between the subsidiary narrative plots ; in the final scene the easily responsive
love of Jessica and Lorenzo, the bolder love of Gratiano and
Nerissa, and Launcelot's unseeing pleasure in his master's
good fortune, all contribute to the judgement on life which is
implicit in the play as a whole.

The reservations which must be made before Jessica,
Gratiano, and Launcelot fit into the general pattern illustrate
an important quality of the play. Shakespeare has not simply
contrived a contrast of black and white, a measured interplay
of abstract figures with every detail fitting neatly into a pre-
determined pattern ; the lovers are not all paragons and Shylock's cry for revenge is not without a 'kind of wild justice'.
Judged against Shakespeare's ideal of love's wealth we
cannot doubt on which side our sympathies should rest, but
such final harmony is only established after we have judged,
as in life, between mixed motives and imperfect responses.
Even when the central theme has been recognized, *The
Merchant of Venice* is not an 'easy' play ; it presents an action
to which we must respond as to a golden ideal, and also as to
a human action.

We have already noticed Shakespeare's achievement of
this double purpose in dialogue ; for example, when Portia
gives herself to Bassanio Shakespeare has not provided a
well-rounded expression of generosity in love for her to
utter ; her speech also embodies modesty, eagerness, and a
gathering confidence, feelings that in a human context must
attend such generosity. Action and dialogue are allied to the
same end ; so Shakespeare presented Bassanio's ill-judged

attempt to justify his venture in commercial terms and followed that by his confused description of Portia's wealth, at first formal, then quickening, glowing, almost boasting, and, finally, blindly confident. Such technique does not simply present a theoretical ideal of love's adventurer, but a human being, fearful and eager, inspired and embarrassed as he realizes the possibilities of love's wealth. In human terms his is a difficult role, for he must feel the confusion of one who asks:

> ... *how do I hold thee by thy* granting *?*
> *And for that* riches *where is my deserving ?*[1]

For the role of Bassanio the 'humanizing' of action and dialogue has been so thorough that its ideal implications are in some danger of being obscured. Some critics have discounted the embarrassment of love's largess and, because of his round-about approach to Antonio, have called Bassanio a heartless 'fortune-hunter'—and in doing so they have failed to see the balance and judgement of the play as a whole.

Shylock is in greatest danger of causing such misinterpretation. This is truly surprising, for in order to bring generosity and possessiveness into intense conflict Shakespeare has made him perpetrate the outrageous deeds of some fantastic villain whom we might expect to see punished without compunction. Moreover Shylock is a Jew and therefore, for an Elizabethan audience, one of an exotic, fabulous race to whom cunning, malice, and cruelty were natural satisfactions; Jews lived obscurely in Shakespeare's London, but in literature and popular imagination they were monstrous bogeys from strange, far-off places and times, fit only to be reviled or mocked.[2] Shakespeare exploited both

---

[1] *Sonn.*, lxxxvii.

[2] cf. C. J. Sisson, *Essays and Studies*, xxiii (1938), 38-51 and J. L. Cardozo, *The Contemporary Jew in the Elizabethan Drama* (1925). It has been argued that Shylock offered his loan in genuine friendship, but Shakespeare has gone out of his way to inform us that, before Jessica eloped and before he had news of Antonio's losses, Shylock had hoped to take 'Antonio's flesh' (III. ii. 289); see also I. iii. 48.

Shylock's irrational, or devilish, motivation and the outrage of his action, but he has presented him in such a way that an audience can find itself implicated in his inhuman demands. Shakespeare seems to have done everything in his power to encourage this reaction. Our revulsion from Shylock's hatred and cruelty is mitigated by the way in which his opponents goad and taunt him; we might suppose that he was driven to excessive hatred only through their persecution. Shakespeare also arranged that he should voice his grievances and plead his case in the play's most obviously lively and impassioned dialogue. This treatment is so successful that when Shylock tries to justify his murderous purpose, some critics have believed that he is making a grand, though tortured, plea for human tolerance. But to go to such lengths of sympathy for Shylock is to neglect the contrasts and comparisons implicit in the play as a whole; we must judge his actions against a purposefully contrasted generosity in love as portrayed by Antonio, Portia, Bassanio, and others. Indeed we may guess that it was in order to make this contrast lively and poignant that Shakespeare has laboured to implicate us in Shylock's hatred, frustration, and pain.

The outcome of the comparison cannot be long in question for judged by Shakespeare's ideal of love's wealth as expressed here and in other comedies, the sonnets and *Romeo and Juliet*, we cannot doubt that Shylock must be condemned. However lively Shylock's dialogue may be, however plausibly and passionately he presents his case, however cruelly the lovers treat him, he must still be defeated, because he is an enemy to love's wealth and its free, joyful, and continual giving; in opposition to this he has 'contrived against the very life' (IV. i. 360) of Antonio, the 'fool that lent out money gratis'.

But this judgement cannot be made lightly; the mirror that Shakespeare held up to nature was unsparing in its truth, and, by presenting his ideal in human terms, he has shown that those who oppose the fortunes of lovers are apt to get more than justice as punishment at their hands. It is Shylock's fate to bring out the worst in those he tries to harm: the 'good Antonio' shows unfeeling contempt towards him, the light-hearted Salerio and Solanio[1] become wantonly malicious when they meet him, and Portia, once she has turned the trial against him, wounds him still further with sarcastic humour. The trial scene shows that the pursuit of love's wealth does not necessarily bring with it a universal charity, a love which reaches even to one's enemies. The balance is fairly kept, for Antonio and the Duke magnanimously spare Shylock's life and this is thrown into relief by the irresponsible malice of Gratiano.

Shakespeare does not enforce a moral in this play—his judgement is implicit only—but as the action ends in laughter and affection at Belmont we know that each couple, in their own way, have found love's wealth. We know too that their happiness is not all that we would wish; as they make free with Shylock's commercial wealth, we remember that they lacked the full measure of charity towards one who, through his hatred and possessiveness, had got his choice of that which he deserved. *The Merchant of Venice* presents in human and dramatic terms Shakespeare's ideal of love's wealth, its abundant and sometimes embarrassing riches; it shows how this wealth is gained and possessed by giving freely and joyfully; it shows also how destructive the opposing possessiveness can become, and how it can cause those who traffic in love to fight blindly for their existence.

Because such judgements are not made explicit in the play, we, as an audience in the theatre, may never become consciously aware of them; we would almost certainly fail in our response if, during performance, our whole attention was given to recognizing and elucidating such judgements. But, consciously or unconsciously, they were in Shakespeare's mind as he wrote the play and helped to control its

[1] So most texts following Q1; the Globe edition, following Q2, names three characters, Salanio, Salarino, and Salerio.

shape, its contrasts, relationships and final resolution, and
to direct and colour the detail of its dialogue; and it therefore follows that as we respond to the action and dialogue
on the stage, as we follow with spontaneous interest and
delight, these judgements will, consciously or unconsciously,
impress themselves on our minds; they are the pattern of the
dance that we are appreciating and in which, imaginatively,
we participate. To understand that dance, to hold it more
fully in our memory, we must also learn to appreciate its
pattern; to understand the full beauty and truth of Shakespeare's comedy we must become conscious of the ideals and
implicit judgements that inform it.

*   *   *

Shakespeare was so deeply concerned with the ideal of
love's wealth in *The Merchant of Venice* that we may presume
that it was fundamental to his thinking and feeling about
human relationships and expect it to inform the selection,
ordering, and treatment of the action and dialogue of all his
romantic comedies.

The chief judgement of *Love's Labour's Lost* lies in a
comparison between affectations, illusions, and 'simplicity';[1]
but in so far as it presents the loves of the king and princess
and of their followers, it is informed by the ideal of love's
wealth. The young king and his courtiers wish, like Rosaline
in *Romeo and Juliet* and the youth of the sonnets, to 'have
traffic' with themselves alone and not to

> ... *stay the siege of loving terms,*
> *Nor bide the encounter of assailing eyes.*[2]

From the first Biron complains against this 'waste in
niggarding':

> *O, these are* barren *tasks, too hard to keep,*
> *Not to see ladies, study, fast, not sleep!*
>
> (I. i. 47-8)

---

[1] See below, pp. 130-4.   [2] *Rom.*, I. i. 218-9.

Study and learning alone cannot bring true increase:

> *These earthly godfathers of heaven's lights*
> *That give a name to every fixed star*
> *Have* no more profit *of their shining nights*
> *Than those that walk and wot not what they are.*
>
> (I. i. 88-91)

When the others find that their affections have grown too strong for their affectation of solitariness, Biron praises the increase and wealth of love:

> *For when would you, my liege, or you, or you,*
> *In* leaden *contemplation have found out*
> *Such fiery* numbers *as the prompting eyes*
> *Of beauty's tutors have* enrich'd *you with?*
> *Other slow arts entirely keep the brain;*
> *And therefore, finding* barren *practisers,*
> *Scarce show a* harvest *of their heavy toil:*
> *But, love, first learned in a lady's eyes,*
> *Lives not alone immured in the brain;*
> *But, with the motion of all elements,*
> *Courses as swift as thought in every power,*
> *And* gives *to every power a* double *power,*
> *Above their functions and their offices.* . . .
>
> (IV. iii. 320-32)

When they hasten to the ladies and present a masque of Muscovites for their entertainment, they are mocked for their pains. In Rosaline Biron finds his match, and can only bring the wealth of love to witness his good intention:

> *We* number *nothing that we* spend *for you:*
> *Our duty is so* rich, *so infinite,*
> *That we may do it still without* accompt.
>
> (V. ii. 198-200)

On this protestation one might expect love's bargain to be clapped up. But as the young men had affected solitariness, so they might be affecting their desire to give in love, and their letters and favours might be merely 'courtship, pleasant jest and courtesy' (V. ii. 790); there has not been a test of their true intentions as in *The Shrew*, nor a hazard of friend, fortune, and other marriages as in *The Merchant*. So when Mercade brings news of the death of the princess's father, the king's suit is rejected because the present moment is

> *A time, . . . too short*
> *To make a* world-without-end bargain *in*
> (V. ii. 798-9)

and the princess decrees a twelve months' trial before the '*reckoning*' (V. ii. 808) of their oaths and constancy.

Indeed the ideal of love's wealth demanded such delay. The Princess could not give in return when her heart was mourning for her father, and the king cannot have truly considered her wishes in pressing his suit at such a time. The king and his fellows have much to learn in their twelve months; love's generosity should reach to all who come in true 'zeal' (V. ii. 518) to do them service, yet they have mocked the pageant of Worthies out of countenance, so that Holofernes, the schoolmaster, could reprove and correct them with 'This is not *generous*,[1] not gentle, not humble' (V. ii. 632). In twelve months their generosity may be stronger and their will more humble, and if Armado, as Hector, should then crave 'Sweet royalty, *bestow* on me the sense of hearing' they may give generously in the words of the Princess—'Speak, brave Hector: we are much delighted' (V. ii. 669-72); recognizing true zeal, they may then take the giver at his word, and in the spirit he desires. Until they know this humility in giving, they cannot expect a 'world-without-end bargain' to be made on the mere protestation of their service; Holofernes' reproof shows that they are, as yet, a 'little o'erparted' (V. ii. 588) in the role of venturers for love's wealth.

[1] In Shakespeare's time the word 'generous' implied the possession of an ideal magnanimity; cf. *N.E.D.*, s.v. 2.

The action of *A Midsummer Night's Dream* is chiefly concerned with enchantments and errors in the wood outside Athens, but reference to the ideal of love's wealth gives a measure of the affections of the young lovers at the beginning of the play. Neither Demetrius nor Lysander is then ready to make love's bargain, for both demand their rights and possessions; so Demetrius pleads:

> *Relent, sweet Hermia: and, Lysander, yield*
> *Thy crazed title to my certain right*
>
> (I. i. 91-2)

and Lysander contests:

> *I am, my lord, as well derived as he,*
> *As well possess'd; my love is more than his;*
> *My fortunes every way as fairly rank'd,*
> *If not with vantage, as Demetrius';*
> *And, which is more than all these boasts can be,*
> *I am beloved of beauteous Hermia:*
> *Why should not I then prosecute my right?*
>
> (I. i. 99-105)

A true lover might take the same line, but he would not speak in the same terms; he would know that his 'rights' to love's wealth could not survive an 'audit by advised respects' and would acknowledge:

> *To leave poor me thou hast the strength of laws,*
> *Since why to love I can allege no cause.*[1]

Knowing so little of love's true wealth, the lovers are fooled, tantalized, and enchanted in the wood.

Such an apprisal of the characters helps towards an understanding of *The Merry Wives of Windsor*. Here Falstaff makes suit to the two wives as a means of getting ready money:

[1] *Sonn.*, xlix.

I will be cheater[1] *to them both, and they shall be* exchequers
to me; they shall be my East and West Indies, and I will
trade *to them both* . . . *we will* thrive, *lads, we will* thrive.
(I. iii. 77-83)

Falstaff's 'French *thrift*' (I. iii. 93) is matched by Shallow's
and Sir Hugh's plan to marry Slender to Anne Page on the
strength of 'Seven hundred pounds and possibilities'
(I. i. 65-6), and Ford's refusal to be a 'secure fool' (II. i. 241)
and his hopes to purchase a knowledge of his wife with
money. These mercenary and possessive loves are contrasted
with Fenton's for Anne Page; in his poverty it seems impossible that he should love her 'but as a *property*' (III. iv. 10)
but he assures her that:

> . . . *wooing thee, I found thee of more value*
> *Than stamps in* gold *or sums in* sealed bags;
> *And 'tis the very* riches *of thyself*
> *That now I aim at.*

(III. iv. 15-8)

So the characters are disposed for the merry action, in which
only Fenton and Anne are clear of all mistaking.

Sometimes the use or abuse of love's wealth helps to
evaluate a single puzzling character. In *Much Ado About
Nothing*, Claudio's love for Hero seems a poor thing against
Benedick's for Beatrice and, when he asks for Don Pedro's
assurance that Hero is Leonato's 'only heir' (I. i. 297), his
motives are open to question. Yet when he speaks in innocence and with more confidence, he voices true generosity
in love: his suit has been made known and Leonato formally
presents Hero to him—

> *Count, take of me my daughter, and with her my* fortunes:
> *his grace hath made the* match,[2] *and all grace say Amen to
> it.* (II. i. 314-6)

---

[1] There is a pun on 'cheater' as the 'officer appointed to look after the
king's escheats' (*N.E.D.*), and on the surviving sense of 'swindler'.

[2] See above, p. 58, note 1.

Claudio is silent at first so that Beatrice interjects 'Speak, count, 'tis your cue', and only then does he confess and refute Leonato's commercial terms:

> *Silence is the perfectest herald of joy: I were but little happy, if I could* say how much. *Lady, as you are mine, I am yours: I* give away *myself for you and dote upon the* exchange.
> (II. i. 318-20.)

Claudio's silence lends emphasis and the impression of sincerity to his assurance; he knows the abundant wealth of love, and our view of his subsequent action must take this into account.

Likewise when we judge Silvius in *As You Like It* we must remember that, however absurd his unrequited love for Phoebe may be, he does stumble forward in the right direction. He knows how much of love lies in the *giving* of faith, service, duty, observance, 'humbleness' (V. ii. 89-105) and he feels something of love's wealth : so he assures Phoebe—

> *So holy and so perfect is my love,*
> *And I in such a* poverty *of grace,*
> *That I shall think it a most* plenteous crop
> *To glean the broken ears after the man*
> *That the main* harvest *reaps: loose now and then*
> *A scatter'd smile, and that I'll* live upon.
>
> (III. v. 99-104)

True lovers agree with his account of 'what 'tis to love' and, with 'measure heap'd in joy' (V. iv. 185), they all join with him in the dance which concludes the play. Silvius is one of the number whom we are invited to judge over against Jaques, the melancholy philosopher who alone refuses to enjoy the dance; Silvius will do and give all for Phoebe's sake, Jaques, who seldom thanks 'any man' (II. v. 25-6), will neglect love's wealth because

> *. . . out of these convertites*
> *There is much matter to be heard and learn'd*
>
> (V. iv. 190-1)

—he is off, not to give, but to gain, to suck more matter, 'as a weasel sucks eggs' (II. v. 13-14).

In the final scene of *As You Like It*, as in those of *Love's Labour's Lost*, the *Dream*, and *Much Ado*, far more is involved than the ideal of love's wealth, for the action and dialogue of these plays have brought other ideas and human conflicts into prominence, and invite other judgements. But this ideal was fundamental to Shakespeare's thought and feeling about love and personal relationships, and therefore in each of the romantic comedies it has its contribution to make to the complex harmony of the whole play.

CHAPTER IV

Love's Truth and the Judgements of
A Midsummer Night's Dream and
Much Ado About Nothing

The search for the way in which Shakespeare's ideal of love's wealth informs *The Merchant of Venice* might begin by tracing recurrent words and images, but it would have to proceed by evaluating the contrasted attitudes of a whole range of characters, and would, at last, be concerned with a wider, and necessarily less precise, account of the characterization and action of the play as a whole. In the sonnets Shakespeare could define and elaborate an ideal of love's wealth—a commerce in which giving is more important than getting and in which the lover's powers of giving appear to be of no account before the wealth of the beloved—but in *The Merchant of Venice* this 'idea' is endowed with 'feature' and 'form and pressure' in a representation of human action. In this comedy the defining words of argument or the images of poetic statement are only part of the complex image of human action, thought, and feeling which is the two or three hours' traffic on the stage; in other words, the poetic 'idea' of love's wealth is here apprehended and presented in terms of a lively and complex dramatic action. Shylock's pungent thrusting dialogue, quickening in malice, triumph, or mockery, and hesitating in calculation or pain, the ordering of his entries and exits, his frequent asides, and the smallest of the actions and gestures which arise from his dialogue are all as representative of his possessiveness and hatred as the actual words with which he claims the forfeit due upon his bond;

and the contrast with the generosity and love of Portia, Bassanio, and Antonio is apprehended in similarly lively and complex dramatic details.

In this sense, all Shakespeare's comedies are truly dramatic poems, and in seeking further knowledge of the ideals which inform them it is well to start with an idea which is expressed in action as well as in speech; we may consider, for example, the notion that lovers, in various ways, 'see' each other.

*   *   *

The commonest form in which Shakespeare presents the mutual recognition of two lovers is the realization of each other's beauty. For the young lovers in *A Midsummer Night's Dream*, such realization carries its own conviction of exclusive truth; Hermia will not 'choose love by another's eyes' (I. i. 140), and, when Duke Theseus orders her to marry Demetrius whom her father favours, she answers in a single line:

> *I would my father look'd but with my eyes.*
> (I. i. 56)

Even if a lover is inconstant he will always demand the use of his own eyes,[1] and neither the authority of a father nor the force of general opinion can displace a conviction based on such experience.[2] Some lovers, like Helena, may live by such a 'truth' even though they recognize that it is exclusive and irrational:

> *Things base and vile, holding no quantity,*
> *Love can transpose to form and dignity:*
> *Love looks not with the eyes, but with a mind;*
> *And therefore is wing'd Cupid painted blind: . . . .*
> (I. i. 232-9)

In this comedy the irrationality of love's choice provides

---

[1] cf. *All's W.*, II. iii. 115.   [2] cf. I. i. 227-9.

sport rather than grief. The action takes place in a wood where moonlight and fairy influence suspend our belief in lasting hardship; sometimes a bush may seem to be a bear, but contrariwise even a bear may seem to have no more awful reality than a shadow and may vanish as easily. Moreover the dialogue of the lovers is light and agile so that we are not allowed to dwell upon frustration or suffering. When the sport natural to blind Cupid is heightened by Oberon's enchantment of the lovers' eyes and when events befall preposterously, we find that, even in the telling of the 'saddest tale', a 'merrier hour was never wasted' (II. i. 51-7).

But our laughter is not thoughtless, for, by bringing Bottom and his fellows to the wood to rehearse a play for the duke's nuptials, Shakespeare has contrived a contrast to the lovers' single-minded pursuit of their own visions of beauty. Once more Shakespeare's comic vision is expressed in contrasts and relationships; Bottom is the sober man by whom we judge the intoxicated. When Lysander's eyes have been touched with the magic herb, he rationalizes his new love for Helena in the loftiest terms:

> *Not Hermia but Helena I love:*
> *Who will not change a raven for a dove?*
> *The will of man is by his* reason *sway'd;*
> *And* reason *says you are the worthier maid.*
> (II. ii. 113-16)

Without the agency of magic but simply because Demetrius scorns her, Helena has come to believe that she is as 'ugly as a bear' (II. ii. 94), and protests, as if it were self-evident:

> *. . . I did never, no, nor never can,*
> *Deserve a sweet look from Demetrius' eye.*
> (II. ii. 126-7)

Helena rationally judges that Lysander's love is a 'flout' for her own 'insufficiency'. And when, in the next scene, Titania is charmed to love Bottom whom Puck has disfigured with

an ass's head, she too declares her love as if she were convinced by the best of reasons:

> *I pray thee, gentle mortal, sing again:*
> *Mine ear is much enamour'd of thy note;*
> *So is mine eye enthralled to thy shape;*
> *And thy fair virtue's force perforce doth move me*
> *On the first view to say, to swear, I love thee.*
>
> (III. i. 140-4)

With more modesty in judgement, Bottom answers the
other lovers as well as Titania:

> *Methinks, mistress, you should have a little* reason *for that:
> and yet, to say the truth,* reason *and love keep little company
> together now-a-days; the more the pity that some honest
> neighbours will not make them friends.* (III. i. 145-9.)

Bottom's modesty in judgement is well placed, for life makes
fewer demands on him—'if I had wit enough to get out of
this wood, I have enough to serve mine own turn' (III. i.
152-4)—he is not asked to love and also to be wise; his
judgement is not at the mercy of his eyes.

When Oberon's spell is broken, Bottom seems to have
had a strange dream, but it does not count for so much as the
helpless game the lovers have played; much as he would like
to, Bottom dares not tell his dream, but the lovers must tell
theirs, even to the sceptical ear of Theseus. As the vagaries
of love and enchantment had seemed perfectly reasonable to
those who were involved, and unreasonable or ridiculous to
those who had only observed, so the whole action in the
wood, once the first sight of day has passed, will seem more
real or more fantastic.

Such reflections are made explicit at the beginning of Act
V, in the dialogue of Theseus and his bride, Hippolyta. And
at this point the play is given a new dimension; previously
we had watched the action as if we were Olympians laughing at the strutting seriousness of mortals; now we seem to
take a step backwards and watch others watching the action:

—'*Tis strange, my Theseus, that these lovers speak of.*
—*More strange than* true : *I never may believe*
These antique fables, nor these fairy toys.
Lovers and madmen have such seething brains,
Such shaping fantasies, that apprehend
More than cool reason ever comprehends.

(V. i. 1-6)

And not content with likening a lover's truth to that of a madman, Theseus equates these with the poet's :

The lunatic, the lover and the poet
Are of imagination all compact :
One sees more devils than vast hell can hold,
That is, the madman : the lover, all as frantic,
Sees Helen's beauty in a brow of Egypt :
The poet's eye, in a fine frenzy rolling,
Doth glance from heaven to earth, from earth to heaven ;
And as imagination bodies forth
The forms of things unknown, the poet's pen
Turns them to shapes and gives to airy nothing
A local habitation and a name. . . .

(V. i. 7-17)

For a moment, the image in the glass of the stage is strangely lightened ; has the action we have witnessed the inconsequence of mere contrivance, or has it the constancy of a poet's[1] imagination? Is it 'more strange than true', or is there some 'truth' in the lovers' visions of beauty, in the moonlight and enchantments, in Oberon's jealousy and Puck's mistaking? Our judgement hesitates with Hippolyta's :

---

[1] In Shakespeare's day 'poet' was used in a general sense after Greek and Latin usage: 'One who makes or composes works of literature; an author, writer' (*N.E.D.*, s.v. Ib); it is used for 'dramatist' in *Ham.*, II. ii. 373. See also B. Jonson, 'To the memory of my beloved, The AUTHOR' prefixed to the Shakespeare 1623 Folio.

> *. . . all the story of the night told over,*
> *And all their minds transfigured so together,*
> *More witnesseth than fancy's images*
> *And grows to something of great constancy;*
> *But, howsoever, strange and admirable.*
>
> (V. i. 23-7)

Possibly we know no more than Demetrius, rubbing his eyes in the daylight:

> *. . . I wot not by what power,—*
> *But by some power it is. . . .*
>
> (IV. i. 168-9)

Our reactions will vary, depending on whether we are stalwart like Bottom, disengaged like Puck, or fanciful like lovers, madmen, and poets. From telling an idle story of magic and love's entangling eyes, Shakespeare has led us to contemplate the relationship between nature and the 'art' of lovers and poets; he has led us to recognize the absurdity, privacy, and 'truth' of human imagination.[1]

Hard on the heels of this questioning moment, comes talk of a masque or a play to 'beguile The lazy time' (V. i. 40-1); this, it seems, is 'where we came in'. But for the 'second time round' the perspective will be changed and we shall watch others watching the play. For us this will be the chief interest of the performance, for, having watched rehearsals, we know precisely the kind of play to expect; again it will be about love and again it will take place by moonlight, but this time the plot will end disastrously. Our interest will lie in whether or not the performance will also be disastrous.

The actors are fully confident; they are so sure of their make-believe that, for fear of frightening the ladies, they must take special precautions before they draw a sword or

---

[1] The beginning of Act V which gives this new perspective, shows signs of revision; Sir Walter Greg believes that it represents Shakespeare's last touches to his play before handing it over to the book-keeper in the theatre (*First Folio* (1955), p. 242).

let their lion roar.[1] But we may doubt whether they will get
any help from their text:

> ... *for in all the play*
> *There is not one word apt, one player fitted.*
> (V. i. 64-5)

As with the pageant at the end of *Love's Labour's Lost*, the
actors are at the mercy of their audience, their success
depending on the audience's ability to be sufficiently
generous, gentle, and humble to 'bestow . . . the sense of
hearing'.[2] We cannot be confident of the outcome. Theseus
has previously 'pick'd a welcome' from the silence of those
who, having prepared entertainment for him, have throttled

> ... *their practised accent in their fears*
> *And in conclusion dumbly have broke off,*
> *Not paying me a welcome.*
> (V. i. 97-9)

but he is also apt to measure lovers' fancies and 'antique
fables' by the comprehension of 'cool reason'. As for the
young lovers, we know that they are inclined to believe their
own dreams, but we have no proof that they will accept in
generosity all that 'simpleness and duty tender' (V. i. 83).[3]

In the event the actors put their faith, as the lovers had
done before them, in the 'truth' of their fiction:

> *Gentles, perchance you wonder at this show;*
> *But wonder on, till* truth *make all things plain.*
> (V. i. 128-9)

and again:

> *This loam, this rough-cast and this stone doth show*
> *That I am that same wall; the* truth *is so. . . .*
> (V. i. 162-3)

---

[1] cf. III. i. 9-47.
[2] *LLL.*, V. ii. 669-70; see above, p. 77.
[3] See above, p. 78.

But the response wavers, and Bottom has to interfere to correct a wrong impression :

—The wall, methinks, being sensible, should curse again.
—No, in truth, sir, he should not. 'Deceiving me' is Thisby's cue: she is to enter now, . . . You shall see, it will fall pat as I told you. (V. i. 183-8.)

Bottom's faith is invincible, but he cannot ensure success, and Hippolyta judges frankly that the play is 'the silliest stuff' that she has ever heard (V. i. 212-13).

At this point Theseus reminds them all of the nature of their entertainment :

—The best in this kind are but shadows; and the worst are no worse, if imagination amend them.
—It must be your imagination then, and not theirs.
—If we imagine no worse of them than they of themselves, they may pass for excellent men. (V. i. 214-20.)

In this spirit, Theseus welcomes the entering actors :

Here come two noble beasts in, a man and a lion.

The actors struggle to the end of their play : Moon, unable to complete his prepared speech by reason of the reception he is given, gamely, if somewhat tetchily, substitutes his own less fanciful words ; Bottom, with even more fortitude, leaves off talking once, as Pyramus, he is supposed to be dead, and he waits until the play is done before he rises to correct his audience and offer an epilogue.

So, unlike the pageant of the Worthies, the 'tedious brief scene' of Pyramus and Thisbe is completed. Theseus refuses the epilogue :

No epilogue, I pray you; for your play needs no excuse. Never excuse; for when the players are all dead, there need none to be blamed. (V. i. 362-5.)

'Truly' it has been a 'fine tragedy' (V. i. 367-8) and the players can celebrate with a Bergomask, a joyful country dance which is natural to their elation and abilities. Then Theseus must recall the lovers from the fiction they have been watching:

> *The iron tongue of midnight hath told twelve:*
> *Lovers, to bed; 'tis almost fairy time.*
>
> (V. i. 370-1)

The 'palpable-gross play' has beguiled the time, and they must now to their own parts. And as they file off in due order for the next scene, the fairies enter from the enchanted wood and, following them, bring blessing on their action.

If one wished to describe the judgement which informs *A Midsummer Night's Dream*, one might do so very simply: the play suggests that lovers, like lunatics, poets, and actors, have their own 'truth' which is established as they see the beauty of their beloved, and that they are confident in this truth for, although it seems the 'silliest stuff' to an outsider, to them it is quite reasonable; it also suggests that lovers, like actors, need, and sometimes ask for, our belief, and that this belief can only be given if we have the generosity and imagination to think 'no worse of them than they of themselves'.

The play's greatest triumph is the manner in which our wavering acceptance of the illusion of drama is used as a kind of flesh-and-blood image of the acceptance which is appropriate to the strange and private 'truth' of those who enact the play of love. By using this living image, Shakespeare has gone beyond direct statement in words or action and has presented his judgement in terms of a mode of being, a relationship, in which we, the audience, are actually involved. And he has ensured that this image is experienced at first hand, for the audience of the play-within-the-play does not make the perfect reaction; one of them describes what this entails but it is left for us to make that description good. The success of the play will, finally, depend upon our reaction to its shadows.[1]

* * *

[1] So Puck assures us; cf. V. i. 430-45.

As an actor, dramatist, and 'sharer' in the finances of a theatre company, Shakespeare was deeply concerned with the ways in which actors and audience accept the 'truth' of dramatic illusion, and, as a poet, he saw in these relationships an image of man's recognition of imagined truths. So the significance of the play-within-the-play in *A Midsummer Night's Dream* is enforced by the use of the same device in other comedies and in history-plays and tragedies.

In *Hamlet*, its use is clear enough. Claudius can witness the murder of Gonzago in the mere outline of a dumb-show without betraying his own guilt, but when *The Mouse-Trap* 'bodies forth' his crime, he rushes from the theatre calling for lights to distract his mind from the truth which lies in his 'bosom black as death' (III. iii. 67); he is forced to manifest his guilt—the 'galled jade' must 'wince'—because his imagination is all too ready to 'amend' the 'shadows' that appear before him. The play's action, acceptable as a fiction, is terrifying when imagination apprehends it as a reality in which one's self is fully involved. In the performance of *The Mouse-Trap* we are not made aware of the actor behind the assumed character as we were made aware of Bottom behind the fiction of Pyramus; this aspect of dramatic illusion has been utilized earlier in the play to show the integrity of Hamlet's imagination as compared with the professional adaptability of the player's. The part which Hamlet is called upon to act is so dreadful in its consequences that faith in its 'truth' must be absolute; its performance must not be in show alone but with the consent and participation of his entire self. This idea recurs later in the contemplation of Yorick's skull: now fully resolved to act his part, Hamlet greets the remembrance of the jester's performances with an assumed humour that dares to 'move wild laughter in the throat of death';[1] with such grim and resolved confidence Hamlet takes his place on the great stage.[2]

In *Titus Andronicus* Tamora and her sons assume the

---

[1] *LLL.*, V. ii. 865.   [2] cf. *Ham.*, V. ii. 345-6.

parts of Revenge, Rapine, and Murder with the object of acting a play to deceive the crazed and maimed Titus.[1] But their performances are not true to his imagination, and seeing through their fiction and disguises, he recognizes only his dangerous enemies. So Tamora's confident dissimulation, her belief that she could 'temper him' by her great cunning in 'art' (IV. iv. 109), is turned into the occasion of her own downfall. This episode has its due place in a formally constructed tragedy because it shows that Titus has his own clear concept of murderous Revenge, that 'shadows' performed by others cannot abuse his own terrible, inward certainty.

In the first part of *Henry IV*, a play-within-the-play is begun in jest, for the actors' gratification rather than the audience's. But the part of the king, which Prince Hal so lightly assumes, fits his imagination and jest turns to earnest; through the spirited dialogue of their fiction—

> . . . *for sweet Jack Falstaff, kind Jack Falstaff, true Jack Falstaff, valiant Jack Falstaff, . . . banish not him thy Harry's company: banish plump Jack, and banish all the world*— (II. iv. 521-7.)

break the hard and simple words 'I do, I will', spoken in the 'truth' of Hal's imagination. We become aware of illusion again when, to give temporary protection to Falstaff, Hal tells a lie and consciously assumes a false part:

> *Now, my masters, for a true face and good conscience.*
> (II. iv. 550-1)

By such means Prince Hal's inward spirit is contrasted with the appearance of a young wastrel.

Shakespeare's significant use of the living image of dramatic illusion in these scenes from *Hamlet*, *Titus*, and *I, Henry IV* suggests that we should examine more casual allusions to the stage with great care.

The image may be evoked without a fully developed

[1] cf. IV. iv. 89 and V. ii. 70.

play-within-the-play. When in *The Two Gentlemen of Verona*, for instance, Julia tells Silvia that she had played a 'lamentable' part in a pageant and that

> . . . *'twas Ariadne passioning*
> *For Theseus' perjury and unjust flight;*
> *Which I so lively acted with my tears*
> *That my poor mistress, moved therewithal,*
> *Wept bitterly. . . .*
>
> (IV. iv. 172-6)

we may readily acknowledge that she would lament from the heart in such a role. This is borne out when, with the Host, she watches Proteus courting Silvia: she is all attention but her companion falls 'fast asleep' (IV. ii. 136) for such a scene does not waken his imagination.

In *As You Like It* Silvius may well be a figure of fun in our eyes, but when his discourse on love is overheard by Rosalind, Celia, and Touchstone, Rosalind listens as at a play in which she recognizes a 'truth':

> *Alas, poor shepherd! searching of thy wound,*
> *I have by hard adventure found mine own. . . .*
>
> (II. iv. 44-62)

Celia, who as yet has never loved a man, is unmoved and turns briskly to more practical matters. Later in the play, Corin invites the others to entertain themselves at Silvius' expense:

> *If you will see a pageant truly play'd,*
> *Between the pale complexion of true love*
> *And the red glow of scorn and proud disdain, . . .*
> *I shall conduct you, . . .*
>
> (III. iv. 55-8)

To the aged Corin, love is like any other drama, but to those whose imaginations are prepared, its 'truth' is compulsive and quickly recognized. The point is made again near the end of the play when Phoebe, Orlando, and Rosalind echo Silvius in his high-flown description of romantic love; they are caught up in the reality of his private play.[1] There is another rudimentary play-within-the-play when Orlando and Ganymede (who is Rosalind disguised as a page), take part in a mock-marriage; so strong are their imaginations that the pretended action seems to draw forth 'real' responses.

* * *

In his developed use of the play-within-the-play, Shakespeare seems to suggest that for dramatic illusion to be complete, the amateur actor must have the imagination to be convinced of the 'truth' of his role, and the audience must have the imagination to amend his 'shadow'. In the comedies, he used the ideal amateur actor as an image of the ideal lover whose every action should perfectly express his imagination, should be a 'true' response to his complex, irrational, and compelling vision of the beloved's beauty. And a man's ability to accept a dramatic illusion performed by others was used by Shakespeare to show the nature of the onlooker's imagination, to show the quality of his inward nature.

In *The Taming of the Shrew* these ideas are of more than incidental importance; they govern the structure of the play as a whole. The first illusion is prepared when the servants agree to their lord's proposals for deceiving Christopher Sly, the drunken tinker:

> . . . *we will play our part,*
> *As he shall think by our true diligence*
> *He is no less than what we say he is.*
>   (Ind. i. 69-71)

On waking, Sly is quick to accept the appearance as reality and readily plays his part:

> *Upon my life, I am a lord indeed*
> *And not a tinker nor Christophero Sly.*
> *Well, bring our lady hither to our sight;*
> *And once again, a pot o' the smallest ale.*
>   (Ind. ii. 74-7)

---

[1] And for good reason; see above, p. 80.

He falls far behind the other actors in 'honourable action'
(Ind. i. 110) but he is happily unconscious of that which all
but he must know. Meanwhile another illusion is being
prepared by professional actors who can 'naturally' and with
modesty (Ind. i. 87 and 94) perform their parts. But Sly,
by his own lights so successful as an actor, makes a poor
audience, and before the first act is finished he is wishing
'would 'twere done' (I. i. 259); nothing more is heard from
him and we may suppose that, like the Host in *The Two
Gentlemen*, he is soon 'fast asleep'.[1]

The play-within-the-play, which holds the stage un-
challenged after Sly dozes off, starts with the entry of
Lucentio and Tranio and they are soon joined by Baptista,
Katharina, Bianca, and Bianca's suitors: 'But stay a while,'
says Lucentio, 'what company is this?', and Tranio answers:
'Master, some show to welcome us to town' (I. i. 46-7). So
they 'stand by'[2] and become an audience. They are both
clear about what they see:

> Tranio. *Hush, master! here's some good pastime toward:*
> *That wench is stark mad or wonderful froward.*
> Lucentio. *But in the other's silence do I see*
> *Maid's mild behaviour and sobriety.*
> *Peace, Tranio!*
>
> (I. i. 68-72)

When the 'show' is finished, Tranio has to explain more
than half the business:

[1] In *The Taming of A Shrew*, a play which is probably a written-up report
of a version of Shakespeare's *Taming of the Shrew*, Sly is eager to watch the
play, takes part in its action, and, when all is done, goes off to tame his own
shrew. Some scholars believe that the play in the 1623 Shakespeare Folio lacks
a similar conclusion, but the last dozing words of Sly in that text (I. ii. 254-9)
seem sufficiently Shakespearian to allow us to assume that if this were so, the
cut and adaptation were made by Shakespeare himself. Hemminge and Condell,
the actors from Shakespeare's company who were responsible for the 1623
Folio, were content with the text as it is printed and the present argument
gives some grounds for believing that Shakespeare was responsible for that
form of the play, even if he also provided an alternative one. See below, p. 98.

[2] Folio stage direction.

> *—Master, you look'd so longly on the maid,*
> *Perhaps you mark'd not what's the pith of all.*
> *—O yes, I saw sweet beauty in her face,*
> *Such as the daughter of Agenor had, . . .*
>
> (I. i. 170ff.)

It is Tranio who understands the situation and calls his master to 'Bend thoughts and wits' to achieve Bianca.

So part of the action is set afoot and the story of the shrew can begin. To Tranio and others she is 'stark mad or wonderful froward', but Petruchio determines to act as though she were mild and kind:

> *Say that she rail; why then I'll tell her plain*
> *She sings as sweetly as a nightingale:*
> *Say that she frown; I'll say she looks as clear*
> *As morning roses newly wash'd with dew: . . .*
>
> (II. i. 171ff.)

At the first meeting, however, he fails to maintain his self-appointed role: when Katharina engages him in jesting and then strikes him in the face, instead of praising her mildness, he answers roundly:

> *I swear I'll cuff you, if you strike again.*
> (II. i. 221)

He gains his point but he has lost confidence in his part; forgetting make-believe, he begs her to put him 'in her books' (l. 225), and when he is told that he is 'wither'd', he replies, simply, that it is 'with cares' (l. 240). By this simplicity, as by Prince Hal's, we know his true heart; in his imagination he is, even now, the anxious suitor. Only when Kate is about to leave him does he recover his pre-determined role, and is able to assure his 'sweet Katharine' that

> *. . . I find you passing gentle. . . .*
> *For thou art pleasant, gamesome, passing courteous,*
> *But slow in speech, yet sweet as spring-time flowers:*

Thou canst not frown, thou canst not look askance,
Nor bite the lip, . . .

(II. i. 244ff.)

Thenceforward he maintains the fiction until, willy-nilly, Katharina is betrothed to him.

Then it is her turn to act a part, for until she will assume obedience and thankfulness, she is given no peace. At length the rough welcome provided by Petruchio has its effect, and grudgingly she who 'never knew how to entreat' (IV. iii. 7) is prepared to act her thanks:

Petruchio. *The poorest service is repaid with thanks;*
    And so shall mine, before you touch the meat.
Katharina. *I thank you, sir.*

(IV. iii. 45-7)

With this acted complaisance she is allowed her wish to return to her father's house, but, to the end, it looks as if all may be marred:

Petruchio. *I say it is the moon that shines so bright.*
Katharina. *I know it is the sun that shines so bright.*

(IV. v. 4-5)

Hortensio, who is accompanying them, prompts Katharina in her role:

Say as he says, or we shall never go.
(IV. v. 11)

She does so and and the crisis is past. When Katharina is tested yet again we see that she is beginning to take pleasure in her role, for she goes beyond her prompting:

Then, God be bless'd, it is the blessed sun:
But sun it is not, when you say it is not;
And the moon changes even as your mind.
What you will have it named, even that it is;
And so it shall be so for Katharine.

(IV. v. 18-22)

To the men, this seems a clear victory, but we cannot be so sure. And our doubts are soon increased for, when Katharina is required to apologize for calling Vincentio a 'budding virgin', she finds further opportunity for reminding Petruchio of his moon-like changes :

> *Pardon, old father, my mistaking eyes,*
> *That have been so bedazzled with the* sun
> *That everything I look on seemeth green:*
> *Now I perceive thou art a reverend father.*
>
> (IV. v. 45-8)

Yet when her real chance comes before a larger audience, she is faithful to the role she has adopted and speaks the unquestioning generosity and obedience of her love with conviction, spirit, and due modesty.[1] Katharina has been shown a role that, to her surprise and delight, answers to the 'truth' of her own imagination ; she can play it to the height of her powers.

Both Christopher Sly and Katharina show the gusto of actors who have been given congenial roles ; but whereas Sly's must soon come to an end, there is no reason why Katharina should not act happily ever after ; for her, appearance has become reality.

And the same may be true for us too. At first Katharina was a character in a fustian, farcical play put on for the entertainment of a tinker, but now we accept her in her own right. There was a 'truth' in the old story of the taming of a shrew which Shakespeare wanted to express, so he used Christopher Sly to introduce this crude fiction. But once the 'truth' has been recognized Sly can be forgotten ; the fiction 'needs no excuse'[2] when it speaks to our imagination, showing us the mystery of Kate, that strange strength of woman which lies, or which seems to lie, in her weakness.[3]

From the play-acting of Sly, Petruchio, and Katharina, and from Lucentio's naïve response to the 'show' that welcomes him to town, stems much of the intrigue and dramatic

---

[1] See above, p. 77.   [2] *MND.*, V. i. 363.   [3] See above, pp. 60-1.

interest of *The Taming of the Shrew*; incidents which, at first
glance, seem to derive solely from the manipulation of an
intrigue plot, are used by Shakespeare to embody his living
image for the acting and recognition of love's truth; and
through them something of the implicit judgement of the
play as a whole may be discerned.

The Comedy of Errors, the earliest of his three intrigue
comedies, has only slight hints of this poetic use of comic
mistakings, but in *The Merry Wives of Windsor* Shakespeare
again related farcical incidents to a play-within-the-play and
again explored the interplay of appearance and reality.

Most of the *dramatis personae* of *The Merry Wives* are
over-confident about appearances: Sir Hugh, Page, and
Shallow forget that Slender's goodwill is not sufficient to
enable him to play a lover's part; Sir Hugh and Dr Caius
are ridiculous in any role because they are too confident of
their ability to speak English; Ford prides himself on his
perspicacity but the 'truth' he sees derives only from his
own imagination. The merry wives themselves are adept as
actors, but Mrs Ford too readily believes that Falstaff
praises only her, and Mrs Page's device of a play at Herne's
Oak fails in half its purpose because she presumes that only
she can manipulate appearances. Falstaff is the prime actor
in this play, but, too confident in his success in a lover's part,
he is ducked, beaten, and publicly mocked for his pains.
His confidence is never greater than in his last adventure; he
recognizes the appropriateness of his absurd disguise of
horns :

> *Remember, Jove, thou wast a bull for thy Europa; . . . O
> powerful love! that, in some respects, makes a beast a man,
> in some other, a man a beast. . . .*

but he does not mind the indignity :

> *When gods have hot backs, what shall poor men do? For me,
> I am here a Windsor stag; and the fattest, I think, i'the
> forest.* (V. v. 3-15.)

He is not in the least discountenanced when two ladies come
to the *rendezvous*; he is happy to be divided between them
and looks for their appreciation of his play-acting :

> *Am I a woodman, ha? Speak I like Herne the hunter?*
> (V. v. 29-30.)

As always Falstaff is carried away by his apparent success
and is ready to believe any fiction; he accepts Mrs Quickly
and Pistol as fairies and is even in terror of the 'Welsh fairy'.
He allows himself to be pinched for his 'corrupted heart'
and crouches in fear as the fairies condemn 'lust and luxury',
sins which we have seen him commit more in intention than
in deed. When the fairies run off and he unmasks, he finds
that he has been 'made an ass' in the eyes of those he had
tried to deceive. But rather than give them the pleasure of
thinking *they* have fooled him, he prefers to blame himself :

> . . . *the guiltiness of my mind, the sudden surprise of my*
> *powers, drove the grossness of the foppery into a received belief,*
> *in despite of the teeth of all rhyme and reason, that they were*
> *fairies.* (V. v. 130-4.)

He speaks all too truthfully, for the actors had condemned
him for the fault that was, in fact, in his mind; his imagination had readily 'amended' the shadows :

> *See now how wit may be made a Jack-a-Lent, when 'tis*
> *upon ill employment!* (V. v. 134-5.)

But before the night is out he has some comfort for those
who had 'ta'en a special stand to strike' at him, find that
their arrow has 'glanced' (V. v. 247-9) and the joke is on
them as well. So they all go off to 'laugh this sport o'er by a
country fire' (V. v. 256-7).

The play-within-the-play which concludes *The Merry
Wives* does not present a recognition of love's truth as the
acting of Katharina does in *The Shrew*, but it shows the
absurdity and the risk of acting a lie. It is the fantastic culmination of a series of false confidences—false in the creation and interpretation of appearances—and the contrasts

which it invites us to make between the various characters suggest that without modesty, generosity,[1] and a regard for love's truth, our dreams will never be given reality.

More than any other of Shakespeare's comedies, *The Merry Wives* aims at making a number of people look ridiculous, but its judgement is not simple. Shakespeare's use of the 'truth' of the theatre as an image for truth in the world has given a strange depth to this last scene. We laugh at Falstaff for the aptness of his role, for his confidence in his powers as an actor, and for his admission that the 'guiltiness' of his own mind has led him to accept the appearance of reproof as a reality; but we have also seen Falstaff preparing for his performances with such a zest that it seems hard that he should be shown up before such an audience and by means of such unsuitable actors. But perhaps there is a double-edged humour in casting Mrs Quickly, Pistol, and Sir Hugh as fairies; not only is Falstaff fooled by the foolish, but the foolish succeed in unlikely roles. The fact that the fairies are solemn enough to speak the praise of the great Order of the Garter which was under the Queen's special patronage[2] suggests that Shakespeare meant them to achieve an illusion which would not only convince Falstaff but also impress others. It is significant that they are all word perfect (the efforts of Sir Hugh, the play's producer, were far less successful when it came to teaching simple Latin) and that all goes to plan as far as reproving Falstaff is concerned; this is in clear contrast to other amateur performances in the comedies, to the pageant of the Worthies and the tedious brief scene of *Pyramus and Thisbe*. By assuming a hatred of 'sluts and sluttery' even these actors might have been acting a 'truth' which lay within them deep and half-forgotten.

[1] See above, pp. 78-9.

[2] It is widely believed that this play was written in its present form for a Garter Feast at Windsor which the Queen honoured (cf. E. K. Chambers, *William Shakespeare* (1930), i. 434-5); if this were so, it seems highly improbable that the passage in praise of that Order should have been inserted in a scene which was meant to be burlesqued.

And after the make-believe has been exposed, a way is suggested for making a profit out of the loss; if the actors are all ready to laugh at each other and at themselves, the human masquerade can always provide mutual, good-natured entertainment.

*　　　　*　　　　*

Shakespeare not only suggests that a lover's 'acting' must be 'true', but also that this can only follow a 'truthful' recognition of beauty. On the moment in which lovers see each other's beauty, the whole secret of their success depends. When this moment of recognition is shown upon the stage, such a stillness, such a poised silence of understanding, may be endowed with mystery and beauty through the bodily grace of the actors and their ability to give to stillness an undefined significance. And Shakespeare doubtless would wish this to be so, even while the play proceeds to explain, or rather to exemplify, the nature of that moment.

To appreciate Shakespeare's ideal of the lover's true recognition of beauty the easiest course is to consider the two main reasons why he thought such a recognition could be false. The first is that beauty of appearance is not always evidence of the inward beauty of the personality or soul. This, of course, was familiar in many 'wise saws and modern instances': in Spenser's *Fairie Queene*, for example, the fair Florimell whom Arthur followed was fair in personality and in looks, but the witch was able to make another Florimell

> *. . . in shape and look*
> *So lively and so like, that many it mistook.*
> (III. viii. 5)

The success of this deception was in accordance with deep and solemn belief: the devil had always been able to appear as an angel of light and, in one of the sonnets,[1] Shakespeare protested:

[1] See also sonnets xcv and xcvi.

> *How like Eve's apple doth thy beauty grow,*
> *If thy sweet virtue answer not thy show.*
>
> (xciii. 13-14)

The false Florimell had led many knights astray.

Such deception is more suitable to tragedy than to comedy and Shakespeare's most sustained treatment of it is in *Othello*: Iago's 'honest' appearance and manner are a cloak for 'hellish' purposes, and he inculcates mistrust in others, suggesting that Cassio puts on

> *the mere form of civil and humane* seeming, *for the better compassing of his salt and most* hidden *loose affection,* . . .
> (II. i. 244-6.)

and persuading Othello that Desdemona is a 'fair devil', a 'weed' which is so 'lovely fair'. The situation is perilous, for Othello's appearance induces fear rather than love, and Desdemona had dared to look behind appearances to see 'Othello's visage in his mind' (I. iii. 253). In more general terms a character's appearance and reality are often contrasted in the earlier tragedies: in *Hamlet* Gertrude is a 'most seeming-virtuous queen' (I. v. 46) and Hamlet has to judge the 'seeming' of Claudius (III. ii. 92); in *Richard III*, Gloucester has nothing to back his suit but 'the plain devil and dissembling looks' (I. ii. 237).

But the deceptiveness of appearance is also directly dramatized in the last act of the early *Two Gentlemen of Verona*. Here Valentine exclaims on the merely outward beauty of Proteus:

> *. . . treacherous man!*
> *Thou hast beguiled my hopes; nought but mine eye*
> *Could have persuaded me.* . . .
>
> (V. iv. 63ff.)

This passionate outburst seems ill-attuned to the quick movements of the comic resolution, but it is kept brief and is meant to provide the shock necessary to reform Proteus.

Proteus had doted first on Julia's outward beauty and then on Silvia's—he eagerly requested the mere 'shadow' of her picture (IV. ii. 131)—but the play concludes only when he recognizes Julia's inward beauty, her 'constancy'; when he sees her thus truly, he prefers her before any rival.

In the majority of comedies, outward beauty is matched by inward beauty and the deceptiveness of appearance is treated in a lighter vein. In *The Taming of the Shrew*, for example, Lucentio responds to Bianca's appearance whose 'sudden sight' has thralled his 'wounded eye' (I. i. 224-5); perhaps he is not wholly deceived in her, but certainly Petruchio's recognition of Kate's true worth has a richer sequel. By arriving as a bridegroom in tattered clothes, Petruchio shows that he scorns mere appearance and, later, he makes his point more explicitly by insisting that Kate returns to Baptista's house in the same manner:

> *For 'tis the mind that makes the body rich;*
> *And as the sun breaks through the darkest clouds,*
> *So honour peereth in the meanest habit.*
> *What is the jay more precious than the lark,*
> *Because his feathers are more beautiful?*
> *Or is the adder better than the eel,*
> *Because his painted skin contents the eye?*
>
> (IV. iii. 174-80)

This idea is presented in another form in *As You Like It*, when Phoebe, 'at first sight' (III. v. 82), loves Rosalind's outward appearance as the page Ganymede. Of course these incidents with tattered clothing and male disguise were meant to provide comic by-play, but they also present a judgement on the love that recognizes beauty in appearances alone. The light-hearted way in which the judgement is presented should not blind us to its importance. Indeed Shakespeare used the very same device—the same dramatic metaphor—in the tragedies; for instance it came to his mind in writing *Hamlet* when he wanted to contrast appearance and inward reality:

> *'Tis not alone my inky cloak, good mother,*
> *Nor customary suits of solemn black,*
> *Nor windy suspiration of forced breath,*
> *No, nor the fruitful river in the eye, . . .*
> *. . . these indeed seem,*
> *For they are actions that a man might play:*
> *But I have that within which passeth show;*
> *These but the* trappings *and the* suits *of woe.*
>
> (I. ii. 77-86)

Hamlet's clothes, like Rosalind's and Petruchio's, are his appearance as compared with the inner reality.

Shakespeare also saw rhetoric, or 'mere words', as a cloak for truth. Again he used the idea in tragedies and comedies alike. In *Hamlet* it is recurrent;[1] so Claudius cries:

> *The harlot's cheek, beautied with plastering art,*
> *Is not more ugly to the thing that helps it*
> *Than is my deed to my most painted word . . .*
>
> (III. i. 51-3)

and again:

> *My words fly up, my thoughts remain below:*
> *Words without thoughts never to heaven go.*
>
> (III. iii. 97-8)

Such passages give greater weight to similar, though more lightly expressed, ideas in the comedies, as, for instance, when Julia, having felt the 'inly touch of love', fondly hopes that the 'words' of Proteus represent his heart (II. vii. 75-6), or when Adriana, in *The Comedy of Errors*, admits 'My heart prays for him, though my tongue do curse' (IV. ii. 28); the quest for love's 'truth' must search behind words and appearances. So in *Love's Labour's Lost* the princess rejects mere protestations of love—she had quoted neither letters nor 'looks' at more than jest—and all must stay

---

[1] See also *Lr.*, I. i., especially ll. 187-8 and 283-4.

> *. . . until the twelve celestial signs*
> *Have brought about the annual reckoning. . . .*
>
> (V. ii. 807-8)

In both tragedies and comedies, Shakespeare used clothes, painting, words, and mere behaviour to suggest the deceptiveness of appearances, and, by contrast, to vindicate 'that within which passeth show'. In the tragedies the judgement is explicit, in the comedies it is almost wholly implicit, bound up with comic business and dialogue.

This is only one aspect of Shakespeare's judgement on the recognition of beauty in love, for, as the 'truth' of love's acting depends on both actors and audience, so the true recognition of beauty in love depends on the truth of beauty and truth of seeing. The confusions of *A Midsummer Night's Dream* have already reminded us that true eye-sight in love is a large demand, that a lover's recognition of beauty is apparently uncontrollable and unreasonable. And, in *The Two Gentlemen*, Speed taunts Valentine with its apparent folly:

> *—I have loved her ever since I saw her; and still I see her beautiful.*
> *—If you love her, you cannot see her.*
> *—Why?*
> *—Because Love is blind. O, that you had mine eyes; or your own eyes had the lights they were wont to have when you chid at Sir Proteus for going ungartered!* (II. i. 73-9.)

At this point we must consider how much is included in Shakespeare's idea of beauty in such a context. Valentine and the lovers of *A Midsummer Night's Dream* are not set by the ears because they are passionately concerned with pure aesthetics—on these grounds there could be nothing to dispute about.[1] A lover's recognition of beauty may include his response to aesthetic beauty and to moral, or inward, beauty, but it will also include his response to what a modern

[1] cf. *MND.*, I. i. 227.

dramatist might call sexual attraction, or, less primly, sex appeal. Shakespeare seldom attempted to isolate this element, but he did not fail to delineate its effects upon human behaviour; Rosaline's outward beauty does not satisfy Biron's conventional aesthetics but her attraction is not purely moral, a mental or spiritual affinity—he insists on asserting an outward beauty which he alone can see.[1] For Shakespeare the 'truthful' recognition of 'beauty' was complex, mysterious, individual, and compelling.

Some unfortunate lovers must be content with only a partial 'beauty'; such is the maid in 'A Lover's Complaint' who knows that the youth's beauty and good words were merely a 'garment of a Grace' with which the 'naked and concealed fiend he cover'd' (ll. 316-7). But Shakespeare held that 'true' seeing in love must combine all elements. *The Merchant of Venice* makes this quite clear. In making his choice of the caskets Bassanio does not hesitate about which motto to choose, for he is prepared to give and hazard; he is only puzzled because Portia seems to be contained in a casket of 'base' lead. In the event he chooses that casket for what it contains rather than for what it looks like; if he has to choose, he is more moved by inward than by outward beauty. This is the whole tenor of his argument before making his choice, the argument which gives symbolic significance to that choice:

> *So may the outward shows be least themselves:*
> *The world is still deceived with ornament. . . .*
> *. . . Therefore, thou gaudy gold,*
> *Hard food for Midas, I will none of thee; . . .*
>   (III. ii. 73-107)

The song which accompanies his earlier, silent deliberations makes much the same point, decrying the 'fancy' which, in contrast to true love, sees only outward beauty:

> *Tell me where is fancy bred,*
> *Or in the heart or in the head?*

[1] cf. *LLL.*, IV. iii. 274.

How begot, how nourished? . . .
It is engender'd in the eyes,
With gazing fed; and fancy dies
In the cradle where it lies.
       Let us all ring fancy's knell. . . .
                  (III. ii. 63-70)

In placing the greater value on inward beauty Shakespeare was accepting a widely current concept of 'ideal' love; for example, John Lyly wrote that

> *the contemplation of the inward quality ought to be respected, more than the view of the outward beauty*

and that one

> *should love those best whose virtue is best.*[1]

But Shakespeare was also concerned to show that Bassanio's recognition of beauty is complete; having chosen the leaden casket and so determined which is the more important beauty, Bassanio delays discovering his success because he feels impelled to express his delight in the mere appearance of Portia as represented in the portrait which he finds in the casket:

> *What find I here?*
> *Fair Portia's counterfeit! What demi-god*
> *Hath come so near creation? Move these eyes?*
> *Or whether, riding on the balls of mine,*
> *Seem they in motion? Here are sever'd lips,*
> *Parted with sugar breath: so sweet a bar*
> *Should sunder such sweet friends. Here in her hairs*
> *The painter plays the spider and hath woven*
> *A golden mesh to entrap the hearts of men*
> *Faster than gnats in cobwebs: but her eyes,—*
> *How could he see to do them? having made one,*

[1] *Euphues*, ed. Arber, pp. 53-4; quoted with other passages to the same effect from Greene, Nashe, Raleigh, etc., C. R. Baskervill, 'Bassanio as an Ideal Lover', *The Manly Anniversary Studies* (1923), pp. 90-103.

> *Methinks it should have power to steal both his*
> *And leave itself unfurnish'd. . . .*
>
> (III. ii. 115ff.)

Clearly Bassanio fully appreciates the compelling power of
Portia's outward beauty and, seeing both inward and outward beauty, sees beauty truly.

       *   *   *

Shakespeare's ideas about love's truth—the imaginative
acting of a lover and the need for our imaginative response to
it, the compulsion, individuality, and complexity of a lover's
truthful realization of beauty, and the distinctions between
inward and outward beauty, appearance and reality, and
fancy and true affection—are all represented in *Much Ado
About Nothing;* they inform its structure, its contrasts,
relationships, and final resolution ; they control many of the
details of its action, characterization, humour, and dialogue.
Indeed, in fashioning these elements into a lively, dramatic
whole, Shakespeare achieved his most concerted and considered judgement upon love's truth.

His device for presenting a lover's imagination, the play-
within-the-play, is used repeatedly in *Much Ado;* almost
every development of the action involves the acting of a
part and an audience's reaction to it. The relationship of
Benedick and Beatrice (the outstanding characters by whose
names the play was sometimes known) is radically altered
by two such play-scenes. First Pedro, Leonato, and Claudio
simulate a concern for Beatrice whom they represent as
pining for love of Benedick, and then Hero and Ursula
'play their parts' (III. ii. 79), simulating a like concern for
Benedick and his 'cover'd fire' (III. i. 77) of love for Beatrice. These two performances are far from convincing to our
eyes—at one point Leonato seems to 'dry' in his performance[1]—but nevertheless they convince their intended
audiences. At the close of the first, Benedick seriously
announces 'This can be no trick', and brings our laughter on

[1] cf. II. iii. 115-9.

himself (II. iii. 228-9); we have seen Claudio's amused relish in his own performance, and yet to Benedick 'the conference was sadly borne' (II. iii. 229). Beatrice, likewise, feels a 'fire' in her ears, and believes the fiction 'better than reportingly' (III. i. 107-16). The 'shadows' have been accepted as 'truth' because they have had audiences whose imaginations were ready to 'amend' them.[1]

This response is surprising to the characters concerned and perhaps to their audience, for hitherto Shakespeare has presented Benedick and Beatrice as gay, light-hearted critics of every illusion. Benedick delights in being an 'obstinate heretic in the despite of beauty' (I. i. 236-7) and when Claudio affirms that Hero is the 'sweetest lady', he coolly replies:

I can see yet without spectacles and I see no such matter.
(I. i. 191-2)

Beatrice likewise takes pleasure in distinguishing good parts from ill in Benedick, Don John, the prospect of Hero's marriage, and in marriage itself; and when she is complimented for apprehending 'passing shrewdly' she thanks her own wit:

I have a good eye, uncle; I can see a church by daylight.
(II. i. 85-6)

Both are convinced of the folly of love on proof of their own observation; for Beatrice men are clearly made of earth and it is therefore unreasonable to 'make an account' of oneself to a 'clod of wayward marl' (II. i. 62-6), and for Benedick man is clearly a fool when he 'dedicates his behaviours to love' (II. iii. 7-12).

But there are some signs which might prepare us for the double *volte-face*. Although Beatrice professes to scorn Benedick, he is the first she inquires after when news comes of the soldiers' return, and in the masked dance they are drawn together, recognizing each other behind visors. For his part, Benedick is strangely insistent about the outward

[1] See above pp. 88-90.

beauty of Beatrice; if she were not 'possessed with a fury' she would excel Hero as the 'first of May doth the last of December' (I. i. 193-5), and again, using clothes as a symbol for mere appearances, she is the 'infernal Ate in good apparel' (II. i. 263-4). To say truth, these wise ones—in spite of sharp eyes and shrewd tongues, in spite of challenging Cupid and scorning matrimony—these wise ones have failed to see or understand their own inward qualities. To see everything except the force of a lover's imagination, to understand everything except the reason why women will make account of themselves and men will become fools, is to be blind in the affairs of love; without this insight, a good eye, even if its owner distinguishes outward from inward beauty, can only see love as the 'silliest stuff'.

After the two play-scenes, Shakespeare causes the seemingly irrational power of their imaginations to be manifested beyond all doubt. The eyes, understanding, and tongue of the 'sensible' Benedick are all affected; he no longer thinks that Beatrice is possessed of a fury but sees 'marks of love' in her manner and 'double meanings' in her curtest message (II. iii. 254-71). When he is taunted by those to whom he had previously boasted of his wisdom, he finds that his tongue dare not speak that which his 'heart thinks' (III. ii. 14 and 73-5); his old role will not answer the truth of his newly awaked imagination. Beatrice also feels that she is out of all good 'tune', but the mere name of Benedick can cause her to disclose, unintentionally, her heart's concern (III. iv. 43 and 77-8). At the beginning of the play we may have laughed with Benedick and Beatrice at their own witticisms and the absurdities of other people; now we laugh *at* Benedick and Beatrice themselves, at the same time as we feel for them; we laugh at their over-confidence and subsequent surprise and discomfiture.

The pattern of the play as a whole becomes clearer when these two lovers are compared with Claudio and Hero. Whereas Benedick thinks he sees and understands everything, Claudio is afraid to trust his judgement and must, to his own embarrassment,[1] ask others for confirmation. Conditions are against certainty ; he had noticed Hero on his way to the wars but it is only when he sees her for a brief moment on his return that he feels 'soft and delicate desires', all prompting him 'how fair young Hero is' (I. i. 299-307). His 'liking' is sudden and seems to be 'engender'd' solely 'in the eyes',[2] to be 'fancy' and not the affection of 'true' love. Because of the attraction of Hero's outward beauty he can say 'That I love her, I feel', but since he can only guess at her inward beauty he is unable to add 'That she is worthy, I know' (I. i. 230-1). Hero is to be a 'war bride'; Claudio must trust his eyes and sudden intuition.

His lack of certainty is not only contrasted with Benedick's confidence but also with Don Pedro's ; although he scarcely knows that Hero is Leonato's daughter,[3] this prince forcefully affirms her worth and readily—perhaps too readily, for he is not asked to do so much—offers to assume Claudio's part in 'some disguise' and woo her in his name. Immediately after this proposal, Claudio's uncertainty is still further contrasted with Antonio's ready certainty ; this old man quickly concludes, from events that merely 'show well outward' (I. ii. 8), that Pedro intends to woo on his own account.[4]

---

[1] Because he approaches Don Pedro with 'your highness now may do me good' and 'Hath Leonato any son?' (I. i. 292-3 and 296), Claudio has often been accused of being mercenary; but he is only embarrassed as Bassanio was embarrassed (see above, pp. 71-2), and approaches his subject indirectly. He may, indeed, be taking his cue from Benedick's cynical response to the naïve avowal of Hero's unpurchasable 'wealth' which he has just made (I. i. 179-84).

In his betrothal to Hero he again asserts that his concern is only to 'give and hazard' for he 'gives away himself' (II. i. 319; see above, pp. 79-80) and dares to do so on the evidence of his eyes alone (see below, p. 116).

[2] *Mer. V.*, III. ii. 67; see above, pp. 107-8. The text of *Ado* gives no indication that Claudio has ever spoken to Hero.

[3] cf. I. i. 103.

[4] The whole of this scene is usually cut in performance; indeed it needlessly confuses the action unless it is justified as a further instance of mistaken overhearing and as further proof that Claudio has seen so little of Hero that his suit is totally unexpected.

Pedro's wooing of Hero in Claudio's name is another of
the 'plays' within this play, and those who overhear it react
in significantly varied ways. Benedick is convinced that
Pedro woos for himself—he has not yet felt the force of a
lover's imagination and could not be expected to distinguish
true from false fire. And on the malicious suggestion of Don
John and his followers, Claudio comes to think so too. If he
had relied on his own eyesight he might have distinguished
Pedro's assumed manner from 'love's truth', but his uncertainty leads him to accept another's interpretation and to
give way to his fears :

> *'Tis tertain so; the prince wooes for himself. . . .*
> *Therefore all hearts in love use their own tongues;*
> *Let every eye negotiate for itself*
> *And trust no agent; for beauty is a witch*
> *Against whose charms faith melteth into blood. . . .*
>
> (II. i. 181ff.)

By means of this play-scene Shakespeare has ensured that,
when Pedro drops his disguise and the matter is cleared up, we
know that Claudio realizes the deceitfulness of appearances
and yet dares to marry Hero on the evidence of his eyes alone.

At this stage we know as little about Hero as Claudio
does, but at their betrothal it seems as if her modesty
matches his. Unlike Benedick, Claudio will not readily trust
'mere words',[1] and so when Beatrice urges him to speak his
happiness, he excuses himself with :

> *Silence is the perfectest herald of joy: I were but little happy,*
> *if I could say how much.* (II. i. 316-18.)

Hero, likewise, needs to be prompted by Beatrice, and then
speaks in private to Claudio alone.

The contrast between the two pairs of lovers is now clear :
Benedick and Beatrice think that they know everything and
consequently misjudge in the affairs of love; Claudio and

---

[1] When Claudio thought Pedro had deceived him he was morosely ill-
tempered in company.

Hero believe they know very little and consequently they are hesitant. Claudio's fears have caused him to misjudge once, but nevertheless he is prepared to venture.

Immediately this main contrast has been established, the action of the comedy quickens and yet another play-within-the-play is prepared. In the wars which had brought the young men to Messina Don Pedro had defeated his bastard brother, Don John, and now one of John's followers, Borachio, conceives a plan to dishonour the victor. The plan is approved and Borachio undertakes to persuade Margaret, Hero's waiting-gentlewoman, to impersonate her mistress and talk with him at the bride's chamber window—

> *there shall* appear *such* seeming truth *of Hero's disloyalty*
> *that jealousy shall be called assurance and all the preparation*
> *overthrown.* (II. ii. 49-51.)

We do not see this played upon the stage but we know that Claudio must witness Hero's 'chamber-window entered, even the night before her wedding-day' (III. ii. 116-17). He will not know that it is Margaret's for he is only sure of the outward beauty of Hero and this Margaret may simulate by her clothes. Nor can he judge the performance by the 'truth' of its action, for the situation it portrays presupposes that Hero does not know a lover's imagination; Margaret's action will be convincingly false. Against such testimony Claudio knows no defence; it answers his worst fears and seems to offer outward proofs where most he lacked them.

When he is assured that Hero will be proved dishonest he swears

> *If I see any thing to-night why I should not marry her to-*
> *morrow, in the congregation, where I should wed, there will I*
> *shame her.* (III. ii. 127-30.)

He chooses to denounce her at the wedding ceremony because there mere words are to stand for deepest thoughts and bridal garments[1] for inward beauty: it will enable

[1] cf. III. iv. 13-25.

Claudio to say effectively that which he can scarcely think. His choice is not due to heartlessness as Beatrice too readily assumes,[1] but to the uncertainty he had always striven against, to the purity of his ideal, and to the blind, destructive rage of his disappointment in which he can pity but not feel for Hero.

In the event Claudio can scarcely bring himself to say the necessary words. When he is asked by the friar if he comes -'to marry this lady', he can only answer 'No', and he does not say even this forcefully; Leonato takes it as a jest and lightly corrects the friar, 'To be married *to* her: friar, *you* come to marry her'. The ceremony proceeds and, when Hero has formally avowed her intention, the friar asks an inescapable question:

> *If either of you know any* inward *impediment why you should not be conjoined, I charge you, on your souls, to utter it.*
> (IV. i. 12-14.)

But once more Claudio evades the issue with 'Know you any, Hero?', and when Hero replies 'None, my lord' he still hangs back. The friar has to ask directly 'Know you any, count?', and even then Claudio is silent. At this *impasse* Leonato speaks for him: 'I dare make his answer, none', and with confident assertion Claudio breaks his reserve and blurts out his passion, exclaiming not against Hero, but against treacherous appearances and false confidence. So haltingly and indirectly he comes, with Pedro's support, to his true theme, and in quickly enflamed language renounces and shames Hero:

> ... *Would you not swear,*
> *All you that* see *her, that she were a maid,*
> *By these* exterior shows? *But she is none:*
> *She knows the heat of a luxurious bed;*
> *Her blush is guiltiness, not modesty.*
> (ll. 32-43)

[1] cf. IV. i. 303-9. Many critics have agreed with this judgement which, in the end, Beatrice must be considered to have reversed.

He is hardly to be understood and Hero asks how she had ever 'seem'd' otherwise than sincere and loving. On this cue Claudio is more explicit, exclaiming on the outward beauty that had deceived him:

> *Out on thee! Seeming! I will write against it:*
> *You* seem *to me as Dian in her orb,*
> *As chaste as is the bud ere it be blown;*
> *But you are more intemperate* in your blood
> *Than Venus,* or those *pamper'd animals*
> *That rage in savage sensuality.*
>
> (ll. 57-62)

He catechizes Hero only to receive further proof of her guilt and he leaves the church resolving never to listen to imagination and never to think that outward beauty can betoken grace.[1]

To examine Claudio's denunciation in detail is to realize part of the judgement lying behind this play. It is basically the same as that presented with tragic intensity in Othello's denunciation of the 'fair devil', Desdemona;[2] both lovers know the 'chaos' which comes when they may no longer look for agreement between inward and outward beauty, and as Othello's forced politeness breaks down in a cry of 'goats and monkeys',[3] so Claudio only finds his voice to denounce the hidden, 'savage sensuality' (IV. i. 62). But not having Othello's confidence in his own power, Claudio does not wish to destroy Hero;[4] he leaves her in impotency and sorrow. The details of Claudio's denunciation—the fearful hesitancy with which he begins, and the remembrance and honour for Hero's outward beauty with which he

---

[1] cf. ll. 101-9.

[2] cf., for example, *Oth.*, III. iii. 385-7 and IV. ii. 67-9, and see above, p. 103.

[3] *Oth.*, IV. i. 274. It may be noted that it is Claudio who most frequently makes the bawdy jokes with which this play abounds; his uncertainty makes him continually aware of the sensuality underlying decorous exteriors; see below, pp. 135-6.

[4] Contrast *Oth.*, IV. i. 211.

continues and concludes—are surely meant by Shakespeare
to be signs of his great inward compulsion and of his sorrow;
it is strange and 'pitiful' to see a lover helplessly vilifying the
'Hero' whom he loves.

When Hero swoons even her father believes that she is
guilty, but Beatrice, who in friendship trusts inward prompt-
ings, and the Friar, who is greater in experience and
wisdom, both believe her innocent. At length they all agree
to hide her away from 'all *eyes*' (l. 245), and, saying that she
is dead, to maintain a 'mourning ostentation'. The Friar
believes that by these means Claudio's intuitions of her
inward beauty will grow in power and outlast the mere
'fancy' engendered by her outward beauty:

> *When he shall hear she died upon his words,*
> *The* idea *of her life shall sweetly creep*
> *Into his study of* imagination,
> *And every lovely organ of her life*
> *Shall come apparell'd in more precious habit,*
> *More moving-delicate and full of life,*
> *Into the* eye *and prospect of his soul,*
> *Than when she lived indeed;* . . .
>
> (IV. i. 225ff.)

If Claudio has truly loved, he will, in due time, believe this
inward vision, even against firm outward evidence of her
guilt.[1]

In order to compare the two stories of this comedy still
further Shakespeare boldly followed these scenes with a
dialogue between Benedick and Beatrice. When these lovers
are alone together they do not abate one jot of their accustomed sagacity and wit; they are, as they learn to say later,
'too wise to woo peaceably' (V. ii. 73-4). Benedick avows
his love for Beatrice and in the same breath asks if that is
not 'strange' (IV. i. 269-70). Beatrice likewise confesses that
she is stayed in a happy hour for she was 'about to protest'
that she loved him (ll. 285-6). But words, even riddling

[1] cf. ll. 232-5.

ones like these, are the easier part of their love. Beatrice, believing that Hero has been wronged, takes Benedick's offer of service at face value and bids him 'Kill Claudio'. She makes this terrifying request in few words but when she is refused she vents her scorn of mere words in many:

> *. . . manhood is melted into courtesies, valour into compliment, and men are only turned into tongue, and trim ones too: . . .*
> (ll. 321ff.)

At length Benedick can put a solemn question, asking

Think you in your soul *the Count Claudio hath wronged Hero?*

and he receives as solemn an answer:

> *Yea, as sure as I have a thought or a soul.*
> (ll. 331-3)

If Benedick truly loves he must—as Claudio must—believe his lady's 'soul' against all outward testimony; he had called her inward spirit a 'fury', but, if he has truly looked upon her with a lover's imagination, he will have seen the beauty of that spirit and will now trust and obey—and will challenge Claudio. The twin stories of *Much Ado About Nothing* turn on the same point; the very wise and the very uncertain must both learn to trust inward qualities, mere nothings to some other eyes; through a lover's imagination each must recognize inward truth and beauty, and must speak and act from a convinced heart.

These scenes in the church might have been unbearably pathetic had not Shakespeare already informed us that Borachio's plot had already been discovered. The device used to this end, the introduction of Constable Dogberry and the men of his watch, also contributes to presenting and widening the underlying theme of the whole play. Dogberry is a great respecter of words—of long words, defaming words, and the phraseology of official regulations—but he respects them only with respect to himself; he interprets the regulations for his own peace of mind and uses words for the little that they mean to himself not for what they mean to others. His watch are 'most senseless and fit' men (III. iii. 23), self-respecting like himself but without his pretensions. By a stroke of irony Shakespeare has directed that Borachio, 'like a true drunkard', tells all to Conrade within their hearing. There is no play-acting in this scene; Borachio tells how the 'fashion of a doublet . . . is nothing to a man' (ll. 125-6) and how the 'appearance' of Hero's guilt has deceived the prince and Claudio. When hidden truth is made so plain, the action of the play must seem as good as over, but Dogberry goes with the news to Leonato, and between the one's busy concern to prepare for his daughter's wedding and the other's happy concern to speak in polite and noble words, the message is never truly delivered. It is still further delayed when Leonato asks Dogberry to act as Justice of the Peace and examine the villains in his place. The Constable's pleasure in his new and elevated role almost perverts justice, but the sexton prompts him in his part and is soon running to inform Leonato.

The comedy moves towards its close but several threads of its pattern are yet to be drawn into place. In his grief Leonato protests that counsel is 'profitless As water in a sieve' (V. i. 4-5); a man who has suffered inwardly as he has suffered must needs rage in his grief, although at other times he may have 'writ the style of gods' (V. i. 37). When Don Pedro and Claudio enter, he and Antonio pretend that Hero is dead indeed and so over-act their parts—it is a fiction they come close to believing—that they nearly involve themselves in a duel. But the prince and Claudio wish to avoid all speech and contact with them; they do not rage in their grief, but having lost all hope and confidence are 'high-proof melancholy'. They welcome Benedick's company so that his wit may beat away their care, but witty words no longer 'suit' their thoughts and the jests go awry, and, before leaving them, Benedick challenges Claudio to a duel for Hero's honour. When Dogberry enters with his prisoners Pedro has the patience and assumed good humour to hear him, but he is cut short by Borachio's confession:

> *I have deceived even your very eyes: what your wisdoms could*
> *not discover, these shallow fools have brought to light. . . .*
> (V. i. 238ff.)

At this point the focus returns to Claudio. Borachio's words run 'like iron' through his blood; he is silent as he remembers Hero's true beauty, but his heart is overcharged and must be uttered in soliloquy:

> *Sweet Hero! now thy image doth appear*
> *In the rare semblance that I loved it first.*
> (ll. 259-60)

This image springs to his mind from the knowledge of Hero's innocence, not from the sight of her outward beauty, but it is important to notice that the image is identical with the beauty he had seen at first. Dramatic interest is forcefully focused on Claudio by his silence and then by his abrupt soliloquy; by these means Shakespeare emphasizes an important turning-point in the action of the play; Claudio realizes that his love for Hero had been true affection all the time, not mere fancy.[1]

Claudio still believes Hero is dead and when he is again confronted by Leonato he knows 'not how to pray his patience'; yet he 'must speak', asking penance for his sin which lay entirely in 'mistaking' (V. i. 281-5). He is asked to write an epitaph for Hero and next morning to marry Leonato's niece. Here again Shakespeare introduces a daring contrast, for Benedick is also writing verses—to Beatrice. He who had been so sure of his tongue is now at his wits' end to fit his lover's imagination to the 'even road of a blank verse' (V. ii. 34). On the other hand, Claudio now seems uncritical of his own utterance, presenting his finished, but not very polished, verses at Hero's tomb, and trusting that they will speak for him when he is 'dumb' (V. iii. 10).

[1] So confirming earlier hints; see above, pp. 79-80.

The comedy is now at its end. Claudio is so hopeless of seeing beauty in love again that he swears to accept the 'penance' of his unseen bride 'were she an Ethiope' (V. iv. 38), and is thereupon, beyond all his hopes, reunited with Hero. Benedick and Beatrice, at the very door of the church, are unwilling—be it through shame or lack of confidence—to assume their 'unreasonable'[1] roles in public. But when Beatrice is shown verses written by Benedick, and Benedick others written by Beatrice, the unreasonable imagination of their love is made evident; their own handwritings appear as strange evidence 'against' their hearts (V. i. 91-2). To prevent yet more ado, Benedick 'stops her mouth' with a kiss; he is now confident in his new role:

> *since I do purpose to marry, I will think nothing to any purpose that the world can say against it; . . . for man is a giddy thing, and this is my conclusion. . . .* (ll. 106-11.)

The joy of the lovers is so complete that it must be expressed forthwith in the harmony of a dance, before the marriage ceremony, and certainly before they spare a thought for Don John, whose deceit was the occasion of so much of their trouble.

Much Ado has been more adversely criticized for its structure than any other of Shakespeare's comedies. This has been largely due to critics who, judging by the 'humanity' of individual characters, have thought that Shakespeare lost interest in the Claudio-Hero story in order to enjoy creating Benedick and Beatrice. But *Much Ado* is, in fact, the most intellectually articulated of the comedies and will not betray its secret to this piece-meal criticism. Its structure depends almost entirely on one central theme, a theme which had already influenced parts of earlier comedies, that of appearance and reality, outward and inward beauty, words and thoughts—in short, the theme of love's truth. When this theme is recognized, the relationships and contrasts between the two main stories, which Shakespeare has been

---

[1] cf. ll. 74 and 77.

at pains to establish, are at once apparent and the play's structural unity vindicated. Then Claudio is seen as a purposeful contrast to Benedick and a character who is interesting—and actable—in his own right.

The theme of *Much Ado* may be simply stated, but its presentation is so subtle that the width and wisdom of Shakespeare's vision can only be suggested. This may best be done, in this comedy as in others, by relating the various characters to each other as the action of play directs. Leonato is one who ordinarily is 'no hypocrite, but prays from his heart' (I. i. 152-3), but he is not always patient enough to disentangle the words and actions of others, and, in sorrow, becomes ludicrously pathetic as the man who can only talk. Margaret, the young waiting-woman, is one who takes pleasure in assuming more apprehension than her experience can lay claim to. Don Pedro is rightly confident in judging Hero's inward worth, but his readiness to speak for Claudio is misjudged and his confidence in assessing the scene acted by Margaret and Borachio is probably culpable, for only a lover who could recognize Hero's inward qualities could possibly judge rightly. Dogberry's self-concerned respect for mere words and for his new and dignified role painfully prolongs the misunderstandings of others; yet he has the wit not to 'like' Borachio's look (IV. ii. 46-7) and blunderingly justice is done. The watch discover the malefactors by chance, but their simple good sense not to trust the words of those who have confessed themselves to be villains—they command them 'Never speak' (III. iii. 188)—prevents still further deceit. Benedick and Beatrice, trusting their eyes, judgements, and power of speech too much, are taught, through the good offices of their friends, to recognize and give sway to their imaginations; so Benedick is 'converted' (II. iii. 23) and finds beauty where he had previously seen a 'fury' and Beatrice learns to look as 'other women do' (III. iv. 92). But even when they are brought, through mutual trust of their own 'souls', to admit their love to each other, it again needs the offices of friends before they will admit the folly of their love to the world. Claudio, fearing, with good enough reason, to trust his eyes alone, is an easy prey to his prince's enemies, and accepts outward proof of inward guilt. In so doing he brings suffering on his lady and on himself, but in the end their love is justified by his imaginative recognition of the 'sweet idea' of Hero's true beauty. Both pairs of lovers take a long road to the same conclusion; in retrospect easier ways recommend themselves, but it is part of Shakespeare's wisdom to suggest that, to those who are engaged in the quest for love's truth, the longest course is often the only one which seems possible to them. It will ever be 'Much Ado'.

It is, perhaps, also a part of Shakespeare's wisdom that the success of *Much Ado* should depend largely on the way in which we receive it, that it should be capable of different, and sometimes destructive, interpretations. The acceptance of 'love's truth' always depends on the imagination of its audience, and the 'truth' of this play is no exception. Even the realization of the main theme of appearance and reality can only explain the dramatic structure, it cannot ensure the play's success. Unless we 'imagine no worse' of Claudio than he is represented as thinking of himself, unless we have the readiness and imagination to 'amend' the shadows of love's truth which are presented on the stage, *Much Ado* will never be for us the lively and human comedy which Shakespeare intended. But given this imaginative response, the implicit judgement of the play and the wisdom of the ideals informing it will, even in our delight, shape our own beings and bring to them something of the life-enhancement inherent in this work of art.

CHAPTER V

Love's Order and the Judgement of
As You Like It

————————————

Shakespeare's history plays are concerned with politics and sociology, but we do not have to be kings or politicians in order to enjoy them; and his comedies, while they are mainly concerned with love and lovers, 'hold the mirror up' to more aspects of 'nature' than those which are peculiar to a lover's experience. In presenting his ideal of love's wealth in *The Comedy of Errors*, *The Taming of the Shrew*, and *The Merchant of Venice*, Shakespeare necessarily presented commercial wealth and aspirations as well, and in his exploration of love's truth in *A Midsummer Night's Dream* and *Much Ado*, he also presented his discoveries about a poet's truth and an actor's. Nor are these contrasts—or dramatic metaphors—seen from a single aspect. The central theme of *Much Ado* is not only expressed through the dialogue and actions of the two pairs of lovers but also through those of Don Pedro, Leonato, Friar Francis, Don John, Borachio, Dogberry, and the watchmen; so in the last scene, when we observe the mazes which the lovers have trod in response to love's imagination, we may also find ourselves reflecting on other mazes, on the vanity of human knowledge and the necessity for it, on the human inability to walk simply, by the shortest route, to the fulfilment of desire. In *The Merchant of Venice* we are shown events through Shylock's eyes as well as through those of the lovers, and in the last act the focus is subtly altered again so that we view Portia and Bassanio as from a distance, against a wider background than that of a mere love story—we judge them as creatures living beneath the stars and we judge their love in comparison with a universal charity.

The comprehensiveness of Shakespeare's mind, his poet's impulse to see the world in a grain of sand, enables us to find our own 'nature' in his 'mirror'. The comedies, seemingly restricted in their scope to tales of wooing and ideal love, are capable of reflecting the form and pressure of far other experiences. We have seen how some of the judgements underlying the comedies may be appreciated by following a simple idea about the lover's realization of beauty, or a more individual idea like the concept of love's wealth, but it is also possible to see something of Shakespeare's judgement —of his shaping and ordering of material and of the contrasts and relationships he effects—by following an idea which is more immediately appropriate to other matters than those of love. We may take, as an example, the ideal of order, an ideal which played such a considerable part in shaping the history-plays.

*   *   *

Shakespeare's history-plays, telling the story of England from the reign of John to the crowning of Henry the Seventh, measure the success or failure of kings and nations against an ideal of order.[1] As God was seen as the ruler and judge of all degrees of creation—spiritual, human, animal, vegetable, material—and as each degree was considered to have a clear ascendancy over inferior degrees, so it was considered that the king, 'god's deputy', should be the 'head' of the state with its various 'members' or degrees in due subservience under him. Political and moral writers found many analogies to this ideal and Shakespeare knew almost all of them ; Menenius, in *Coriolanus*, uses the comparison of the head's rule over the body,[2] the Archbishop of Canterbury,

[1] E. M. W. Tillyard's *Shakespeare's History Plays* (1944) traces the influence of this ideal in the plays. His *Elizabethan World Picture* (1943) and A. O. Lovejoy's earlier *The Great Chain of Being* (1936) demonstrate its prevelance and comprehensiveness in Elizabethan thought and feeling.

[2] I. i. 99-164.

in *Henry V*, that of a hive of bees where 'obedience' or 'order' enables many creatures to 'work contrariously' yet in harmony and fulfilment,[1] and Henry the Fourth calls on rebels to imitate the constellations and

> *. . . move in that* obedient *orb again*
> *Where you did give a fair and* natural *light,*
> *And be no more an exhaled meteor,*
> *A prodigy of fear and a portent*
> *Of broached mischief to the unborn times.*[2]

Those who rebelled against the king or his officers were 'unnatural', or as the Elizabethans often put it, 'un-*kind*';[3] they were like animals, 'monsters'[4] not men. Without due order a nation would grow to 'savagery' and unnatural 'wildness';[5] it would be like a diseased body,[6] a 'disordered' or unweeded garden,[7] a river overflowing its banks,[8] a 'vast confusion' and 'tempest'.[9]

The ideal of order influenced men's thoughts in many other matters. Each man had to order his faculties as a king ordered a nation; so Prince Hal's personal reformation is described as the unthroning of 'Hydra-headed wilfulness',[10] and Richard the Second comes to recognize that there should be a 'concord' or 'music' in men's lives as in the state, a keeping of time and due 'proportion'.[11] In its widest expression in political, social, human, and religious terms, the ideal of order helped to shape and inform Shakespeare's greatest tragedies, especially *Hamlet*, *Macbeth*, and *Lear*. Its influence is most apparent in *King Lear* where we are shown a sequence of tyranny, revolt, disorder, judgement, and renewed order, experienced in a nation, in families, and in individuals. Analogies to an ordered state suggested far-ranging images for these actions—images of health, music,

[1] I. ii. 183-213.   [2] *IH4*, V. i. 17-21.
[3] cf., for example, *IH6*, IV. i. 193.   [4] *H5*, II. ii. 85.
[5] *H5*, V. ii. 47ff.   [6] cf., for example, *IH6*, III. i. 73 and 192-4.
[7] *R2*, III. iv. 40-66.   [8] cf. *John*, V. iv. 52-7.
[9] *John*, IV. iii. 152-6.   [10] *H5*, I. i. 35-6.   [11] *R2*, V. v. 42-8.

wisdom, civilization, constellations, and the natural succession of days and seasons—and Shakespeare used these images to universalize the action of this tragedy, to show in this one 'mirror' the whole state of 'nature'.[1]

As the influence of this ideal of order upon the writing of *King Lear* may be detected by the recurrence of its associated images and similes, so may its influence upon the writing of the comedies.[2] For example, the portrayal of villains called for images of discord and bestiality. When Shylock demands the pound of flesh he is likened to the sea encroaching upon the land, to a wolf, and to 'mountain pines ... fretten with the gusts of heaven'.[3] When Shylock demands the right of killing, he justifies it as a right over an animal, not over a man.[4] In *Much Ado*, Don John is 'out of *measure*' sad; he 'had rather be a *canker* in a hedge than a rose' in Don Pedro's 'grace', and he wishes to use his mouth only to 'bite', his 'liberty' only to do his own 'liking'.[5] Images of disorder are especially prevalent in *A Midsummer Night's Dream* where they describe the fairy kingdom divided against itself; 'brawls' disturb their dances and in consequence:

> ... *the winds, piping to us in vain,*
> *As in revenge, have suck'd up from the sea*
> *Contagious fogs; which falling in the land*
> *Have every pelting river made so proud*
> *That they have overborne their continents....*
>
> (II. i. 88ff.)

Through this 'distemperature', or lack of order, even the sequence of seasons has been disturbed. Disorder is again suggested when, in his spite, Oberon plans to make Titania love some loathsome animal.

[1] Professor John F. Danby has used these images as a key to an appreciation of *King Lear* in his *Shakespeare's Doctrine of Nature* (1949).

[2] G. Wilson Knight's *Shakespearian Tempest* (1932) traces many of these images in the comedies in an attempt to show that an 'opposition' between 'tempest' and 'music' is 'the only principle of unity in Shakespeare' (p. 6).

[3] *Mer. V.*, IV. i. 71-80; see also IV. i. 128, 133-8, 217, 287, and 292.

[4] *Mer. V.*, IV. i. 69.   [5] I. iii. 1-41.

But even when they are not directly suggested by a villain or a divided kingdom, the images of order and disorder are used in the comedies to picture human relationships. This may be illustrated from the early *Comedy of Errors*. The Antipholi and Dromios accept an habitual order in their relationships with other people as any men might do, but when they are involved in a series of misunderstandings with their twin counterparts the seemingly irrational occurrences suggest a nightmare disorder. Antipholus of Syracuse imagines a world of

> *Dark-working sorcerers that* change *the mind,*
> *Soul-killing witches that* deform *the body,*
> *Disguised cheaters, prating mountebanks,*
> *And many such-like* liberties *of sin.*
>
> (I. ii. 99-102)

Both master and man believe they are 'transformed' (II. ii. 197-8) and for Dromio disorder takes shape in Luce, 'a very *beastly* creature', who lays claim to him; she seems to be a 'witch' who would 'transform' him to a 'curtal dog'.[1] When Antipholus of Ephesus is shut out of his own house, his Dromio swears it would 'make a man mad as a *buck*' (III. i. 72), and his own subsequent 'incivility' (IV. iv. 49) makes everyone—his wife, sister-in-law, friends, and doctor— believe that he is mad indeed; he foreswears 'most *monstrously*', is no longer a 'formal' man, and demeans himself 'rough, rude and wildly'.[2]

Images of disorder are also used for describing Adriana's mismanaged marriage; she will not accept her husband's lordship, seeing obedience as mere 'servitude'; and not trusting her husband she fears that he is an 'un*kind* mate', a 'too *unruly deer*';[3] she sees their life together as a disordered garden, her husband as an elm 'usurped' by 'ivy, brier, or idle moss' (II. ii. 179-82). We have already observed that the final scene is attended by a spirit of generosity,[4] but we

---

[1] III. ii. 88 and 148-51. [2] V. i. 11, 105, and 88.
[3] II. i. 26, 38, and 100-1. [4] See above, pp. 56-7.

may also note that for Adriana generosity has to be expressed in a willing acceptance of the 'order' of matrimony. At the beginning Luciana had reminded her of an ideal order in marriage:

> There's nothing situate under heaven's eye
> But hath his bound, in earth, in sea, in sky:
> The beasts, the fishes and the winged fowls
> Are their males' subjects and at their controls:
> Men, more divine, the masters of all these, . . .
> Are masters to their females, and their lords: . . .
>
> (II. i. 16-25)

and at the close the abbess, with more experienced voice, rebukes her in the same vein:

> The venom clamours of a jealous woman
> Poisons more deadly than a mad dog's tooth. . . .

Such behaviour invites

> . . . a huge infectious troop
> Of pale distemperatures and foes to life.
>
> (V. i. 69ff.)

Both recommend patience,[1] and Adriana is shamed into vowing that Antipholus is 'lord' of her and all she has (V. i. 137). The disorders arising from mistaken identities are resolved on visual proof of the mistakes, but Shakespeare seems to suggest that the disorders arising from 'intemperate' hostility between man and wife must be resolved by the generous recognition of an order which permits them both to 'work contrariously' in harmony and fulfilment.

*   *   *

As Shakespeare thought of marriage in terms of an ideal order so he also thought of a lover's wooing; this is shown in

---

[1] In some of his most mature plays, as *Lear*, the last comedies, and *Henry VIII*, Shakespeare returns to a call for patience in face of the world's disorders; cf. J. F. Danby, *Poets on Fortune's Hill* (1952), pp. 74-127.

another early comedy, *Love's Labour's Lost*. At first the King of Navarre and his followers believe that love leads only to disorder, and so they decide to make war against their affections, boasting that they are 'brave conquerors' (I. i. 8) and that they are removing the 'weeds' from growing corn (I. i. 96). In this way they try to establish order in themselves, swearing 'Not to see ladies', to study, fast, and sleep but three hours a night (I. i. 48). But Shakespeare at once proceeds to show that theirs is an arbitrary and imperfect order. First Biron criticizes it:

> *Why should I joy in any* abortive *birth?*
> *At Christmas I no more desire a rose*
> *Than wish a snow in May's new-fangled mirth;*
> *But like of each thing that in* season *grows.*
>
> (I. i. 104-7)

As all true order must be in accordance with natural order, so Biron insists that a young man's personal regimen must allow the pleasures appropriate to the 'season' of his life. A second criticism follows immediately in a description of Armado—

> *One whom the* music *of his own vain tongue*
> *Doth ravish like enchanting* harmony; . . .
>
> (I. i. 167-8)

His 'harmony', or order, is in words and not in deeds, and it convinces only himself; and so indeed the King's may prove, for 'necessity' has already compelled him to welcome the princess against the dictates of his own fine-sounding pledges of order.

A third criticism of the King's new order is implicit in the person of the swain Costard who is the first new character to be introduced on the stage. He enters under the charge of Constable Dull, for, in defiance of the King's decree, he has 'sorted and consorted' with a wench, Jaquenetta. He has no defence for his action, only a reason—that 'it is the manner of a man to speak to a woman', that it is 'the simplicity of man to hearken after the flesh' (I. i. 211-12 and 219-20). He suffers 'for the truth', for, as he readily acknowledges, he 'was taken with Jaquenetta, and Jaquenetta is a true girl' (I. i. 313-15). He is philosophically content:

and therefore welcome the sour cup of prosperity! Affliction may one day smile again; and till then, sit thee down, sorrow! (I. i. 315-17.)

Costard is well aware of just that element which the King has tried to ignore in ordering his life; as true order in the state gives freedom to all subservient members, so true order in a man must realize his full potential, must allow man to act in 'the manner of a man'.

The young men soon learn that their arbitrary order is easier to decree than to obey. The King recognizes its faults almost as soon as he sees the princess; at first glance his self-composure is disturbed,[1] and soon he must be riding his horse for all it is worth.[2] Before long he acknowledges what has happened and he does so in a new formulation of order; for him the princess now brings the blessings of sun and moon, and no order is now conceivable unless she, as 'queen of queens' (IV. iii. 40) accepts his love and service. For Longaville, Maria becomes an 'empress' (IV. iii. 56); she is a 'goddess' whose 'grace being gain'd cures all disgrace' (IV. iii. 65-7). For Dumain, Kate would make Jove turn 'mortal' in order to woo her (IV. iii. 120). The demands of their new order are quite contrary to those of their previous one, and Biron chides them for their apparent disorder:

O me, with what strict patience have I sat,
To see a king transformed to a gnat!
To see great Hercules whipping a gig,
And profound Solomon to tune a jig, . . .
                 (IV. iii. 165ff.)

But as we already know, he, who had laughed to see Cupid's power, has now found that he also must accept his demands.

[1] cf. II. i. 234-49.　　　　[2] cf. IV. i. 1-4.

Soon all four lovers know each other's plight. In his 'sim-plicity' even Costard can mock them as he and Jaquenetta are hurriedly ordered away: 'Walk aside the true folk', he comments, 'and let the traitors stay' (IV. iii. 213).

Biron encourages the others to accept Costard's valuation; they are 'traitors' to their self-appointed order but 'true ... as flesh and blood can be' (l. 215). After this new realization, they see their earlier oaths as 'Flat treason 'gainst the kingly state of youth' (l. 293) and know that order can now only be truly attained if each acknowledges his 'fair mistress' (l. 376). To Biron, this new order seems able to draw all things into its own harmony:

> ... when Love speaks, the voice of all the gods
> Make heaven drowsy with the harmony.
> Never durst poet touch a pen to write
> Until his ink were temper'd with Love's sighs;
> O, then his lines would ravish savage ears
> And plant in tyrants mild humility.
>
> (IV. iii. 344-9)

Their new order is at once tested, for all four lovers are mocked for their past mistakes and are asked to prove their new loyalty by a year's service. It must be more enduring than an 'offer made in heat of blood' (V. ii. 810); it must include the mere 'simplicity of a man' but it must also be more than that; it must be an ordering of the whole man.

The play started with the young men seeking fame by trying to establish an order within themselves, and it draws towards its close with a pageant of Worthies, of those who have achieved fame. Thereby all the *dramatis personae* are brought together, their relationships established, and Shake-speare's overall judgement most clearly discerned. Armado has been forced to forget his fanciful, self-created nobility and to recognize a plain man's desire for a plain 'Maid', the 'base wench', Jaquenetta (I. ii. 62 and 139-40). This leads him to find his true degree in society, for, after he has attempted to play his part as a Worthy, he leaves the stage to follow the plough with the 'simple' folk : 'You that way', he seems to tell the courtiers, and 'we this way'.[1] Costard 'proves the best Worthy' (V. ii. 564), for he who had known the 'manner of a man', assumes his role with a just diffidence :

> *It pleased them to think me worthy of Pompion the Great: for mine own part, I know not the degree of the Worthy, but I am to stand for him.* (V. ii. 506-9.)

The other actors, with more determination not to be 'put out of countenance' (V. ii. 611), find that 'their form'—their outward appearance or, perhaps, their assumed 'rank or quality'[2]—is quickly 'confounded' (V. ii. 520) ; they are foolish, mild, honest men, good bowlers perhaps,[3] but no Worthies. As for the other characters, the young nobles, we know that they are on probation ; they have a new ideal of order, of service and honour to those who seem well worthy in their own eyes. If this new order is truly and fully realized, they will be judged worthy and their 'humble suits' (V. ii. 849) will be accepted. This will be a comprehensive order,

[1] V. ii. 941-2. These words occur only in the Folio; some editors consider them to be an unintelligent correction of the abrupt conclusion of the Quarto text, but, if the ideal of order is recognized in this play, their appropriateness may attest their authenticity.

[2] *N.E.D.*, s.v. 6. Or possibly 'form' means 'good order'; cf. *John*, III. iv. 101-2: 'I will not keep this form upon my head, When there is such disorder in my wit.' 'Confound' often had the meaning 'disorder'; cf. *N.E.D.*, s.v. 5.

[3] When Costard calls Sir Nathaniel a 'good bowler' (V. ii. 587) he may well mean that he drinks deep (cf. *N.E.D.*, s.v. 2); this would be appropriate to the theme of order and worthiness, for the 'natural' Costard would be praising worthiness in its lowest degree (cf. *Mer. V.*, I. ii. 92-6 and *Oth.*, II. iii. 290-312). There is an earlier allusion to Sir Nathaniel's deep drinking in the talk of 'piercing a hogshead' (IV. ii. 84-90; cf. *LLL.*, ed. R. David (1951), p. 85), and, possibly, in his willingness to fall to his 'recreation' (IV. ii. 174).

R. Greene's *A Quip for an Upstart Courtier* (1592) gives a portrait of a country parson, Sir John; he is made to claim for himself—'I am indeed none of the best scholars yet I can read an homily every Sunday and holiday, and I keep company with my neighbours, and go to the alehouse with them, . . .' (G2ᵛ). If 'bowler' does mean 'drinker' in *LLL.*, then Sir John sounds as if he were, like Sir Nathaniel, a 'marvellous good neighbour, faith, and a very good bowler'.

giving freedom to every faculty, and in it the 'simplicity of man' will find its true place and true fulfilment.

The play ends with songs of the cuckoo and owl, the one a reminder of the flesh, the other of death;[1] theirs is the annual reckoning of spring and winter against which all order must be tried.[2]

*   *   *

In Shakespeare's view the 'simplicity of man to hearken after the flesh' can lead to order or disorder, to a unified, free, and worthy life in relationship or to a mere bestiality. The disorder of one extreme is a subject for tragedy rather than comedy : in *Hamlet*, for example, the prince cries out against treachery in love and against the ensuing discord, madness, mutiny, bestiality, sickness, rankness, and corruption.[3] In *Othello*, the theme is explored still further; the Moor, secure in his love for Desdemona, can restore order with a word of command, but once he has seen corruption where he had looked for purity, he himself rages on the floor like an uncontrolled monster. But the most simple and explicit presentation of love's disorder is probably in the narrative poem, *The Rape of Lucrece:* Tarquin's journey through the night is accompanied by 'owls' and wolves' death-boding cries' (l. 165) and Lucrece—

> *. . . the picture of pure piety,*
> *Like a white hind under the gripe's sharp claws,*
> *Pleads in a wilderness where are no laws,*
> *To the rough beast that knows no gentle right,*
> *Nor aught obeys but his foul appetite.*

(ll. 542-6)

---

[1] cf. *IH6*, IV. ii. 15, *R3*, IV. iv. 509, and *Mac.*, II. ii. 3, &c.

[2] cf. V. ii. 809-17; the young men had attempted their arbitrary order to 'grace' themselves 'in the disgrace of death' (I. i. 3), but they had forgotten the song of the cuckoo; and as soon as they had recognized her song, their insistence on clapping up their 'bargain' immediately, despite the French King's death, suggested that they had now forgotten the song of the owl.

[3] cf. III. iv.

The comedies are chiefly concerned with the establish-
ment of love's order, but, unless we realize the possibility of
chaos, the full force of their harmonious conclusions will be
lost. Occasionally there are direct remembrances of it:
Falstaff's transformation to a Windsor stag—a 'beastly
fault' (V. v. 10)—is a comic example, and Claudio's outcry
that Hero is more 'intemperate in her blood' than

> ... *pamper'd* animals
> *That rage in* savage *sensuality*
> (IV. i. 61-2)

is a passionate example.[1] For such glimpses of love's disorder, Shakespeare used images which are able to evoke the
whole intellectual and emotional force of the history-plays
and major tragedies.

Other reminders of the possibility of disorder are found
among the bawdy jokes and *doubles entendres* which run
throughout the comedies. Allusions to horns, tails, geese,
savage bulls and the like constantly touch upon the essenti-
ally beastlike element of love, the element which must either
disorder all, or be ordered with all in due degree; they carry
the thread of animal appetites into the woven pictures of a
full and triumphant love. The 'gross' speaking[2] of the last
act of *The Merchant of Venice* reminds us, for example, that
compounded in the generous and golden love of Bassanio
and Portia is the 'simplicity of man'. Unless Shakespeare
wished to celebrate the romantic elements of their love and at
the same time to insist on its full complexity, it is hard to see
why he concluded this entrancing scene with a bawdy
allusion to the pains of married chastity. One might argue
that this was a sallet for the groundlings, but that does not
explain why he gave it this position of prominence. We must
either think that Shakespeare had lost interest in his play by
this time—and the quality of the writing argues against that
—or else we must conclude that he relished this joke, and

---

[1] For a comparison with Othello's disorder, see above, pp. 116-7.
[2] V. i. 266.

many another like it, for its own sake and also for the sake of his ideal of love's order.

The significant use of bawdry may be further illustrated by the manner in which one particular joke about horns and savage bulls is repeated at intervals throughout *Much Ado*. In the first scene Don Pedro tells Benedick that he too may fall in love, reminding him that 'In time the *savage* bull doth bear the *yoke*'. Benedick scorns such bestiality:

> *The* savage bull *may; but if ever the sensible Benedick bear it, pluck off the bull's* horns *and set them in my forehead: and let me be* vilely *painted, and in such great letters as they write* 'Here is good *horse to hire', let them signify under my sign* 'Here you may see Benedick the married man.' (I. i. 264-70.)

Pedro and Claudio remember his boast and, later in the play, they are quick to quote his words against him.[1] Then, in the very next scene Benedick tries to rhyme out his love for Beatrice only to find that the word 'horn' occurs all too readily to his mind.[2] As he is about to marry, Claudio again reminds him of his earlier scorn of beastlike servitude. This jibe and Benedick's reply are harsh and brutal,[3] but when their loves are successfully resolved, Benedick's acceptance of his 'yoke' leads him to turn the joke, in gay and confident mood, upon Don Pedro and his single state.[4] Both Falstaff and Benedick remember Jove's transformation into a bull; the difference between these two lovers lies not in the presence or absence of bestiality, but in the use—the order or disorder—to which that 'simplicity' is put. In the very conclusions of his comedies Shakespeare did not care to celebrate a 'platonic' love which ignores or supersedes man's 'hearkening after the flesh'; the love which triumphs is a full one, established at the risk of disorder and compounded of beast, man, and spirit.

*   *   *

To picture the order of this love Shakespeare not only

[1] cf. V. i. 183-4.   [2] cf. V. ii. 38.   [3] cf. V. iv. 43-51.
[4] cf. V. iv. 124-6.

used verbal images and associations but also a few traditional
devices or stage symbols, actions which celebrated the creation of order. Their significance may easily be understood:
the only difficulty is that familiarity may blind us to their
importance. The simplest of these stage devices is the hero
and heroine concluding the play by walking off-stage arm-
in-arm with each other. This can only be effective with such
special preparation as it is given in *The Taming of the Shrew*.
After the discordant action of most of this play, Katharina
expresses her belief in an ideal of mutual service and order in
love; she explicitly invokes the comparison of a well-
ordered state:

> *Such duty as the subject owes the prince*
> *Even such a woman oweth to her husband....*
> (V. ii. 155ff.)

Petruchio and Katharina ratify their mutual obligations with
a kiss;[1] and then, instead of the '*Exeunt omnes*' which concludes all the other comedies, the folio text of *The Shrew*
directs Petruchio to exit alone, calling Kate to come with
him.[2] The rest of the *dramatis personae* are left standing, to
follow as best they may after two final speeches of wonder-
ment. By an explicit statement of its significance and by
contrast with the actions of the other characters, the final
exit of this hero and heroine implies and celebrates the
achievement of love's order.

In other comedies Shakespeare did not rely upon a long
explication like Katharina's speech; he used concluding
devices of stage action which are sufficiently eloquent in

[1] See above, p. 61.

[2] There is no other comedy for which an authoritative early edition
directs hero and heroine to leave the stage before the rest of the *dramatis
personae*. In *A Midsummer Night's Dream*, mechanicals, courtiers, and fairies
leave at different times, but they all leave in company. *The Comedy of Errors*
comes nearest to *The Shrew*, directing the two Dromios to remain after
'*Exeunt omnes*' and then to go out 'hand in hand, not one before another'
(V. i. 425); see above, p. 57.

themselves. One of these is the communal departure for a banquet or feast, the traditional celebration of unity and concord. This action embraces not only the lovers, but all the other characters who can share the celebration : so at the end of *The Comedy of Errors*, the Abbess bids duke, husband, children, and servants to join together in a 'gossips' feast' (V. i. 405); at the end of *The Two Gentlemen*, Valentine looks forward to 'One feast, one house, one mutual happiness' (V. iv. 173); and at the end of *The Merry Wives*, everyone goes to 'eat a posset' at Page's house, accepting the general invitation of his wife :

> *Good husband, let us every one go home,*
> *And laugh this sport o'er by a country fire;*
> *Sir John and all.*
>
> (V. v. 255-7)

For Shakespeare the banquet was more than a conventional ending for a comedy, being a recurrent stage device, or dramatic metaphor, for concord, order, and peace. It is found in the earliest tragedies; the action of *Titus Andronicus* culminates in a feast 'ordain'd to an honourable end' (V. iii. 22) and Capulet, in *Romeo and Juliet*, fears a 'mutiny' among peaceful guests (I. v. 82). Later, in *Macbeth*, the guests of the newly crowned king are invited to sit at a banquet as if order and decorum were natural to them—'You know your own *degrees*; sit down' (III. iv. 1)—but when the king remembers his guilt he is 'unmann'd' and the feast is broken 'With most admired *disorder*' (III. iv. 110)—the guests are bidden :

> *Stand not upon the* order *of your going,*
> *But go at once.*
>
> (III. iv. 119-20)

In Shakespeare's last plays this stage image returns with added significance: in *Cymbeline*, for example, feasts celebrate the reunion of Imogen and her husband, the restoration of families, and the 'harmony' of the nation's peace :

138

> *Publish we this peace*
> *To all our subjects. . . .*
> *And in the temple of great Jupiter*
> *Our peace we'll ratify; seal it with feasts.*
>
> (V. v. 478-83)

But in the early comedies dancing is the most eloquent stage action which Shakespeare used to celebrate concluding order and harmony. Sir Thomas Elyot and Sir John Davies[1] have both described its significance for Shakespeare's contemporaries; in common with many other writers in the Renaissance tradition, they saw dancing as an analogy to the movement or 'music' of the spheres, a human figure of heavenly order and harmony. Davies went further, calling it a 'model of the world's great frame' (st. 33), an imitation of the pristine order of all created things. It was also a figure of order in society; for Elyot it entailed the 'intimation of sundry virtues', and, in certain forms, it 'signified matrimony';[2] for Davies, likewise:

> *Concord's true picture shineth in this art,*
> *Where divers men and women ranked be,*
> *And every one doth dance a several part,*
> *Yet all as one, in measure do agree,*
> *Observing perfect uniformity; . . . .*

> *If they whom sacred Love hath link't in one,*
> *Do as they dance, in all their course of life,*
> *Never shall burning grief nor bitter moan,*
> *Nor factious difference, nor unkind strife,*
> *Arise betwixt the husband and the wife;*
>   *For whether forth or back or round he go*
>   *As the man doth, so must the woman do.*
>
> (sts. 110 and 111)

[1] cf. Sir T. Elyot, *The Book Named the Governor*, published in 1531 and reprinted some seven times by 1580, and Sir J. Davies, *Orchestra, or a Poem on Dancing* (1596).

[2] *The Governor*, ed. H. H. S. Croft (1883), i. 233.

For an age that delighted in emblems and symbols, dancing signified concord and order between male and female.

Shakespeare used this symbolic action most subtly in the masque of *The Tempest*. In its formal dialogue, music, and dancing, Prospero figures the ideal of love and fruitfulness, but the concluding dance of Nymphs and Reapers is never completed. This is because Prospero remembers 'that *foul* conspiracy Of the *beast* Caliban and his confederates' (IV. i. 139-40); with this remembrance of disorder, Prospero is 'distemper'd' and 'to a strange, hollow, and *confused noise*', the dancers 'heavily vanish'.[1]

The associated symbols of dance, music, and discord give significance to many incidental details of action and dialogue in the early comedies; Shylock hates the 'vile squealing of the wry-neck'd fife' and forbids Jessica even to see the dancing;[2] the enmity between Oberon and Titania disturbs the fairies in their dancing;[3] in *The Two Gentlemen*, music can give no pleasure to Julia because the singer is 'false', and unless Silvia is with him Valentine can hear 'no music in the nightingale';[4] in *Much Ado*, Don John and his followers do not join the banquet or the masked dance, but go their own discordant ways.[5] The ideas associated with these actions are most explicitly expressed in one of the first group of sonnets; here the image of music is used to describe love's 'concord' or 'mutual ordering' as clearly as it describes moral and political order in *Richard II*:

> *If the true concord of well-tuned sounds,*
> *By unions married, do offend thine ear,*
> *They do but sweetly chide thee, who confounds*
> *In singleness the parts that thou shouldst bear.*
> *Mark how one string, sweet husband to another,*
> *Strikes each in each by mutual ordering,*
> *Resembling sire and child and happy mother*
> *Who all in one, one pleasing note do sing. . . .*[6]

[1] Folio stage direction. [2] *Mer. V.*, II. v. 30.
[3] cf. *MND.*, II. i. 86-7 and 140-2. [4] IV. ii. 54-72 and III. i. 179.
[5] cf. I. iii. 35 and 73-5, and II. i. 161ff. [6] *Sonn.*, viii. 5-12.

This sonnet and the other allusions to music and dancing indicate the significance of the stage action when the mechanicals and then the fairies conclude *A Midsummer Night's Dream* with dancing, when Oberon and Titania 'new in amity'

> . . . *solemnly*
> *Dance in Duke Theseus' house triumphantly*
> *And bless it to all fair prosperity.*
> (IV. i. 91-4)

The same symbolic action is used again when Benedick calls for music and *Much Ado* concludes with a patterned dance, the expression of high-spirited harmony of 'hearts', 'hands', and 'heels'. In *Love's Labour's Lost* there is a significant variation; though the stage seems fully set the lovers are not ready for their dance in unison, nor do those who act the 'Worthies' perform their jig as Constable Dull had expected;[1] the only harmony is in the songs of winter and spring, the alternation of the seasons, to which all must tune their individual harmonies.

    *   *   *

The comedy which culminates in the fullest celebration of the ideal of love's order is *As You Like It*. As 'still music'[2] sounds, Hymen is drawn mysteriously to this place and time, and links earthly and heavenly harmony:

> *Then is there mirth in heaven*
> *When earthly things made even*
> *Atone together. . . .*
> (V. iv. 114ff.)

'Atone' means 'to achieve unity or concord',[3] and so, when wonder has become more familiar, when the eight lovers have taken hands, and when news has come of the tyrant duke's abdication, music is called for and

[1] cf. V. i. 160-1.   [2] Folio stage direction.   [3] cf. *N.E.D.*, s.v. 2.

. . . brides and bridegrooms all,
With measure heap'd in joy, to the measures fall.
(V. iv. 184-5)

In the circumscribed steps of the dance, the abundance of their joy finds full expression. The exceptional elaboration of this conclusion—its formal groupings, music, song, dancing, and attendant god—suggests that *As You Like It* is informed to an exceptional degree by Shakespeare's ideal of love's order ; we may expect to discover a fuller appreciation of its peculiar delightfulness by following throughout its development the images, words, and actions associated with this ideal.

Alone among the comedies, *As You Like It* starts with a single prose speech of over two hundred words ; the words are simple enough but the speech is so involved with parenthetical qualifications and elaborations that it has to be delivered slowly and deliberately. Before the play can quicken into action, the audience must hear Orlando reiterate how Oliver, his guardian and eldest brother, keeps him in 'servitude', 'bars' him the 'place of a brother', and treats him as one of his 'hinds' or 'animals'. Oliver's entry interrupts this protestation, but only momentarily, for the two brothers start at once to quarrel in earnest. When Adam, an old servant, begs them, in their father's name, to 'be at *accord*' (I. i. 68), Oliver orders him away as an 'old dog' (I. i. 85). The whole exchange is a picture of disorder in a family. Left alone, Oliver asks for Charles, the 'duke's wrestler', and in direct terms—'what's the new news at the new court?' (I. i. 101-2)—calls forth still more direct exposition. There follows a second picture of disorder in society, for 'the old duke', says Charles, 'is banished by his younger brother the new duke' (I. ii. 104-5) ; our attention is turned from a 'tyrant brother' in the country, to a 'tyrant duke' at the court (I. ii. 300).

It is clear that, in this comedy, Shakespeare is concerned with society as well as with love, and at this point anyone who knows Shakespeare's history-plays might expect some criticism of these two disorders. It comes at once from Charles, the professional wrestler,[1] who in his dispassionate, professional way tells how 'three or four loving lords' have given up 'lands and revenues' to go to the forest of Arden and live there with the old duke in 'voluntary exile' (I. i. 106-8). Objectively he recounts the common notion of this other court:

> they say many young gentlemen flock to him every day, and fleet the time carelessly, as they did in the golden world. (I. i. 123-5.)

After this momentary contrast, the action continues with Oliver persuading Charles to attempt the life of Orlando who intends to wrestle for a prize at court. But when the scene changes there is a further contrast and we are shown Celia, the tyrant duke's daughter, promising Rosalind, the banished duke's daughter, that she will restore all as soon as she is able—she would count herself a '*monster*' if she failed to do this (I. ii. 24).

After these contrasts the tyrant's court is presented more directly. First Touchstone talks, jestingly as befits a clown, of its lack of true honour and wisdom, and then the duke himself enters to watch the wrestling match between Charles and Orlando. Orlando wins but when he says that he is the youngest son of Sir Rowland de Boys, he receives no honour for his victory; although the 'world esteem'd' Sir Rowland 'honourable', the tyrant had found that he was always his enemy and therefore he cannot welcome the son (I. ii. 237-8). This example of court life comes pat upon Touchstone's moralizing.

The action of the comedy is now well under way, for Rosalind and Orlando have fallen in love, but Shakespeare is still not finished with social disorder. Into the story which he found in Lodge's *Rosalynde*, he has already introduced two characters; the first, Touchstone the clown, has been

---

[1] He fights for his professional 'honour'; cf. I. i. 137.

used to comment on the corruptions of the court, and the second, Le Beau the courtier, is now used likewise. As a messenger from the tyrant, he had spoken with marked lack of feeling about the sport which, for his master's entertainment, had killed the three sons of an old father—the incongruity of this entertainment was quickly underlined with a jest from Touchstone—but now, in his own person, he feels such warm friendship for Orlando that he neglects attendance on the duke to counsel him to leave the court. Le Beau recognizes the 'malice' of his master, but, as Touchstone had hinted earlier, the 'little wit' that he has has been 'silenc'd' at court (I. ii. 95); he breaks off his hurried meeting with—

> Sir, fare you well:
> Hereafter, in a better world than this,
> I shall desire more love and knowledge of you.
> (I. ii. 295-7)

From this world, Rosalind and Celia escape to Arden, and, because she fears the unordered 'thieves' of the forest (I. iii. 110-12), Rosalind decides to disguise herself as a page, Ganymede, and they agree to ask Touchstone to accompany them. Thus weakly and foolishly protected, they leave the court's travesty of order and security, going—

> . . . in content
> To liberty and not to banishment.
> (I. iii. 139-40)

On this cue the scene changes for the first time to the forest of Arden, and, at once, our expectations are dashed; it is neither the careless golden world of the people's imagination nor the ruffian world of Rosalind's. We do indeed find contentment there, but it has only been won by *searching* for

> . . . tongues in trees, books in the running brooks,
> Sermons in stones and good in every thing.
> (II. i. 16-17)

There is an 'adversity' (II. i. 12), or 'stubborness of fortune', which has to be 'translated' into peace and quiet (II. i. 19-20);[1] order and tranquillity are subjective only, and not easily maintained. The banished duke has deliberated so curiously that he is 'irked' because the deer, 'poor dappled fools' and 'native burghers of this desert city', have to be 'gored' to provide him with sustenance (II. i. 22-3). This appears to be a new scruple—there's nothing to suggest that he had thought of being a vegetarian while at court—but he is immediately echoed by a jesting report of how Jaques, a lord who seeks to 'pierce' to the truth about life in 'country, city, court', has found that in killing deer the duke does 'more *usurp*' than did his brother who banished him (II. i. 25-63). This short scene concludes with the duke going to hear Jaques' philosophizing. The pastoral and courtly worlds had been compared a thousand times before Shakespeare wrote this play, but here the comparison is unexpected and strangely baffling; it raises issues without answering them, issues clearly related to those of earlier scenes by the direct comparison of the 'woods' with the 'envious court' (II. i. 3-4).

The action returns to the court to show the usurping duke hearing of the princesses' escape and reacting with nervous suspicion and vindictiveness. Then Adam is seen encountering Orlando and persuading him to fly from his brother who is again plotting to take his life. Adam laments in words that partly echo and partly amplify those of Le Beau:

> O, *what a world is this, when what is comely*
> *Envenoms him that bears it.*

> (II. iii. 14-15)

Under Oliver's unnatural tyranny, his 'house is but a *butchery*' (II. iii. 27-8), but Orlando swears that he would rather stay there than beg or—

---

[1] The duke's acceptance of the 'winter wind' as a counsellor that 'feelingly' persuades him of what he is (ll. 5-11) is a foretaste of Lear upon the heath, and a development of the princess's advice to the king in *Love's Labour's Lost*, V. ii. 802-17.

> ... *with a* base *and* boisterous *sword* enforce
> *A* thievish *living.* . . .

(II. iii. 32ff.)

As Rosalind found comfort in Celia and Touchstone, so
Orlando does in Adam who, trusting in the One who 'pro-
vidently caters for the sparrow' (l. 44), gives to his master all
the savings of his thrifty, well-ordered youth, and offers to
go with him into exile. Like Le Beau and Adam, Orlando
now remembers another 'world', where order, service, and
duty were all respected:

> *O good old man, how well in thee appears*
> *The* constant service *of the antique world,*
> *When service sweat for duty, not for meed!*
> *Thou are not for the fashion of these times,*
> *Where none will sweat but for promotion,*
> *And having that, do* choke *their service up*
> *Even with the having:* . . .

(II. iii. 56ff.)

Together they leave Oliver's tyranny and seek, instead,
'some settled low content' (II. iii. 68).

The preliminary pictures of disordered society are now
almost complete—there is only one more direct view which
comes four scenes later and shows the tyrant sending Oliver
'out of doors' to seek his brother while seizing into his own
hands the lands and revenues which Oliver had sought to
augment. Shakespeare has created these pictures in 'primitive' outline and colour, a technique which has enabled him
to isolate and contrast significant and typical actions. By a
series of recurrent words, actions, and images, and by additions to his source, he has shown how generous loyalty and
affection cannot purge a disordered world but can at least
give to fugitives some measure of personal order and content.

The 'primitive' technique of these early scenes has led
some critics to think that Shakespeare was only interested in

getting to Arden as quickly as possible, but once the action is centred in the forest, he is still not wholly concerned with its delights; repeatedly these early scenes are echoed in theme if not in manner, and their careful contrasts and emphases are made to contribute to the final resolution. For example, the preliminary scene in Arden had stressed the need for a personal acceptance of the 'stubbornness of fortune'—the pastoral world was not an easy substitute for the corrupt court—and this is the point which Shakespeare reiterates as each fugitive enters the forest. Rosalind, Celia, and Touchstone are the first to arrive, weary in body and spirit. The clown says frankly that it were better to be at court, while Rosalind, asking the old shepherd Corin for help, hardly dares to hope that such a 'desert place' can yield 'entertainment' (II. iv. 72). When Corin rejoins that he is a 'shepherd to another man', a master of *churlish* disposition' who

> . . . *little recks to find the way to heaven*
> *By doing deeds of hospitality.* . . . .
>
> (II. iv. 78ff.)

their fears seem confirmed. But Rosalind discovers a kinship with the suffering, amorous shepherd, Silvius, and Corin promises to help them, and at once their spirits rise; Rosalind offers to buy the master's cottage and Celia forgets both her weariness and the unfriendly aspect of Arden—she will 'mend' Corin's wages and 'willingly could waste' her time in the forest (II. iv. 94-5).

This double aspect of Arden, at one moment forbidding and at the next welcoming, presents problems which no modern scene-designer is fully able to solve; indeed its beauty, lying only in the eye of the beholders, cannot be represented objectively. When Orlando enters the forest with Adam, he almost despairs of comfort:

> *If this* uncouth *forest yield any thing savage, I will either be food for it or bring it for food to thee.* (II. vi. 6-8.)

But if a scene-designer listened to Orlando and painted a 'desert' (l. 19) visited by 'bleak' winds (l. 16), he would have to prepare—the lighting expert would help him—an entirely different setting for the very next moment when we are shown the banished duke and his followers taking their ease and feeding plentifully in the open air. And even this quick change would not fully serve, for Orlando soon rushes in and tries to force the others to give him food; not only has 'bare distress' taken from him all 'show of smooth civility' (II. vii. 95-6),[1] but to him the forest is still a 'desert inaccessible' and the duke is incongruously at ease under 'melancholy boughs' (II. vii. 110-11).

The duke replies to Orlando with true 'gentleness',[2] and, having sheathed his sword, Orlando goes to fetch Adam and then joins 'the good man's feast', the visible token of order and concord in Arden.[3] Thenceforward he complains no more of Arden's 'unkindness'; he lies under its oaks, roams through its glades, and thinks, writes, and talks of Rosalind's perfections :

> *Why should this a* desert *be?*
> *For it is unpeopled? No;*
> *Tongues I'll hang on every tree,*
> *That shall* civil *sayings show:*
> *Some, how brief the life of man*
> *Runs his erring pilgrimage. . . .*
> *Some of violated vows*
> *'Twixt the souls of friend and friend:*
> *But upon the fairest boughs,*
> *Or at every sentence end,*
> *Will I Rosalinda write,*
> *Teaching all that read to know*

[1] cf. Orlando's earlier boast that he would not 'enforce a thievish living' (II. iii. 32-3).

[2] The words 'gentleness' (i.e. courtesy, courtliness, '*kind*ness', civilized or ordered sentiment and action), 'good manners', 'nurture', 'civility' are used many times within some thirty lines.

[3] See above, p. 138-9.

The quintessence of every sprite
Heaven would in little show. . . .
Heaven would that she these gifts should have,
And I to live and die her slave.

(III. ii. 133-62)

The verses are lame, but the reconciliation they attempt to
celebrate is complete; if he cannot *find* 'tongues in trees,
books in the running brooks' by means of the duke's philosophy, he will at least *give* them his own tongue, his 'civil
sayings'; he can now have order and joy in Arden.

Oliver flying, in his turn, to the forest is threatened by
a lionness and a snake, but he is rescued by Orlando,
motivated by '*kind*ness, nobler ever than revenge' (IV. iii.
129). This effects a 'conversion' (l. 137) in him, and the two
brothers make their peace and go to the 'gentle duke' at
whose hands Oliver receives 'fresh array and entertainment'
(ll. 143-4). The earlier pattern is repeated, for Oliver soon
falls in love with Celia and is content to resign all his wealth
and 'live and die a shepherd' in the forest (V. ii. 14); we
hear no more of wild beasts or deserts.

Arden is not necessarily or unequivocally the 'golden
world' of the people's imagination, but 'gentleness', '*kind*-
ness', the duke's philosophy, or the willingness to serve
submissively and patiently for love can translate the 'stubbornness of fortune' into a sweet and quiet style. This is the
point at which the pictures of social disorder and of new-
found order in Arden are contrasted and related, and thereby
illuminate each other. At court or in Oliver's household,
affection and faith could only bring 'content' in the 'liberty'
of banishment, but once in Arden, content is at command:
the forest mirrors one's mind; if peace and order are found
there, the forest will reflect them.

And at this point too, order and disorder are related to the
love stories which are about to take the main focus in the
drama. Contentment in love is, like content in Arden, subjective; it is as one's self likes it. Phoebe's eyes have power

to act against Silvius as 'tyrants, butchers, murderers'
(III. v. 14), but that is only because Silvius sees her in that
way; when she tries to 'entame' Ganymede, she is for
Rosalind a 'tyrant' who 'exults' in a power which only
Silvius recognizes: ''Tis not her glass, but you, that flatters
her', she tells the youth—

> *And out of you she sees herself more* proper
> *Than any of her lineaments can show her.*
>
> (III. v. 36-56)

This private, subjective truth is sufficient for the lovers, as
the subjective order must be for the fugitives in Arden;
Silvius can only answer Phoebe's refusal with renewed vows
of generous service.[1]

And as each of Arden's citizens and each of its lovers finds
content in his or her own manner, so both citizens and lovers
find it in terms of the 'gentleness', service or order which
has been neglected in the world outside. For Silvius love is

> *. . . to be all made of faith and service . . .*
> *All adoration, duty, and observance,*
> *All humbleness, all patience and impatience,*
> *All purity, all trial, all observance.*
>
> (V. ii. 95-104)

As in the 'antique world' of good order, he 'sweats for duty
not for meed'. And when Phoebe finds she has been fooled
by the appearance of a man in Ganymede,[2] she accepts the
suit of Silvius because of his belief in an order in which
she herself believes:

> *Thy* faith *my fancy to thee doth combine.*
>
> (V. iv. 156)

Oliver and Celia establish their mutual content more rapidly
and confidently, but it is still in terms of order; as Caesar
established his kingdoms, so they both 'came, saw, and
overcame' (V. ii. 35). Rosalind and Orlando had met for the

---

[1] See above, p. 80.   [2] See above, p. 104.

first time at court but their love was not fully expressed there. They had done what they could—Rosalind had given him a favour to wear and both had confessed that they were 'thrown down', 'overthrown', disordered by a new 'master' and new duties of service[1]—yet more was expressed in their hesitations than in words or deeds, and it is only in Arden that they learn the full strength of their new order, of their mutual defeat and mastery. In the forest they learn to make their love explicit in the very words by which Silvius vows his service, observance, and faith.[2] On one level the story of Rosalind and Orlando is easily appreciated, but it should be seen in the context of the whole play, of the tyrannies outside Arden, of the subjective content which can be won within Arden, and of the other love stories; all these are informed by Shakespeare's ideal of order and all these contribute to the implicit judgement of the play, and to the full significance of any part of it.

Arden's pleasures and love's order do not recommend themselves to all comers. Touchstone does not readily give way to such enthusiasms: he is 'Nature's natural' (I. ii. 52) who cares not for his 'spirits' if his legs are not 'weary' (II. iv. 2-3). The excitement of a lover, the zeal of a scholar, the business of a lawyer do not affect, for him, the pace of Time;[3] for him, Time travels regularly:

> *'Tis but an hour ago since it was nine,*
> *And after one hour more 'twill be eleven;*
> *And so, from hour to hour, we ripe and ripe,*
> *And then, from hour to hour, we rot and rot....*
>
> (II. vii. 24-7)

Determined to treat a spade only as a spade, Touchstone will not be carried away by any subjective idealization of life in Arden:

[1] I. ii. 262, 266, and 271-2.

[2] cf. V. ii. 89-108; the addition of this chorus of lovers is among the most significant modifications to Lodge's *Rosalynde*.

[3] cf. III. ii. 320-51.

*in respect of itself, it is a good life; but in respect that it is a
shepherd's life, it is naught. . . .* (III. ii. 13ff.)

In the affairs of love he reckons, like Costard, on the
'simplicity of man';[1] he notices the 'strange capers' which
lovers run into (II. iv. 55), but he quickly accounts for such
vagaries :

> *If a hart do lack a hind,*
> *Let him seek out Rosalind.*
> *If the cat will after kind,*
> *So be sure will Rosalind. . . .*
>   (III. ii. 107ff.)

Yet once Touchstone finds Audrey his attitude changes ;
the desire to possess involves him, by degrees, in the mutual
order of love. The first time we see them together, he is
offering to 'fetch up' her goats and is already impatient of
Time, questioning 'Am I the man yet? doth my simple
feature *content* you?' (III. iii. 1-4). He cannot contemplate
his actions without misgivings, but he rallies his courage :

> *. . . As horns are odious, they are necessary . . . as a walled
> town is more* worthier *than a village, so is the forehead of a
> married man more* honourable *than the bare brow of a
> bachelor; and by how much defence is better than no skill, by
> so much is a horn more precious than to want.* (III. iii. 48-62.)

When Jaques tells him that Sir Oliver Martext can only wed
them like badly joined wainscot, Touchstone professes himself content, for, in due time, this will give him the better
excuse to leave his wife. But he is further in than he admits,
and, to Audrey's surprise, he fails to take advantage of Sir
Oliver but goes with Jaques to find a 'good priest that can
tell . . . what marriage is' (ll. 86-7). He now remembers, not
merely that 'cat will after kind', but also something which is
above man's apparent 'simplicity' ; he recollects that

> *As the ox hath his* bow, *. . . the horse his* curb *and the falcon*

[1] *LLL.*, I. i. 219; see above, pp. 130-1.

her bells, *so man hath his desires; and as pigeons bill, so* wedlock *will be nibbling*. (III. iii. 80-3.)

The 'yoke', 'curb', or order of love also seems to be 'necessary', even for a man of 'a fearful heart'.

Touchstone falls in with the ordered dance of the lovers as best he may. First he jousts with William a youth of the forest who lays claim to Audrey and, asserting his new-found possessiveness, routs the complacent, good-natured clown. Then he is ready to press in 'amongst the rest of the country copulatives' (V. iv. 57-8). Knowing that 'marriage binds and blood breaks', he expects to 'swear and to forswear' (ll. 58-60), but he makes what show he can. Audrey may not cut a fine figure in the eyes of other people but love is ever 'as you like it'; 'a poor virgin, sir', he explains, 'an ill-favoured thing, sir, but mine own' (ll. 60-1). And as he is now disposed to dignify any complaisance with the formality of honour and good manners, so he commands Audrey—and his concern for this draws laughter from everyone—to 'bear' her 'body more seeming' (l. 72).[1] Touchstone may yet find the 'pearl' in his 'foul oyster'; at least he knows something of the terms —the mutual order of love—on which such treasure is discovered.

By adding Touchstone to the story that he had found in Lodge's *Rosalynde*, Shakespeare has emphasized the implicit judgement of this play; by contrast and relationship with other characters, Touchstone illuminates the main theme in each of its three branches—social disorder, Arden's subjective order, and love's order. And Shakespeare's preoccupation with these ideas becomes even clearer when we notice that Jaques, his other major addition to Lodge, is used in the same threefold manner.

Jaques' talent is for the exposure of disorder, not the affirmation of order; we first hear a report of his whimsically extravagant denunciation of the duke's 'tyranny' over the deer, and then we see him 'sucking' melancholy from

---

[1] For Shakespeare's age, 'seeming' meant suitably, becomingly, beseemly.

Amiens' song, as 'a weasel sucks eggs' (II. v. 12-14).
Jaques rightly uses a destructive image to describe his
pleasure, for he finds no joy in the song's harmony nor in
its simple, complaisant reconciliation with Arden:

> *Under the greenwood tree*
> *Who loves to lie with me,*
> *And turn his merry note*
> *Unto the sweet bird's throat,*
> *Come hither, come hither, come hither:*
> *Here shall he see*
> *No enemy*
> *But winter and rough weather.*
>
> (II. v. 1-8)

The 'young'[1] foresters join in with Amiens' second stanza
but Jaques thinks of the 'grossness', the lack of complexity,
which their song represents. He offers another stanza of his
own:

> *If it do come to pass*
> *That any men turn ass,*
> *Leaving his wealth and ease,*
> *A stubborn will to please,*
> *Ducdame, ducdame, ducdame:*
> *Here shall he see*
> *Gross fools as he,*
> *An if he will come to me.*
>
> (II. v. 52-9)

Observing the circle in which the young men have gathered
to ask what 'ducdame' means, Jaques uses it as a token of
their easy-going acceptance of order in Arden: ''Tis a
Greek invocation', he explains, 'to call fools into a circle'
(ll. 61-2).

Jaques will not risk being a fool on his own account—he
prefers to rail against others—but he feels a kinship with
the clown Touchstone who sees life as a mere 'simplicity' of

[1] cf. I. i. 123.

ripening and rotting. He is at once ambitious for a fool's licence to speak his mind and so, as he believes,—

> ... *through and through*
> *Cleanse the* foul *body of the* infected *world.*
>   (II. vii. 59-60)

Given his liberty he would sing no song, but rail against disorder, against the city woman who bears the 'cost of princes on *unworthy* shoulders' and against the upstart courtier of '*basest* function' (ll. 74-82). When Orlando enters, desperate with hunger, Jaques has only 'reason' to offer as a cure (ll. 100-1);[1] and then, while Orlando goes to fetch Adam at the duke's invitation, he proceeds to amplify Touchstone's wisdom and to speak of the seven ages of man as of a mere mutation in response to Time's ordering—of man's own ordering vision, he makes no account. At this point Shakespeare fully demonstrates Jaques' limitations, for as soon as he has called old age a 'second childishness and mere oblivion' (l. 165), Orlando re-enters with the aged Adam whose 'constant service' has made him the 'venerable burden' which the duke at once recognizes. Following this reminder of all that Jaques had forgotten, Amiens sings of man's ingratitude; respect for virtue is not forgetfulness.

Jaques' negative, reasonable, and unenthusiastic attitude towards men and society, which decries disorder but neglects to praise and appreciate such order as men have achieved, is matched by his attitude to lovers. With Orlando, conversation is almost impossible. Jaques reproves him for 'marring' the trees by 'writing love-songs in their barks', and Orlando reproves Jaques for reading them so 'ill-favouredly' (III. i. 276-9). Jaques does not like the name of Rosalind, and Orlando does not defend it; these matters are 'as you like it' and there was 'no thought of pleasing [him] when she was christened' (ll. 283-4). Jaques invites him to rail 'against our

---

[1] There may be a pun on reason/raisin for Orlando has just demanded some fruit; such a pun would tend to emphasize the single word, the rational purgative which is Jaques' only medicine.

mistress the world and all our misery', and Orlando, mindful of another mistress, answers that he will 'chide no breather in the world' but himself, against whom he knows 'most faults' (ll. 295-300). Orlando's love leads him into absurdities which appear as 'faults' to others, but they are faults that Orlando would not change for the 'best virtue' that Jaques can boast of (ll. 301-2).

Jaques has more to say to Touchstone, for he must denounce the iniquities of Martext, but with Rosalind he can only once more manifest his ignorance of love's inward order and joy. He is neither scholar, musician, courtier, soldier, lawyer nor lover, and he feels none of their emotions ; he merely contemplates their exploits and failures, and gains a 'most humourous sadness' (IV. i. 20). This is his only possession. Orlando interrupts his talk with Rosalind, or rather with Ganymede, by addressing the seeming boy with 'Good day and happiness, dear Rosalind' ; to Jaques this is doubly nonsense and he leaves, baffled by their mutual, private pleasure.

When the duke is restored to his true place in society by the sudden conversion of his tyrant brother, Jaques cannot join the dance which celebrates the new order of the lovers ; unappeased, he must seek more matter for his contemplation. But having seen them all endure 'shrewd days and nights' (V. iv. 179), he accepts this as testimony of their inward virtues, and, for the first time in the play, sees promise of order, not of disorder. He speaks formally and in due order—to the duke:

> *You to your former honour I bequeath;*
> *Your patience and your virtue well deserves it:*

then to Orlando, Oliver, and Silvius in turn, dismissing them:

> *You to a love that your true faith doth merit:*
> *You to your land and love and great allies:*
> *You to a long and well-deserved bed.*
>
> (V. iv. 192-6)

For Touchstone he foresees 'wrangling', for the clown has only given proof of 'victual' for some two months of 'loving voyage' with Audrey (V. iv. 197-8). This is a rational appraisement of their several chances of creating love's order in the more complex, less subjective, world of society at large.

A detached critic who rails at the follies or 'disorders' of others sounds a tiresome character for any comedy, but even when Jaques criticizes those who affirm individual visions of order, the effect on them is only to add to their happiness; his 'sullen fits' (II. i. 67) are sport for the philosophical duke, his encounters with Rosalind and Orlando encourage them to be more confident in their own happiness, and his mockery of the young foresters for 'conquering' the deer, sends them singing through the forest.[1] His strictures on corrupt society can give pleasure by the seasoned wit with which he, like a true satirist, affirms the value of order by recognizing and describing disorder; as he himself says, his 'sadness' is one, limited, kind of 'good' (IV. i. 7). Without Jaques, *As You Like It* would be a far less subtle play, for besides showing the limitations of his own disinterested judgement, he makes us aware of the limitations of subjective order and content; he shows us that the philosophical duke is 'too disputable' for some company (II. v. 36), that the young foresters are content because they are easily so, that Orlando does not care to mend his most obvious absurdities. And indirectly Jaques affirms the complexity of love's order, for as the couples come together at the close of the play, he reminds us that they are not merely servants of each others' excellencies, but also 'couples . . . coming to the Ark', some of them very 'strange beasts' (V. iv. 36-7).

To follow Jaques through the play is to become aware of Shakespeare's preoccupation with the ideal of order in society, in Arden, and in love, and of the subtlety and range of his consequent judgements. But Jaques alone cannot suggest the light-footed gaiety, the warmth, and the

[1] cf. IV. ii.

confidence with which this comedy is written. Some of these qualities derive from the apparently easy interplay between the varied and individually conceived characters; for example, the absurdly single-minded Silvius is first introduced talking to the simply and sensibly satisfied Corin, and overheard by Rosalind and Touchstone, and then, later, Touchstone and Corin meet and compare their individual 'simplicities'. But the play's generosity and confidence spring chiefly from the characterization of Rosalind. She ensures that Shakespeare's ideal of love's order is not presented as a cold theorem; in her person love's doubts and faith, love's obedience and freedom, co-exist in delightful animation.

The lively characterization of Rosalind is not an added, irrelevant pleasure, but arises from, and continually illuminates, the thematic structure of the whole play. This is perhaps Shakespeare's greatest triumph in *As You Like It*: from the moment when she is disordered by the claims of love to the moment when she makes Orlando reiterate their 'compact' (V. iv. 5) for the last, unnecessary time, she invites our understanding as well as our enthusiasm. She delights to 'play the knave' with Orlando (III. ii. 314-15), for the more she casts doubts upon whether he is truly 'sick' of an unsatisfied love the more assurance she receives that he is indeed so, and the more outrageously she pictures women the more strongly he affirms his faith in her own virtue. Yet while his faith permits her to enjoy this freedom, she is careful to offer no more alluring 'cure' for his 'sickness' than the prospect of living 'in a nook merely monastic' (III. ii. 440-1). Love's order has its justice, and Rosalind must pay for the advantage she delights to take; Orlando, protected by the belief that she is Ganymede, can come 'within an hour' of his promise and be quite easy in mind (IV. i. 42-3), but for Rosalind, to 'break but a part of the thousandth part of a minute' has its torments. She may 'disable' all the fabled heroics of other lovers, but that is only because her own love is too great to be spoken, because she 'cannot be out of the sight of Orlando' (IV. i. 223-4).

In the two central scenes between Orlando and Rosalind, Shakespeare shows us the growing assurance of their mutual love, its generosity, truth, and order. And at the close of the play, he directs that they should take hands in the forefront of the other lovers and, after the final dance affirming the creation of mutual order, that they should go back with the duke to the court, away from purely subjective content—they go to play their part on the great stage of society and to affirm order and harmony there.

And then Rosalind steps forward:

It is not the fashion to see the lady the epilogue; but it is no more unhandsome than to see the lord the prologue. . . .

She will not beg for applause for the play; her 'way is to conjure':

I charge you, O women, for the love you bear to men, to like as much of this play as please you: and I charge you, O men, for the love you bear to women—as I perceive by your simpering, none of you hates them—that between you and the women the play may please.

'Between the men and the women' the play *can* please, for it mirrors the 'mutual ordering' of love. If we answer its 'conjuration', we shall, consciously or unconsciously, be 'pleased' with its ideal of harmony. We may, of course, allow the trick to retain all its mystery, but if we wish, by tracing the implicit judgements of the play, we may realize that it succeeds not merely by some sleight of hand, but also by reason of the ideals which inform it.

CHAPTER VI

Twelfth Night or What You Will

In the previous three chapters we have assumed that Shakespeare's comedies are informed by his attitude to life and, in particular, to love and personal relationships. We have proceeded on the understanding that one of the prime tasks of criticism is to define that attitude and the way in which it has been 'bodied forth' in the drama. Clearly the task is endless; we must aim at a full appreciation of Shakespeare as a man and also as a poetic dramatist, of his wisdom and human sympathy and of his technical accomplishments. In the last resort our difficulties are due to the nature of Shakespeare's mind; this was not characterized by any startling originality or idiosyncrasy, but by an extraordinary comprehensiveness and unity. Once the reader, actor or audience is prepared to give the comedies the same humility of attention as he accords to the history-plays or tragedies, he will find that the vision they express and the subtlety of its expression are always eluding a completely satisfactory definition. He will discover many speeches and actions which, viewed in the context of a whole comedy, are liable to call up every cliché of criticism; for lack of better terms one must discuss their truth to nature, their currents of association, their width of reference, complexity of meaning, universal validity, the various levels of possible interpretation.

The attempt to discuss the comedies in the light of three of Shakespeare's ideas about love has entailed drastic simplifications. In the first place, these are not the only ideas implicit in the comedies; Shakespeare was also concerned with time, destiny, and patience, with old age and youth,

with the individual and society, with ignorance and knowledge, confidence and melancholy, with contrasts between
love and friendship, nature and art, justice and mercy. But
to illustrate the implicit judgement of the comedies and to
show Shakespeare's growing power over his material, it was
expedient to select the three main ideas and follow them
singly throughout the whole sequence of the early comedies.
For those plays in which one of these ideas is so dominant
that it might be called Shakespeare's theme or preoccupation
—the choice between these terms depending on our estimate
of Shakespeare's conscious artistry—this procedure can give
some idea of their complexity, of the freedom with which
the central theme is treated so that it illuminates a wide
range of human thought and feeling. In *Much Ado*, for
example, the theme of love's truth led Shakespeare to contrast the old age of Leonato and Antonio with the youth of
Claudio and Benedick, to show in Benedick and Beatrice
the difference between recognizing and acknowledging a
truth, to alternate confidence and melancholy in Don Pedro
and Claudio, to contrast ignorance and knowledge in
Leonato, Claudio, Benedick, Pedro, Margaret, Dogberry,
and the watchman, to be concerned in Benedick's and
Claudio's speeches and verse-making with nature and art, in
the relationships of Pedro, Benedick, and Claudio to show
the strength and weakness of friendship. Because of the unity
of Shakespeare's mind, to consider the basic themes of the
comedies is to become aware of all the other themes as
well.

To discuss the implicit judgement of the comedies under
three heads is a simplification in yet another direction : three
are too many as well as too few. Although *As You Like It* is
largely inspired by the ideal of order, one must also be aware
of the judgements and emotions associated with the ideals of
love's wealth and love's truth, and while *The Merchant of
Venice* is chiefly concerned with love's wealth, the casket
scenes and Shylock's proferred friendship cannot be rightly
appreciated without an awareness of Shakespeare's ideal of

love's truth, nor the bawdy jokes of the last act without remembering his ideal of love's order. No comedy is governed *wholly* by one of the three themes which we have discussed. In some, not one of the three is clearly dominant; the conclusion of *The Shrew*, for example,[1] celebrates love's truth in Katharina's acceptance of her new role, and love's order in the mutual giving and obedience of the two lovers. In the final analysis the three basic themes of the comedies, or the three hundred minor themes which might be enumerated, are only aspects of one single theme—Shakespeare's comprehensive and unified vision of human life.

To make this point in a practical manner, and to try to do justice to this particular play, *Twelfth Night* has been reserved for separate treatment. None of the three themes or preoccupations is dominant here, but they all work together, in conjunction with further ideas, towards a new and comprehensive effect. It has often been remarked that *Twelfth Night* repeats characters, situations, and dramatic devices from earlier comedies; it also repeats their implicit judgements, and modifies and enlarges them by new associations. This play cannot be fitly considered in the light of any one of the three basic ideas; the three threads must be held in the hand all the time.

* * *

Twelfth Night begins with music, but it does not express an ordered harmony; Orsino, the lord of Illyria, longs for an 'excess' of it, hearkens after one particular strain, and then abruptly sends the musicians away. Orsino speaks of love, but it is not that love which

---

[1] The year's probation required of the young men at the end of *Love's Labour's Lost* must be explained by reference to all three themes; they must show that their new order can withstand winter and the cry of the owl (see pp. 132-4 above), they must learn to be 'generous, gentle, and humble' in their acceptance of the performances of true zeal (see p. 77 above), and they must prove that their own words are not mere outward tokens, mere 'courtship, pleasant jest and courtesy' (see p. 105 above).

> *. . . gives to every power a double power,*
> *Above their functions and their offices. . . .*[1]

His spirit of love is 'quick and fresh', but notwithstanding its 'capacity', it

> *Receiveth as the sea, nought enters there,*
> *Of what validity and pitch soe'er,*
> *But falls into abatement and low price,*
> *Even in a minute. . . .*
>
> (I. i. 10-14)

His love knows no 'order', and it knows no 'wealth'; he is far from Valentine who can feed upon 'the very naked name of love',[2] from Portia who would be 'trebled twenty times' herself only to 'stand high' in Bassanio's account,[3] or from Juliet who likens her love to the sea as Orsino does, but in a far different sense:

> *My bounty is as boundless as the sea,*
> *My love as deep; the more I give to thee*
> *The more I have, for both are infinite.*[4]

Orsino's love is not 'boundless as the sea', but

> *. . . all as hungry as the sea,*
> *And can digest as much. . . .*
>
> (II. iv. 103-4)

Instead of finding love's wealth, he finds 'abatement and low price'. Nor does he pursue his unrequited love in the same active way as the headstrong lovers in *A Midsummer Night's Dream*, or as Silvius in *As You Like It* who thinks it

> *. . . a most plenteous crop*
> *To glean the broken ears after the man*
> *That the main harvest reaps.*
>
> (III. v. 101-3)

---

[1] *LLL.*, IV. iii. 331-2.   [2] *Gent.*, II. iv. 142.
[3] *Mer. V.*, III. ii. 154-7.   [4] *Rom.*, II. ii. 133-5.

He mars no trees with his verses, attempts no tasks of 'faith and service'; he does not find a new and comprehensive 'order' in love, but in solitariness[1] indulges his fancy, leaving the stage with:

> *Away before me to sweet beds of flowers:*
> *Love-thoughts lie rich when canopied with bowers.*
>
> (I. i. 40-1)

Instead of seeking opportunities to 'give and hazard', he passively takes what seeming pleasures can be his.

The first scene also contains a picture of Olivia, Orsino's beloved. She has been left sorrowful and unprotected by the death of her brother, and, not returning Orsino's love, she has resolved to shut the gate upon the world and—

> *. . . like a cloistress, she will veiled walk*
> *And water once a day her chamber round*
> *With eye-offending brine.*
>
> (I. i. 28-30)

Olivia is like the young men of *Love's Labour's Lost*, or like Romeo's Rosaline, all of whom swear to live alone and 'in that sparing' make 'huge waste';[2] in the words of the sonnets, Olivia has determined to be a 'profitless usurer', to 'abuse The bounteous largess' given her to give;[3] she has determined to hazard nothing of her potential 'wealth' in love.

This first scene is a mere forty lines and it is followed by one only slightly longer, but with an immediate contrast in tone; the dialogue is now brisk, the characters active. Viola, like Olivia, has lost her twin brother and only guardian, and is even more unprotected, being shipwrecked and friendless on the strange shore of Illyria. But unlike Olivia, she takes comfort, and later she hears that her brother, Sebastian, has, unlike Orsino, been 'Most *provident* in peril' (I. ii. 12) and may have survived the wreck. Viola could wish to 'abjure'

---

[1] cf. I. iv. 40-1.   [2] *Rom.*, I. i. 224.   [3] *Sonnet*, iv.

the company and sight of men as Olivia has done (ll. 40-4), but, trusting the sea captain's 'fair and outward character' (l. 51), she determines to disguise herself as an eunuch and serve Orsino of whom she has heard her father speak. Viola's entry upon the scene, rising mysteriously from the sea, is strange, and her sudden 'intent' to serve Orsino is strange also ;[1] but her activity, her willingness to trust the outcome to 'time' (l. 60), and her brisk exit—'I thank thee : lead me on.'—are all in clear contrast to the earlier scene. On her next appearance as Cesario, Orsino's page, the contrast is clearer still, for she is one who will generously give and hazard for love—she will do her best to woo Orsino's lady though she herself 'would be his wife' (I. iv. 45). On her third appearance she is one who knows love's true wealth ; to her way of thinking, Olivia 'usurps' herself, for what is hers to 'bestow' is not hers 'to reserve' (I. v. 200-2). When Olivia asks what Cesario would do in Orsino's predicament, Viola's ardent description of a lover's restless and possibly absurd activity is in direct contrast to her master's indulgence, and in Olivia it awakens admiration, generosity, and the willingness to hazard.

Shakespeare has not presented Orsino and Olivia in a directly satirical manner ; indeed the warmth of Olivia's affection for her brother and the richness and ardency of Orsino's fancy have led some critics to think that Shakespeare wholeheartedly approved of their actions.[2] But the judgement which Shakespeare's ideal of love's wealth leads us to expect, is implicit in the dialogue, and is made dramatically apparent by the contrast of Viola ; the first two scenes

[1] It is just possible that Shakespeare intended her ready remembrance of Orsino's name and her immediate recollection that he was a 'bachelor' (I. ii. 29) to suggest that her father had mentioned his name with the purpose of interesting her young affections in a desirable husband.

[2] For example, Dr L. Hotson thinks that Orsino is a complimentary portrait of a Count Orsino who visited Queen Elizabeth in 1600, and that Olivia is 'a romanticized and youthful shadow of "the most excellent and glorious person" of the Queen herself'; cf. *The First Night of 'Twelfth Night'* (1954), p. 121 and *passim*.

leave the audience delighted and charmed, and also uncertain; youth, beauty, and the wealth of love are already in question.

Sir Toby Belch begins the next scene with

What a plague means my niece, to take the death of her brother thus? I am sure care's an enemy to life. (I. iii. 1-3.)

and, at once, there is another contrast. Sir Toby is a hanger-on in Olivia's household, indulging in wine and good fellowship at the buttery-bar. The cares of either mourner or lover are not for him. He does, however, profess friendship, and his 'love' for the foolish knight, Sir Andrew Aguecheek, contrasts him directly with the more courtly characters. The ideals of love's wealth are doubly outraged in this friendship, for he encourages Sir Andrew to recoup his fortune by paying court to Olivia and uses this as a pretext to fleece his 'friend' on his own account. Later when Fabian, one of Olivia's servants, remarks that Sir Andrew is a 'dear manakin' to Sir Toby, the latter replies, delighting in the ducats which have come from his purely commercial bargain—

I have been dear *to him, lad, some two thousand strong, or so.* (III. ii. 56-9.)

This travesty of love's wealth in friendship is immediately contrasted in a scene between Sebastian and Antonio, the friend by whose help he has survived the shipwreck. Unknown to the others, they have reached Illyria where Antonio, having in the past fought against the Illyrians, dare not show his face. As Sebastian goes to look at the sights of the city, Antonio freely and without prompting offers his purse. 'Why I your purse?' queries Sebastian and he is immediately answered:

Haply your eye shall light upon some toy
You have desire to purchase; and your store,
I think, is not for idle markets, sir.

(III. iii. 43-6)

These true friends delight to give before they are asked, and demand no surety or promises.

The characters of this play seem to take up formal relationships to each other in the light of their attitudes to love's wealth. Malvolio, Olivia's steward, is another instance; he affects to love Olivia, but truly he loves only himself. He is first encountered calling Feste, the fool, a 'barren rascal', and putting him out of his merry humour. Olivia, who sees the faults of others more readily than her own, rebukes him in words that echo Armado's rebuke to his audience in *Love's Labour's Lost*:

> *O, you are sick of self-love, Malvolio, and taste with a distempered appetite. To be* generous, *guiltless and of* free[1] *disposition, is to take those things for bird-bolts that you deem cannon-bullets:* ... (I. v. 99ff.)

Malvolio shows his lover's disposition in soliloquy; he indulges the fancy—somewhat like Orsino—that his dreams have come true, and we hear his wildest hopes. In these he thinks only of the wealth and importance which love will bring to himself; Olivia doesn't even come into the picture, nor the service that he can do for her. 'Having been three months married to her', he muses—

> *sitting in* my *state,* ... *Calling* my *officers about* me, *in* my *branched velvet gown; having come from a daybed, where* I *have left* Olivia *sleeping,* ... *And then to have the humour of state* ... *telling them* I *know* my *place as* I *would they should do theirs, to ask for* my *kinsman Toby,* ... *Seven of* my *people, with an obedient start, make out for him:* I *frown the while; and perchance wind up* my *watch, or play with* my——

—here he pauses, for momentarily he has forgotten that he would have more than one ornament about him; he corrects it to '*some* rich jewel', and then continues about extending

---

[1] For 'generous' see p. 77 above, n. 1, and for 'free' see pp. 48-9 above.

'*my* hand', about '*my* familiar smile' and '*my* fortunes' (II. v. 49-88). If in courting Olivia, Sir Andrew strives for 'that which many men desire', Malvolio is fool enough to 'assume desert' and to choose 'as much as he deserves';[1] loving only himself, thinking only of what will accrue to him, failing to be '*generous*' and 'of *free* disposition', he is unable to realize the true 'wealth' of love.

* * *

Having presented these characters in terms of love's wealth, Shakespeare developed the action by many of the devices associated with the ideal of love's truth. Most obvious is Viola's disguise as Cesario. When Olivia falls in love with the seeming boy, Viola at once suspects that she has been charmed merely by her 'outside' (II. ii. 18). Viola is constantly aware of the difference between appearance and reality; in judging the sea captain she remembers that a 'beauteous wall' may 'oft close in pollution' (I. ii. 48-9), and she tells Olivia that although she is beautiful she may also be proud, for even devils can be 'fair' (I. v. 270). Nevertheless she may misjudge Olivia's infatuation for herself, for Olivia is also well aware that the 'eye' may be 'too great a flatterer' to the mind (I. v. 328), and her concern for Cesario seemed to start from his ardour as well as from his fair 'outside'.[2]

Viola's disguise shows love's truth in another way, for it means that she must act a part. Viola is not that she 'plays' (I. v. 195-8), and so in praising Olivia she must use her art, remembering a well-penned speech. Eventually she has to improvise and becomes Olivia's 'fool' (III. i. 156), 'dallying nicely with words' (III. i. 16-17). Yet when she is asked how she herself would love, she can speak clearly and freely although such a speech is 'out of her part' (I. v. 191); her lover's imagination takes over and she acts with complete 'truth'. It is the same in Orsino's presence; when she says that a tune

[1] cf *Mer. V.*, II. vii, and ix. [2] cf. I. v. 311-2.

> *...gives a very echo to the seat*
> *Where Love is throned. ...*

Orsino recognizes 'truth' at once, and says she speaks it 'masterly' (II. iv. 21-3).

As one good actor on a stage will make bad ones more conspicuous, so Viola's 'acting' shows up that of others. Olivia has to appear disinterested, but she cannot maintain the part and at last declares her passion for Cesario. Even Orsino, who believes that he loves Olivia completely and ardently, is liable to seem a poor actor when he speaks of her, and a 'truthful' one when he speaks of Cesario.[1] When commanding Cesario to entreat Olivia once more, he boasts that no woman's love can be compared with his, yet when Viola simply interjects 'Ay, but I know——', he stops abruptly and asks 'What dost thou know?'; after a pause,[2] Viola quietly answers:

> *Too well what love women to men may owe.*
> (II. iv. 104-8)

This gives Viola the cue to speak of her own love, under the veil of speaking of Cesario's sister; and the tale so holds her master that it is she who has to draw his attention back to immediate concerns:

> *—But died thy sister of her love, my boy?*
> *—I am all the daughters of my father's house,*
> *And all the brothers too: and yet I know not.*
> *Sir, shall I to this lady?*
> *—   Ay, that's the theme.*
> *To her in haste; give her this jewel; say,*
> *My love can give no place, bide no denay.*
> (II. iv. 122-7)

He finishes abruptly; it might seem, to an observer, that he

---

[1] Contrast II. iv. 33-6 and 96-9.

[2] So the lining suggests: Orsino's question is a short line of four syllables; Viola continues with a complete decasyllabic.

had been prompted in a role that was no longer true to his imagination.

Malvolio is one to whom life has never given a part answerable to his imagination; as we witness, he can only rehearse in soliloquy his favourite role of 'Count Malvolio' (II. v. 40); lacking an audience he must always be 'practising behaviour to his own shadow' (II. v. 20-1). But when Maria, Olivia's waiting-gentlewoman, writes a letter in her mistress' handwriting addressed 'To the unknown beloved' and leaves it where he must find it, Malvolio is encouraged to bring his performance before the world. So powerful is his imagination that he can see no trick; he believes that Olivia loves him because he had always imagined that she must. This, he thinks, is no longer acting, this is the real thing:

> *I do not now fool myself, to let imagination jade me. . . .*
> (II. v. 178-9.)

He will never more lack an audience and his performance need never come to an end. He rises to the occasion, his vocabulary jetting with 'what should that alphabetical position portend', and 'there is no consonancy in the sequel; that suffers under probation' (II. v. 130-1 and 141-2). Success goes to his head and he is unaware that he is being ridiculous in the eyes of others, that the 'truth' of his imagination, though strong, is also absurd. He cannot even hear when Olivia says that he is mad;[1] when she calls him 'fellow' (III. iii. 67), the word he had used in contempt of Cesario,[2] he believes that she is singling him out for special favour. When all's done he is a 'poor fool', 'baffled' by others (V. i. 377); the lack of 'generosity', the failure to recognize his own faults, a disposition not 'free' in his dealing with an allowed fool, have made him, in his turn, a laughing-stock for others; to get 'what he deserves', to act to the height of his imagination, is to choose a fool's head. He gives the performance of his career, and, at the last, is forced to see that his audience does not admire; if it were 'played upon

[1] cf. III. iv. 61.   [2] cf. I. v. 145.

a stage', it would be condemned 'as an improbable fiction'
(III. iv. 140-1).

Malvolio's is not the only absurd performance. Following
the subjective truth of their imaginations, each of the lovers
may appear foolish or mad in the eyes of those who have not
the imagination to 'amend' their performances. Antonio,
exclaiming against the seeming perjury of Sebastian, seems
'mad' to disinterested observers (III. iv. 405); Olivia
acknowledging her love for Cesario thinks she is as 'mad' as
Malvolio could ever be (III. iv. 15); Sebastian surprised by
Olivia's welcome and beauty thinks likewise that he himself
is 'mad' (IV. i. 65). The essential difference between these
follies and Malvolio's is in the imagination that prompts
them. True lovers are willing to hazard their reputation to
affirm the truth they see; so Sebastian affirms:

> *What relish is in this? how runs the stream?*
> *Or I am mad, or else this is a dream:*
> *Let fancy still my sense in Lethe steep:*
> *If it be thus to dream, still let me sleep!*
>
> (IV. i. 64-7)

Malvolio cannot do this; to call him madman when he is
affirming his own greatness is to defeat his very object.

There are some follies that have little imagination to
support them. Throughout the play Sir Andrew takes his
cue from Sir Toby, repeating his jokes, claiming the same
exploits, and continually failing to get his performance
right. He knows that many think him a 'fool' (II. v. 89-90),
yet his pathetic faith in Sir Toby's encouragement keeps
him at the game. On his own initiative he is willing to
quarrel, but here his natural cowardice lets him down; he
suggests challenging Malvolio, but at the same time he
suggests that it would be sport not to turn up for the
engagement.[1] Nevertheless he challenges and prepares to
meet the mild-looking boy Cesario. Their duel renders them
both ridiculous; they are so sure that their roles are beyond

[1] cf. II. iii. 135-8.

them that they accept, without question, a mere report of valour in their opposites. Viola cannot now remember that a brave 'outside' may 'oft close in pollution', and her inglorious attempt to avoid combat shows how much she lacks of a man; the role she so readily accepted has led her into a situation where she can perform neither by imagination nor by mere artifice; in this she is as foolish as Sir Andrew.

Our laughter is immediately checked, for Antonio enters and, thinking that it is Sebastian who is in danger (for Cesario looks exactly like him), parts the combatants at the cost of being discovered and apprehended by Orsino's officers. As he is taken off under guard, he asks for the purse he had given Sebastian and, when Viola disclaims all knowledge of it but offers half her present possessions, he reproves her for ingratitude. In the person of Cesario she disclaims the charge:

> *I hate ingratitude more in a man*
> *Than lying, vainness, babbling, drunkenness,*
> *Or any taint of vice whose strong corruption*
> *Inhabits our frail blood.*

(III. iv. 388-91)

In his desperation Antonio cannot believe her; in his eyes the 'truth' of her assertion is only a 'beauteous evil' (ll. 403-4), an appearance of truth. But we must believe her; from laughing at her weakness in the role of a man, we are brought to a renewed remembrance of her strength, of her generous courage and patience in adversity, and in Orsino's service.

The others are unashamed and the trail of mistakings continues; Aguecheek, seeing that Cesario is a coward, engages with Sebastian and is quickly worsted, and then Sir Toby, thinking that Sir Andrew is vanquished through his own weakness, takes on Sebastian who defends himself stoutly. The fight is stopped by Olivia's entrance and her dismissal of Sir Toby:

Will it be ever thus? Ungracious wretch,
Fit for the mountains and the barbarous caves,
Where manners ne'er were preach'd! out of my sight!

(IV. i. 51-3)

To Olivia, Sir Toby's scrape only shows his true nature.

*　　　*　　　*

In *Twelfth Night*, as in Shakespeare's other comedies, 'barbarous' disorder may always threaten the ordered peace of society. So Sir Toby's indulgent roistering is liable to disturb the 'peace' of Olivia's household. Yet we can scarcely judge him harshly, for in contrast Olivia's cloistered good order seems zestless; when Maria, knowing Olivia's displeasure, tells him to 'confine' himself 'within the modest limits of order', there is some justice in his incorrigible evasion:

> *Confine! I'll confine myself no finer than I am; these clothes are good enough to drink in. . . .* (I. iii. 8-12.)

Olivia believes that he is in the 'third degree of drink, he's drowned', but Feste answers that he is but 'mad' and that he, the fool, will 'look' to him (I. v. 145-8). Since Sir Toby has few aspirations above a very lowly level, he would be happy under this tutelage; this is the level on which he can be 'in admirable fooling' (II. iii. 86-7) and excellent company.

When Sir Toby is at the height of his powers, Shakespeare directed Malvolio to enter and reprove him for 'disorders' and 'uncivil rule' (II. iii. 105 and 132). But Malvolio is only a seeming-virtuous man—Maria says he is only 'a kind of puritan', a hypocrite or 'time-pleaser' (II. iii. 151-60), and to Viola's quick eyes he is merely some '*churlish* messenger' (II. ii. 24)—and again few in the audience will not side with Sir Toby. He continues to take his pleasures in his own way until he finds himself in serious combat with Sebastian and reproved with full authority by Olivia. He is last seen with a 'bloody coxcomb' (V. i. 179), a

fool among fools; he is loudly reviling a drunken doctor—
'I hate a drunken rogue'—and is calling his chosen companion 'an ass-head and a coxcomb and a knave . . .' (V. i.
207-14). He enforces judgement on himself.

Shakespeare's ideal of order is implicit in the affairs of
love as in those of society; Sir Toby's thirst is not the only
appetite to threaten good order. Olivia has no sooner
rebuked him than she herself becomes 'much out of quiet'
(II. iii. 144); the enchantment of Cesario's beauty and
eloquence has released a new disordering element within her
and she finds her honour

> . . . *at the stake*
> *And* baited . . . *with all the* unmuzzled *thoughts*
> *That* tyrannous *heart can think.*
>
> (III. i. 129-31)

Orsino suffers the same disorder; when he first saw Olivia
her beauty seemed to 'purge the air of pestilence', but within
him disorder ensued:

> *That instant was I turn'd into a hart;*
> *And my desires, like fell and cruel* hounds,
> *E'er since pursue me.*
>
> (I. i. 20-3)

As Cesario the page, Viola understands her master's disordered state, for she, 'poor *monster*, fond[s] as much on
him' (II. ii. 35). By these turbulent, animal images, Shakespeare has shown at what risk of disorder love's order is
finally established; he has shown the force behind the lovers'
desire to 'live at peace' (IV. iii. 28).

He is also at pains to show that, as love's truth may be
'madness' in the eyes of society, so love's order may cut
across society's notions of decorum. This comedy is called
Twelfth Night to good purpose, for during the festivities of
that night, the lowliest persons may become as lords, acting
for general merriment the role of the Lord of Misrule. Its
title is a figure of Olivia's lovemaking; she who manages her

household with 'smooth, discreet and stable bearing' (IV. iii. 19), for the sake of her notion of love's truth must acknowledge the lordship of the 'man' and not the 'master' (I. v. 313), must sue to her 'servant's servant' (III. i. 113). It is a figure too of Orsino's love and Viola's; she who called him 'master' for so long, becomes her 'master's mistress' and his 'fancy's queen' (V. i. 332-4 and 397). The order of love is 'what you will', the assumption of the roles of master and servant according to the individual, subjective truth of love's imagination.

Not every one who claims love's truth is able to establish such an order. Malvolio knows that there is 'example' (II. v. 44) for 'Twelfth Night' reversals in the name of love, but, seeking the greatness and not the service, seeking to honour himself and not his mistress, he attempts to assert love's order only to give further proof that he lacks the warrantry of a lover's imagination. He is not only absurd in the unquestioning way in which he follows the directions detailed by Maria, or in his over-weening self-confidence; he is also absurd as indecorum is absurd. For courtly address he can only summon 'Sweet lady, ho, ho'; for conversation he can only remark on his own discomfort; and for a love sonnet he can only quote a common ballad. His interview with his lady ends in a delighted recitation of his own greatness.[1] The antithesis to this performance is Antonio's willing offers of service when he discovers that his friend is one whom the world would call his master.[2] Malvolio is put in a dark house for a madness and indecorum that has no authority beyond his own love of himself; since he only wishes to 'lime' his lady (III. iv. 82), the mutual order of love can never justify his folly.

*　　　*　　　*

With the interplay of generosity and possessiveness, of subjective truth and order and subjective folly, and of good-humoured disorders and natural fooling, Shakespeare has

---

[1] cf. III. iv. 18-60.　　　[2] cf. II. i. 36, and III. iii. 1-4.

mingled the artful wisdom of Feste the fool ; here is another
contrast :

> *For folly that he wisely shows is fit;*
> *But wise men, folly-fall'n, quite taint their wit.*
>
> (III. i. 74-5)

He *seems* to be a 'merry fellow' who cares 'for nothing', but
in fact he makes it clear that he does 'care for something'
(III. i. 30-2). It is not at all obvious what that 'something' is ;
it might be the money he so often begs for his fooling, or it
might be his skill, 'As full of labour as a wise man's art'
(III. i. 73) ; but it is most likely to be his attempt to find that
'foolish thing' (V. i. 400) which would content himself
rather than his audience. In the meantime he fulfils his
calling ; he 'walk[s] about the orb like the sun' (III. i. 43-4)
and by the light of his folly discovers kinship with other
mortals.

But as well as showing the follies of others, Feste is used
by Shakespeare to introduce a new theme to this comedy, or
rather to give greater prominence to a subsidiary theme which
he had hinted at in earlier comedies. In *Love's Labour's
Lost*, the lovers are attentive to the cuckoo and the owl, and
are willing to test their 'world-without-end' bargains by
submitting the 'gaudy blossoms' of their love to the 'frosts
and fasts' of time's reckoning. In *As You Like It*, Jaques, the
detached critic, brings to the enjoyment of simple pleasures
the remembrance of the seven ages of man, the 'strange
eventful history' all must fulfil. So Feste, the professional,
detached jester, is also time's remembrancer. As Ariel, the
airy spirit, alone can sing of summer as Prospero draws men
together for forgiveness and resignation, so Feste, the professional fool, sings in the youthful[1] Illyria of death and the

---

[1] The youth of the two main pairs of lovers is often missed in modern
productions of this play. Viola and Sebastian are twins; they must be at least
thirteen years old, for their father had died when they were that age, and they
cannot be more than about nineteen, for Sebastian is still beardless enough to
be imitated—'An apple, cleft in two, is not more twin' (V. i. 230)—by his

passage of time; the shadow of the cypress falls across the Twelfth Night merriments when he sings that

Youth's a stuff will not endure.
(II. iii. 53)

This note is echoed several times in the course of the play. Sir Andrew, so unsuccessful in his present endeavours, remembers that he 'was adored once, too' (II. iii. 197), and, at the outset, Olivia reminds us of time by her contempt or ignorance of it. Olivia believes that she can keep her brother's love 'fresh And lasting in her sad remembrance', and that her own beauty will 'endure wind and weather'; she does not heed Feste's warning that 'As there is no true cuckold but calamity, so beauty's a flower', but defies time in cutting seven years from her life in the world.[1] But her contempt is changed to concern; although the clock 'upbraids' her 'with the waste of time', she stays to speak her love and to vow by 'the roses of the spring' (III. i. 141 and 161), and later she is forced to excuse her haste to be married.

A poignant echo of Feste's songs is heard when Viola and Orsino speak of the tune for 'Come away, come away, death'. Viola, who is serving Orsino as Cesario the page, has to hear her master say:

> ... *women are as roses, whose fair flower*
> *Being once display'd, doth fall that very hour.*
> (II. iv. 39-40)

---

twin sister. Orsino is of 'fresh and stainless' youth' (I. v. 278) and since while wooing Olivia he believes that the man should be older than the woman, we may suppose him a little older than Olivia. By the same token Olivia should be younger than Sebastian and hence younger than Viola; this may be pushing consistency too far, yet she must surely be very young indeed to be willing, even for the death of a brother, to cloister herself for seven years; if Olivia is the youngest of the four, her timidity and disregard of time at the outset of the play become more acceptable. We may therefore suppose that Orsino, the oldest, is as little as 19 or as much as 30. Viola and Sebastian about 18, and Olivia 17.

[1] I. i. 31-2, I. v. 256, and 56-7.

She can only affirm the truth of this; she cannot tell him, as
she told Olivia, that a 'copy' of that beauty is able to cheat
the grave (I. v. 261); nor can she explain that

> . . . *flowers distill'd, though they with winter meet,*
> *Leese but their show; their substance still lives sweet.*[1]

In her generous love for Orsino she does what he desires and
forwards his suit to Olivia; 'giving' is her only resource and
the rest she commits 'to time' (I. ii. 60).[2] She must 'sit like
patience on a monument' while concealed love, 'like a worm
i'the bud', feeds on her own beauty (II. iv. 113-18). Knowing all this and thinking of the passage of time, she can only
answer Orsino with:

> *And so they are: alas, that they are so;*
> *To die, even when they to perfection grow!*

*   *   *

Twelfth Night is based on *Gl'Ingannati*, an Italian comedy
of mistaken identities, and its last scene retains something
of the rapid cumulative dénouement of this source; of
Shakespeare's earlier comedies, only *The Comedy of Errors*
and *The Merry Wives* have so many unmaskings, recognitions, and reversals in their last scenes. Yet *Twelfth Night* is
also distinguished for its ardent poetry. Benedick and Beatrice, Rosalind and Orlando had wooed chiefly in prose, and
one must go back to *A Midsummer Night's Dream* or *The
Merchant of Venice* to find heroes and heroines who speak so
consistently in poetry—and their poetry, except for set
pieces like the casket scene or trial scene in *The Merchant*,
is much lighter and quicker than that which springs from
'unpremeditated' dialogue in *Twelfth Night*. As Viola
acknowledges that beauty is a flower, a deeper and more
sustained lyrical note is heard than in any of the previous
comedies.

These two characteristics, combined with the judgements

---

[1] *Sonn.*, v. 13-4.   [2] cf. also, II. ii. 41.

inherent in any expression of Shakespeare's ideals, give a strange intensity and beauty to the end of *Twelfth Night*. Although its dialogue is almost wholly in verse, the rapidity of this last scene allows no opportunity for the full expression of thought and feeling; nevertheless our interest and feelings have already been engaged and, as the characters take up their final relationships, the merest word can be charged with meaning. In the light of Shakespeare's threefold ideal of love, the contrasts and conflicts of this comedy are resolved like the last inevitable moves in a game of chess; implicit in each swift alteration there is a tally of earlier successes and failures. But this simile will not fully hold, for the object is not to defeat pieces of a certain colour; it is rather to range all in due order; the only 'defeat' is an inability to find a place in that order.

Lightheartedly, save for a disguised purposefulness in Orsino, the characters begin to take up their places; but as Antonio enters under arrest, bloodshed, envy, and disorder are remembered from his half-hidden past; the violent words—'Vulcan', 'smoke of war', 'scathful grapple', '. . . That took the Phoenix', '. . . that did the Tiger board'— seem to tear apart the fabric of the dialogue. But Antonio's concern is with the more immediate past, with the 'rude sea's enraged and foamy mouth' from which he had redeemed Sebastian, and with the 'witchcraft' which has drawn him into new danger. Explanations are prevented by Olivia's entry and Orsino's subsequent discovery of disorder and danger within his own heart. Because Olivia is concerned for Cesario and not for him, Orsino asks why he should not 'kill' the one he loves; but he prefers that she should live the 'marble-breasted tyrant still':

> *But this your minion, whom I know you love,*
> *And whom, by heaven I swear, I tender dearly,*
> *Him will I tear out of that cruel eye,*
> *Where he sits crowned in his master's spite.*
> *Come, boy, with me; my thoughts are ripe in mischief:*

I'll sacrifice the lamb that I do love,
To spite a raven's heart within a dove.
(V. i. 128-34)

Orsino's heart is as disordered as seafight or tempest, and Viola can only continue to 'give and hazard'; she merely reiterates her love and her willingness to die a thousand deaths to give him 'rest' (V. i. 136). And Olivia must acknowledge her new order which will seem but a 'Twelfth Night' folly to others; so she calls Cesario 'husband' before the contemptuous glance of Orsino. She brings the friar to witness, and he acknowledges the 'contract of eternal bond of love' in formal words and measured sentences.

Quickly the action moves forward with Sir Andrew and Sir Toby entering to protest their own folly and hence their own place in the order of things. Then Sebastian enters and full recognitions ensue. Olivia finds that she was contracted to a man who had dared to trust the dream-like truth he had found; however much her eye had proved a 'flatterer for her mind', she had not formally given and hazarded until she found one who could answer fully to her 'soul' (IV. iii. 27). And Orsino's perturbation is quieted; instead of desiring 'the dove' whom he had loved for that which 'nature pranks her in' (II. iv. 89), he learns to value 'the lamb' whom he had loved even in 'masculine usurp'd attire'—Viola's generous and patient love is thus attractive.[1] Orsino's jealous savagery towards Cesario in this last scene had betrayed his true bias, even as, earlier, his close attention to Cesario's tale had shown where his imagination truly lay. Viola again reiterates her love and duty, but now she knows that winter's ragged hand cannot deface her summer; she is able to—

Make sweet some vial; treasure . . . some place
With beauty's treasure, ere it be self-killed.[2]

As these characters join hands in mutual accord, others

---

[1] cf. V. i. 329-34.   [2] *Sonn.*, vi. 3-4.

take up their due places. We hear that Sir Toby has married Maria in recompense for the trick she had played on Malvolio. He would claim this as a generous impulse for he asks 'no other dowry . . . but such another jest' (II. v. 202-3), but he could scarcely hope for a greater; the best of his bargain is that he has become a 'bond-slave' (II. v. 208-9) to one who he believes 'adores' him (II. iii. 196) and one who tries to confine his habits 'within the modest limits of order'. Then Malvolio enters having been released from the dark room in which Sir Toby has bound him; his kind of love has proved the most foolish, the most a prey to the mockery of others, and now it appears to be incurable. Still believing that Olivia wrote the letter, he seeks redress for the 'madly-used Malvolio', yet when he is disabused he is silent, unable to accept his own absurdity. When injuries on both sides are considered, the 'sportful malice' of his persecutors 'May rather pluck on laughter than revenge' (V. i. 374); but Malvolio's self-love will not allow this. When Feste reminds him that he had previously mocked a fool as a 'barren rascal' and that 'the whirligig of time brings in his revenges', Malvolio still cannot accept the judgement; he must, in his own right, be 'revenged on the whole pack' of those who had mocked and tormented him. He cannot be taught to have a generous, guiltless, and free disposition.

In earlier comedies, the characters who rejected the ordered conclusions have left the stage without the lovers sparing much thought for them; so, in the eyes of others, Shylock has 'but justice' and no one but the Duke asks Jaques to stay; and so Don John is thought on only so that the morrow may devise brave punishments for him. But in *Twelfth Night*, Malvolio is considered; Olivia remembers a 'most extracting frenzy' of her own (V. i. 288) and Orsino's violent disorder is still in his mind. There is no move in the last scene which is so inevitable as Malvolio's exit thinking of revenge, but nevertheless Olivia, echoing his own words, acknowledges that he has been most 'notoriously' abused

(V. i. 388),[1] and Orsino commands that he should be sent after and entreated 'to a peace' (V. i. 389). There is no communal feast, music, or dance to close this play—that must wait until 'golden time convents' (l. 391); but as the lovers leave the stage together we know that their generosity and desire for harmony can, after the realization of their own follies and disorders, reach to one who has 'had but justice', and that but a kind of wild justice.

We must do more than delight in this conclusion of the lovers' wooing. Feste is left alone on the stage to sing of man's folly and disorder, of the passing of time, and of 'the wind and the rain'. The theme of the comedy moves beyond that of particular love-making and its key is transposed from a major to minor; Feste's professional, disinterested view brings us to a contemplation of the whole course of man, and of the need for a generous, guiltless, and free acceptance of all things. And his song ended, Feste is a lonely figure requiring our applause.

[1] Almost certainly there is laughter in Olivia's voice; Malvolio has been given to long words and 'notorious' is one of his favourites; he has just used it twice (ll. 337 and 351), and in his previous scene he had used Olivia's very phrase (IV. ii. 94-5).

CHAPTER VII

Love's Ordeal and the Judgements of *All's Well that Ends Well*, *Measure for Measure*, and *Troilus and Cressida*

Most scholars believe that during the five or six years that followed the completion of *Twelfth Night*, Shakespeare wrote the major tragedies and three more comedies—*Troilus and Cressida*, *All's Well that Ends Well*, and *Measure for Measure*.[1] There is no need to search for implicit judgements before arguing that these comedies are not simply carefree, escapist entertainments. Even on a very superficial level, their overt moralizing, in didactic or gnomic speeches about justice, order or true nobility, marks them apart from earlier comedies. They have been distinguished as 'comical satires', but together with a more direct exposure of vice and folly, they have a more intense dramatic focus, an immediacy of feeling in moments of doubt or suffering which unites the audience in sympathy with individual characters; such a shifting response is alien to pure satire and the audience is forced to search for some other mode of reaction which can respond to both elements. Because of the moral issues which they so clearly raise, the three comedies have also been called 'problem plays'. But again this title has only a specialized application, for each play has a last scene which most pointedly does not explicitly resolve the issues raised earlier. *All's Well* and *Measure for*

[1] So E. K. Chambers, *William Shakespeare* (1930), i. 443, 451, and 453. See also J. G. McManaway, *Shakespeare Survey*, iii (1950), 29.

Measure seem to conclude with precipitous theatricality, as if in the middle of a battle some one came along and said that the soldiers were only toy soldiers and must be fitted back into their box; and in neither play is the presiding figure portrayed with the impressive simplicity or mystery which would make him readily acceptable as a *deus ex machina*. So much is unresolved at the end of *Troilus and Cressida* that it has been suggested that the surviving text is merely the first part of a two-part play.[1] One might argue that these comedies are simply failures, but recent productions have vindicated their stage-worthiness and recent criticism has pointed out the subtlety of much of their dialogue and characterization. Many critics prefer to believe that they are perplexing because they were meant to be so, that they are not merely didactic but designed to vex and disturb. For the present it is sufficient to say that no one can read or see these plays without being involved with, and in some measure perplexed by, deep and serious issues.

This reaction is so different from that which is usually evoked by earlier comedies that it is necessary to stress the considerable similarities between the two groups. *All's Well* and *Measure for Measure* have obvious similarities in structure and dramatic technique—they have several inter-related plots, several kinds of characterization, and elements from both narrative and intrigue comedies. Because *Troilus* is concerned with warfare and politics as well as with love it is usually compared with the history-plays, yet many of the technical devices it shares with the histories are also to be found in the early comedies. Moreover these technicalities are bound up with similarities in theme; like their predecessors these three comedies are informed by Shakespeare's ideals of love's wealth, love's truth, and love's order. They introduce other political, social, and moral themes, but in so far as they deal with stories of love-making and love, they clearly spring from the same creative vision of life; that vision is manifested under changing forms and is now more

[1] cf. Variorum edition (1953), pp. 450-4.

sympathetic to the imperfections of humanity than elated with the joy of its successes, but its judgements remain unaltered. These three comedies refine and extend Shakespeare's comic vision, they do not replace it.

To appreciate these plays is to increase our appreciation and understanding of the earlier ones; their more explicit moralizing and their greater intensity and closer involvement may help to clarify the issues which are implicit in the other comedies—plays which are possibly more puzzling to interpret because they are less obviously puzzling.

*　　　*　　　*

The interdependence of the two groups of comedies is clearest in *All's Well*, for of the later three this has the most romantic setting and is the most wholly concerned with love. Helena, a physician's daughter, loves Bertram, the young count of Rousillon. In Shakespeare's source, which was William Painter's translation from the *Decameron*, her father's death had left this girl so rich that she had many suitors, but Shakespeare has widened the distance from Bertram by making her poor as well as lowly. It seems to her that:

> *'Twere all one*
> *That I should love a bright particular star*
> *And think to wed it, he is so above me. . . .*
> (I. i. 96ff)

For his part Bertram scarcely sees her; we learn later that his eye has already been caught by fair Maudlin, daughter of the lord Lafeu.[1] Helena's situation is like Viola's in *Twelfth Night* who, shipwrecked in Illyria, falls in love with the Count Orsino whose fancy has already been won by Olivia's beauty; as Viola can only give generous service to Orsino, so Helena knows that she

> *. . . cannot choose*
> *But lend and give where she is sure to lose.*
> (I. iii. 220-1)

[1] cf. V. iii. 44-55.

In words that mock and pervert the wisdom of the sonnets,[1]
the braggart Parolles reminds her of the full wealth or
usury of love:

> *Loss of virginity is rational increase. . . . That you were
> made of is metal to make virgins. Virginity by being once
> lost may be ten times found: by being ever kept, it is ever lost:
> 'tis too cold a companion; away with't!* (I. i. 139-45.)

Helena answers that she is determined to 'stand for' her
virginity 'a little', though therefore she may die a virgin
(ll. 146-7). As Parolles continues about the 'goodly increase'
which follows the loss of virginity, Helena, despairingly or
involuntarily, or perhaps merely to prevent further talk,
touches her true dilemma:

> *How might one do, sir, to lose it to her own liking?*
> (ll. 165-6)

Viola was content to 'lend and give' and leave the rest for
time to 'untie', but Helena, when the opportunity presents
itself, cannot resist forming a plan to *enforce* a return; she
decides to cure the fistula from which the King is dying by
using a remedy she has inherited from her father, and to ask,
as a reward, for her choice of husband from all the young
noblemen of France. She rationalizes her decision by
arguing that no one ever strove to 'show her merit, that did
miss her love' (I. i. 242), but what in fact has happened is
that, in face of seeming hopelessness, her patience has
broken down and she has determined to do more than
'lend and give' and leave the rest to time.

The effect is soon apparent, for having followed her plan
with mingled trepidation and courage, and having succeeded, all her confidence deserts her. Confronted with
Bertram she finds that, after all, she can only continue to
give. So she addresses him:

---

[1] See above, pp. 47-50.

I dare not say I take you; but I give
Me and my service, ever whilst I live,
Into your guiding power. This is the man.
                    (II. iii. 109-11)

When Bertram protests that in 'such a business', he should
have the use of his 'own eyes' and scorns her as a 'poor
physician's daughter' (ll. 114-23), Helena is silent until, at
length, she is able to tell the king:

> *That you are well restored, my lord, I'm glad:*
> *Let the rest go.*

                    (ll. 154-5)

To the king and to other old people, Lafeu and the Countess,
Bertram's mother, Helena's 'merit' clearly 'deserves' more
than Bertram's love: 'there is more owing her than is paid;
and more shall be paid her than she'll demand'(I.iii. 107-9);
her potential wealth in love is such that 'virtue and she Is
her own dower' (II. iii. 150-1) and outweighs inherited
wealth or nobility. But however simple it may seem to wise,
old heads, the young must find love's wealth for themselves.
The king exerts his authority and forces marriage on
Bertram, but having relied on her father's cunning and not
on her own generous giving and hazarding, Helena finds
that she has won a husband in name but not in substance.
When she determined to 'show her merit', she 'assumed
desert',[1] and chose wrongly; she now realises that
she has acted against the nature of 'love's wealth', and
has tried to '*take*' by right that which can only be '*given*'
in return for '*giving*'.

Bertram's scornful, self-protective arrogance—he greets
her with 'Here comes my clog' (II. v. 58)—does not dimin-
ish her estimate of his worth but rather enforces her sense
of guilt: she knows she is 'not worthy of the wealth' she
owns, but wishes 'like a timorous thief' to 'steal' that which
the law has already given her (II. iii. 84-7). They part without even a kiss; Helena at her husband's command goes to

[1] *Mer. V.*, II. ix. 51.

Rousillon, and Bertram, asserting his independence against the king's command, goes to the wars in Florence. Soon Helena receives a letter vowing:

> *When thou canst get the ring upon my finger which never shall come off, and show me a child begotten of thy body that I am father to, then call me husband: but in such a 'then' I write a 'never'. . . .*
> *Till I have no wife, I have nothing in France.* (III. ii. 59-63 and 77.)

Helena blames only herself and leaves France as a pilgrim to Saint Jaques. She writes to the Countess:

> *Ambitious love hath so in me offended,*
> *That barefoot plod I the cold ground upon,*
> *With sainted vow my faults to have amended . . .*
> *He is too good and fair for death and me;*
> *Whom I myself embrace, to set him free.*
>
> (III. iv. 5-17)

When Giletta, the Helena of the *Decameron*, heard Beltramo's vow, she boldly made up her mind to retrieve him; Helena's self-blame is entirely Shakespeare's addition to his source. Neither in letter, dialogue, nor soliloquy does Helena show any intention of regaining Bertram, nor any hope of it.

After this subtle and pathetic picture of Helena's impatience, shame, and repentance, the action moves on rapidly. Leaving France she goes disguised as a pilgrim to Florence where she finds that Bertram is ignobly asserting his independance and soliciting Diana, a Florentine of lowly birth, to his 'unlawful purposes' (III. v. 72-3). With the permission of the girl's widowed mother, Helena arranges for Diana to beg Bertram's ring and make an assignation at her chamber for midnight; and when this is successfully accomplished, she herself takes Diana's place. Although we may presume that Helena went to Florence in order to see Bertram, she could hardly have foreseen this opportunity and, however readily she accepts it, there is no sign that she had sought it. With a necessary dramatic tact, Shakespeare has allowed no time for the expression of Helena's motives and feelings; the centre of the stage is now held by Parolles and Bertram.

At first glance the showing-up of Parolles as braggart and coward may seem irrelevant to the main plot of the play. If this were so it would be a considerable fault, for in the theatre Parolles can almost 'steal' the play; Charles I called it by his name and during the eighteenth century it was frequently produced in order to give comedians a chance of performing this role.[1] Because of their liveliness and ability to hold an audience, and because they are one of Shakespeare's main additions to his source, the Parolles scenes must be essential to any true interpretation of the play as a whole. In fact, lest we should miss their relevance, Shakespeare has prefaced the actual showing-up with a dialogue between two Lords which points its moral. They talk first of Bertram and his dealings with Helena and Diana, and then they moralize generally:

–*Now, God delay our rebellion! as we are ourselves, what things are we!*
–*Merely our own traitors. And as in the common course of all treasons, we still see them reveal themselves, till they attain to their abhorred ends, so he that in this action contrives against his own nobility, in his proper stream o'erflows himself.* (IV. iii. 23-30.)

Bertram, they say, is rebelling against his true nature, and, that leading them to the business in hand, they wish he would come to—

see his company [that is Parolles] anatomized, that he might take a measure of his own judgements, wherein so curiously he had set this counterfeit. (ll. 37-40.)

[1] cf. H. Child, *The Stage History of 'All's Well'*, New Cambridge Shakespeare (1929), pp. 187-8.

While every one else sees through Parolles, Bertram is 'taken in' by his mere appearance of soldiership and court-liness. This is the first point of contact between Parolles and the rest of the play; by deluding Bertram he shows how inexperienced Bertram is, how young and how ready to accept at *outward* value all he hears and sees. To his un-trained eye the most accessible or the most obvious may seem to be the most true, or the most beautiful; he accepts the mere 'words' of Parolles at their 'face value' and has seen nothing in Helena besides her modest appearance; we may presume that he has never yet seen anyone 'truely', with a lover's imagination.

The farcical showing-up of Parolles soon disabuses Bertram about his companion, but its contribution to the play as a whole does not stop there. With a sudden and effective change of focus, it is followed by a short soliloquy in which Parolles admits that if his 'heart were great' it would 'burst' at this indignity. But he prefers to be thankful and so gathers courage and accepts his shame and true status:

> *Captain I'll be no more;*
> *But I will eat and drink, and sleep as soft*
> *As captain shall: simply the thing I am*
> *Shall make me live. . . .*
> *Rust, sword! cool, blushes! and, Parolles, live*
> *Safest in shame! being fool'd, by foolery thrive!*
> *There's place and means for every man alive.*
> (IV. iii. 366-75)

He promises himself a soft option but in the event he dis-covers otherwise; he is harboured only by Lafeu, who had mocked him as a braggart but now is prepared to employ him as a fool and to give him food and a few coppers. This also has a general significance in the play, for Bertram, in his turn, is shown-up in public, and, after 'boggl[ing] shrewdly' (V. iii. 232) and aggravating his 'treasons' as any Parolles might do, he also is forced to acknowledge his own faults.

As Parolles had been a traitor to his true self, so had Bertram; the one should have been a fool, the other truly noble.

Bertram should be played as a brilliant young man endowed with all the outward graces of his father, but too young to have proved his own virtue; he is deceived by appearances and even his ignoble faults may be excused because the 'boldness of his hand' has acted before his heart could learn to give 'consent' (III. ii. 79-80). When he understands that Helena is still living and not dead as he had thought, he asks for pardon in very few words; this has been considered a last outrage, but it may rather be construed as a new modesty and self-knowledge—he will no longer trust mere 'words'.

The reunion of Helena and Bertram is not easy to portray. Helena, acting the part of Diana and therefore with none of her own 'merit' to recommend her, has accepted Bertram's love at the lowest level. A short but poignant scene shows that she recognizes this:[1] speaking to the widow and Diana (and therefore not as freely as in soliloquy), she blames the men whom she is yet content to follow:

> *O strange men!*
> *That can such sweet use make of what they hate,*
> *When saucy trusting of the cozen'd thoughts*
> *Defiles the pitchy night: so lust doth play*
> *With what it loathes for that which is away.*
> (IV. iv. 21-5)

Helena puts such thoughts out of their talk, but not out of her own mind; she comforts the others with 'All's Well that Ends Well', but, as she looks forward, she only hopes that her brier will have 'leaves' as well as 'thorns'; she dares not hope for flowers. As soon as she sees Bertram again, before claiming that she has fulfilled the riddle, she tells him:

[1] See also III. vii. 44-7.

SHAKESPEARE AND HIS COMEDIES

> *. . . when I was like this maid,*
> *I found you wondrous kind.*
>
> (V. iii. 310-11)

For his part, Bertram claims that having lost Helena, he had found, like Claudio in *Much Ado*, that the sweet 'idea of her life' had crept into his 'study of imagination'[1]—that having 'lost', he had 'loved' (V. iii. 54); if this be true, such inward love must be stronger than any of his outward fancies. But for the moment there can be no confidence in words; the play does not end jauntily with 'All's Well that Ends Well';[2] the king who has presided helplessly over events he could not control, draws all to a close with:

> *All yet seems well; and if it end so meet,*
> *The bitter past, more welcome is the sweet.*

*   *   *

At the beginning of *All's Well*, Helena is measured against the ideal of love's wealth and falls short in her refusal to give and hazard and leave the rest to time, in her attempt to 'take' as well as to 'give'. Then Bertram is measured against the ideal of love's truth and is shown to be deluded by mere words and mere appearances, and to be acting without the consent of his heart. The consequences of these failures show Shakespeare's continuing belief in the ideals implicit in his earlier comedies, and at the conclusion, under the eyes of the King, Helena and Bertram are ready to take up a new relationship in love which must be judged by the standards they have previously violated.

In a similar way *Measure for Measure* reasserts the ideal of love's order. This comedy is chiefly concerned with justice and mercy, deeds, intentions, authority, and power, but, in

---

[1] *Ado*, IV. i. 226-7; see above, pp. 117 and 120.

[2] In the *Decameron*, Beltramo does not aggravate his 'treasons' in the last scene but, acting as his own judge, he perceives Giletta's 'constant mind and good wit' and receives her as his wife; in contrast to *All's Well*, the *Decameron* tells a story of 'virtue rewarded'.

so far as it is concerned with love, it follows the same kind of pattern as *All's Well*. At the beginning the various characters are measured against the ideal of love's order, and at the end the duke pardons their lapses and a new start is made.

As in *All's Well*, the immediacy of the dialogue, in situations which are often strange and sometimes fearful, keeps the audience continuously questioning the rights and wrongs of the various conflicts. In *All's Well* this questioning is accentuated and guided by the comments of the old, experienced characters who are continually at variance with the young lovers. There is no such chorus in *Measure for Measure* but the way in which Shakespeare has presented the duke serves much the same purpose. The duke attempts to act as counsellor and justicer, and the manner in which he governs the action raises difficulties at almost every turn. Although he knows that

> *He who the sword of heaven will bear*
> *Should be as holy as severe. . . .*
>
> (III. ii. 275-6)

the readiness with which he applies '*craft*[1] against vice' (III. ii. 291) and racks so many minds with grief and fear, makes us suspect the end which is meant to justify such doubtful means. The duke provokes our doubts to the very close,[2] for then, in a characteristically cold and self-important way—'I have a motion much imports *your* good' (V. i. 541) —he suggests that Isabella may join with him in the concord which the lovers are about to attempt once more.

Shakespeare's characterization of the duke serves another purpose in making us aware, as he had so often done in

---

[1] In Shakespeare's works 'craft' usually carries the implications of cunning and deceit; cf. *Meas.*, II. iv. 75 and III. ii. 10. See also *Troil.*, III. ii. 160 and IV. iv. 105.

[2] To Angelo the duke appears as 'power divine', but this tells us more about Angelo's guilty imagination than about the duke himself (V. i. 374); it is the 'galled jade' that winces (see above, pp. 91-4 and 100-1).

earlier comedies, of the lovers' need for imaginative understanding. The duke is one who boasts that the 'dribbling
dart of love' is unable to pierce his 'complete bosom'
(I. iii. 1-3) and he is therefore without the 'imagination' to
think 'no worse' of the lovers 'than they of themselves'.
The contrast between his unimaginative wisdom and the
lovers' imaginative concern is frequently insisted upon ; in
his guise of heavenly comforter he sees no need to prepare
Juliet for the news that Claudio, her lover, must die on the
morrow, and no need to help her sustain this new cause of
grief ;[1] his 'consolation' to the condemned Claudio[2] paints a
life as empty of affection and idealism as Jaques' account of
the seven ages of man. We question the duke's judgements
as we question those of Jaques, for neither can fully appreciate either the sufferings or the merits of those who are
pierced by love's 'dribbling dart'.

The subjectivity of the lovers' experience is also implied
in the omission of some of the characters from the last scene.
This is a tacit recognition that the ennobling order of love
is not for all, and that any attempt to legislate cannot
prevent, but only hinder, disordering abuse. There will
always be those like Pompey, the bawd, and like Parolles,
Armado, and Costard from other plays, who require nothing
more than some indulgence for man's 'simplicity', who are
willing to accept the mere ability 'to live' (II. i. 234-9) as
sufficient matter to build their hopes upon.

So among the many moral and social issues in *Measure
for Measure*, a lover's subjective imagination is again presented and the judgements dependent on the ideal of love's
order are again implicit in its action : the duke believes he is
'complete' without love, but at the end asks for love ;
Angelo and Isabella attempt to establish some order in the
affairs of love by 'restraint', the one by caring about the
appearance of a strict chastity and righteousness, the other
by entering a nunnery, and both regimens are tested and
found wanting ; Claudio, impatient of the 'denunciation . . .

---

[1] cf. II. iii. 37-9.　　　　[2] III. i. 5-41.

of outward order' (I. ii. 152-3) has erred by 'too much liberty' (I. ii. 129); the disorders of Lucio, Froth, and Mrs Overdone are shown for what they are worth to the state and to the individuals; only Juliet shows, in her generous repentance, a full and proper understanding of love's mutual order—she silences even the duke's good advice. Earlier comedies had celebrated the fulfilment of love's order, but this play explores the difficulty with which any such order is attained, and the good intentions of those who fail to achieve it.

Yet its conclusion presents no alternative ideal. At the end of *Measure for Measure*, as at the end of *All's Well*, the focus alters and we are told almost nothing of inmost thoughts and feelings; the characters become strangely silent and inscrutable as they take up their final positions as lovers—Claudio with Juliet, Angelo with Mariana, the duke with Isabella. We are left knowing that the hearty and generous acceptance of love's mutual and fulfilling order is the only way to make this conclusion acceptable, but we have no certainty that it is so. If they are about to fail again Shakespeare has no more to say; but at the best, if we think well of them—and their dispensing and accepting of mercy is a good augury—their silence and formal gestures of assent represent a new humility before an ideal, the shame-fastness of those who must return.

In *All's Well* and *Measure for Measure* Shakespeare has not affirmed and celebrated love's wealth, truth and order in the ideal fulfilment of romantic stories; he has rather presented imperfect responses. So Lucio commonsensically chides Isabella who had sought for some 'more strict restraint' (I. iv. 4):

> *Our doubts are traitors*
> *And make us lose the good we oft might win*
> *By fearing to attempt.*

(I. iv. 77-9)

And so, at the conclusion, Escalus the old Justicer continues to lament that:

> *. . . one so learned and so wise*
> *As you, Lord Angelo, have still appear'd,*
> *Should slip so grossly, . . .*
>
> (V. i. 475ff.)

In the very first scene of *All's Well*, the Countess remembers that :

> *where an unclean mind carries virtuous qualities, there commendations go with pity; they are virtues and traitors too.* (I. i. 48-50.)

And again before the trial of Parolles and Bertram, the 'First Lord', speaking chorus-like, asserts :

> *The web of our life is of a mingled yarn, good and ill together: our virtues would be proud, if our faults whipped them not; and our crimes would despair, if they were not cherished by our virtues.* (IV. iii. 83-7.)

The settings for Shakespeare's plays are still romantic— youth, wealth, and beauty are still at stake—but instead of fulfilling romantic expectations, he has shown men and women as 'merely their own traitors'.

Such emphasis is not entirely new : at the end of *Love's Labour's Lost*, the impetuous lovers are as yet a 'little o'erparted' and so 'Jack hath not Jill' (V. ii. 885) ; at the end of *A Midsummer Night's Dream*, the perfect response to Bottom's fiction is only suggested ; at the end of *The Merchant*, we are made aware that the harmony of the lovers falls short of universal charity ; and at the end of *Twelfth Night* 'golden time' does not 'convent'—Antonio has been 'unsound' enough to 'upbraid' Sebastian with the kindnesses he has done for him (III. iv. 384-6), and Orsino, Olivia, and even Viola and Sebastian, are so lately fortunate that their follies and ignorances cannot yet be forgotten. It is just these details which Shakespeare brings into full focus in *Measure for Measure* and *All's Well*. But still his ideals of love remain the same, and at the conclusions of these plays he can only show the characters dwarfed by the mere possibility of perfection in generosity, truth, and order. It would take yet another play to make their thoughts explicit in repentance, forgiveness, and renewal, or even in a final destructive refusal.

*   *   *

Troilus and Cressida, which deals in the manner of a history-play with the course of the Trojan wars, does not conclude, like *All's Well* and *Measure for Measure*, with a neat but merely formal resolution of all preceding conflicts. But it bears very much the same relationship to earlier comedies; in its presentation of the love of Troilus for Cressida it invokes the same ideals and in its conclusion it even more clearly rejects any alternative ideals.

Its reliance on the same ideal of love's wealth that is implicit in *Romeo and Juliet* and *The Merchant of Venice* is evident in Troilus' first soliloquy:

> *Tell me, Apollo, for thy Daphne's love,*
> *What Cressid is, what Pandar, and what we?*
> *Her bed is India; there she lies, a pearl:*
> *Between our Ilium and where she resides,*
> *Let it be call'd the wild and wandering flood,*
> *Ourself the merchant, and this sailing Pandar*
> *Our doubtful hope, our convoy and our bark.*[1]
>
> (I. i. 101-7)

When Cressida receives his suit, Troilus expresses his sense of joy and wonder in words which closely echo the scene in which Portia and Bassanio discover their mutual love:

> *I am giddy; expectation whirls me round. . . .*
>
>   *. . . what will it be,*
> *When that the watery palate tastes indeed*
> *Love's thrice repured nectar? death, I fear me,*

---

[1] cf. *Rom.*, II. ii. 82-4 and *Mer. V.*, I. i. 167-72 and III. ii. 242-4.

Swooning destruction, or some joy too fine,
Too subtle-potent, tuned too sharp in sweetness,
For the capacity of my ruder powers:
I fear it much; and I do fear besides,
That I shall lose distinction in my joys; . . .

My heart beats thicker than a feverous pulse;
And all my powers do their bestowing lose,
Like vassalage at unawares encountering
The eye of majesty.

You have bereft me of all words, lady.[1]
(III. ii. 19-58)

But here there is a feverish quickening of the senses which is not in *The Merchant of Venice*, for Troilus is eagerly anticipating with 'imaginary relish' (III. ii. 20). When he actually meets Cressida the dialogue is less like that of the earlier play; he senses the 'monstruosity in love, . . . that the will is infinite and the execution confined, that the desire is boundless and the act a slave to limit' (ll. 87-90). When they are forced to part, he doubts Cressida's 'truth' (IV. iv. 60-99).

He soon has proof that Cressida is indeed false to him in the Greek camp, and that he has loved her in 'fancy' (V. ii. 165), not in the true 'imagination' that sees into the heart.[2] However fervently he may wish to 'invert the attest of eyes and ears' (V. ii. 120-2), when the 'poor girl' sends him a letter he must recognize:

Words, words, mere words, no matter from the heart;
The effect doth operate another way.

(V. iii. 108-9)

However generous his love might be, however fully he was

---

[1] cf. *Mer. V.*, III. ii. 145, 111-14, 177-85. Cf., also *Troil.*, III. ii. 125-37 and *Mer. V.*, III. ii. 8 and 16-18.
[2] See above, p. 118.

ready to hazard for love's wealth, without 'truth' nothing is possible for him. The 'virtue' of Troilus' generosity and sense of love's wealth has been 'betrayed' by his impatience, by his too ready acceptance of the appearance of steadfastness and 'truth' in Cressida.

The action of this play provides no propitious event, no benevolent king or fortunate substitute to make the end all even. Its conclusion can be paralleled from a tragedy, not from a comedy. As King Lear finds that 'the justice' and 'the thief' have become indistinguishable from each other (IV. vi. 153-8), so Troilus finds truth and falsehood:

> *This she? no, this is Diomed's Cressida:*
> *If beauty have a soul, this is not she; . . .*
> *If there be rule in unity itself,*
> *This is not she. . . .*
> *. . . this is, and is not, Cressid.*
> (V. ii. 137-46)

And as Lear, alone and helpless on Dover Beach, plans to steal

> *. . . upon these sons-in-law,*
> *Then, kill, kill, kill, kill, kill, kill!*
> (IV. vi. 190-1)

so Troilus, resolute on the battlefield after the death of Hector, thinks only of destruction:

> *You vile abominable tents,*
> *Thus proudly pight upon our Phrygian plains,*
> *Let Titan rise as early as he dare.*
> *I'll through and through you! and, thou great-sized coward,*
> *No space of earth shall sunder our two hates:*
> *I'll haunt thee like a wicked conscience still,*
> *That mouldeth goblins swift as frenzy's thoughts.*
> *Strike a free march to Troy! with comfort go:*
> *Hope of revenge shall hide our inward woe.*
> (V. x. 23-31)

With music, nature's cures, and the kiss of Cordelia, Lear was to awaken to a new, humble, and suffering life, but there is no such renewal for Troilus; we are forced to take leave of him here. When Shakespeare presented one who, venturing for love's wealth, was shipwrecked by his failure to live up to the ideal of love's truth, he presented his story without a propitious ending; for the faithful Troilus he did not care to replace the lost possibility of love's wealth, its merely fanciful fulfilment, with any other kind of love.

CHAPTER VIII

The Criticism of Shakespeare's
Early and Mature Comedies

───────────────

The same ideas, preoccupations, or themes inform Shakespeare's comedies from the very earliest to the three 'dark' or 'problem' comedies. On first acquaintance, the early comedies up to and including *Twelfth Night* invite such a rich and light-hearted enjoyment that it seems inappropriate to search in them for themes or judgements ; indeed Shakespeare has not explicitly indicated any theme, nor invited any clear judgement. Nevertheless by tracing the recurring words, images, actions, and sentiments which are associated with Shakespeare's ideas in other more explicit works, and by regarding the contrasts and relationships invited by the interweaving of the comedies' multiple plots, it becomes evident that these comedies have been created around certain unifying ideas or themes, and that these themes have been manifested in the situations, development, and final resolution of their dramatic narratives, and in all the richness, humanity, and subtlety of Shakespeare's dialogue and characterization. Three main themes may be distinguished—the ideals of love's wealth, love's truth, and love's order—but they are combined and emphasized in many different ways, and alongside them, or rather, within them, many other themes are explored. They represent, in effect, a comprehensive and developing view of love and personal relationships, and of life itself as experienced through such relationships.

The persistence of these themes, or of this vision, is a

fact of prime importance for the appreciation of Shake-speare's comedies ; indeed, even for the greatest of them, for *Much Ado*, *As You Like It*, and *Twelfth Night*, the identifica-tion of these themes is a necessary prerequisite for a full understanding of Shakespeare's comic art. Without such a compass, the constellation of romance, laughter, and humanity will amaze and entertain us, but it will remain incomprehensible ; its individual lights may be enjoyed and studied, but their relevance to each other and to us—the delight, mystery, and wisdom of their conception—may be missed. Each particular star in the constellation is well worthy of individual scrutiny and enjoyment, but a full appreciation of the music of the spheres, to which every star contributes, requires a wider understanding.

*   *   *

It is often regretted that Shakespeare's comedies 'have been accorded far less attention than his tragedies or history plays',[1] but, in fact, the volume of work which has been done on some of the individual comedies equals or even surpasses that on individual histories or tragedies. What is lacking is a continuous and comprehensive critical argument, a com-munity of critical and interpretative thought. This is prob-ably due to a tendency to examine the detail before a sufficient understanding has been grasped of the ideas behind the comedies as a whole, and of the way in which every detail of them depends on this essential vision. It is possible to discuss Shakespeare's treatment of his sources without discovering why those stories or plays originally appealed to him from among the infinitude of possibilities, to appreciate individual characters or lyrical passages, to analyse comic situations, to note the presence of 'tragic' elements within the comedies, or even to discuss Shake-speare's manipulation of multiple plots, without coming to an understanding of his aims and achievements in any single comedy. It is in this wider, interpretative work that the

[1] A. Nicoll, *Shakespeare Survey*, viii (1955), v.

study of the comedies lags behind that of other plays.

The overall 'meaning' of individual comedies, and of the whole *corpus* of the comedies, needs to be discussed with the same particularity as the 'meaning' of the tragedies, histories, 'last plays' and 'problem comedies'. If we could be more or less agreed on this 'meaning', or, to put it in the terms that we have been using, on Shakespeare's informing ideas, the individual studies of lyricism, characterization, sources, influences, and so forth could be related to each other, and scholars and critics could begin to develop a community of critical opinion around Shakespeare's comedies as around his other plays.

*   *   *

To define the 'meaning', ideas, or themes of the comedies up to and including *Twelfth Night* was the main purpose of this present book. It has been an essay in interpretation rather than in appreciation or criticism; using only the most immediate means, it has tried to describe a complex vision which Shakespeare never explicitly stated and may never have consciously formulated. Such a description must tend to simplify Shakespeare's creative purposes—were a full description possible it would have to be many times longer than the texts of all the comedies—but such a simplification is a necessary step towards a fuller appreciation of the plays in all their richness. Indeed, while this book does not set out to appraise the comedies, the recognition of the essential elements of their underlying vision must at once add to our powers of appreciation; on returning to the plays themselves and on admiring once more their characters, humour, and lyricism, we shall be able to give a fuller and more precise meaning to the age-old critical epithets of 'good-natured', 'rich', 'lively', 'true to nature', and 'humane'.

And with a knowledge of Shakespeare's comic vision, we may also realize more fully the nature of the ever-lasting appeal of these plays. The dialogue and action which give us such delight are not casual fancies, but a lively celebration of ideals about life. These plays do not seek to convict us of specific faults or to persuade us to hold any stated opinion ; if that had been Shakespeare's intention he would have provided explicit judgements upon their actions, or would have written different, satiric comedies. These plays are rather concerned with ideals, with wooing and wedding rather than with marriage, and they are set in Illyria rather than in London ; in them Shakespeare sought to affirm a generous, true, and ordered mode of existence, and to their harmony, integrity, humour, and beauty we may respond and, in responding, may affirm for ourselves. In such an affirmation there is a judgement upon life, a judgement which is only implicit but which may receive a wider hearing than the reproofs of a satirist or the precepts of a moralist. To such plays we may return again and again, with profit and delight.

Shakespeare seems to have found the affirmation of his ideals in comedy particularly congenial to his creative mind. The comedies form the largest single group of his plays, and his writing in this mode is noticeably free and unconstrained. In comedy he found that he could be at once positive and unassertive, that he could work upon the imaginations of his audience without raising their purely intellectual responses, their prejudices or predispositions ; and he could write without limiting his width of reference by explicit moralizing. Tragedy with its focus on a single hero, its greater intensity and intellectual clarity, could offer other opportunities, but in his own kind of comedy Shakespeare was able to affirm his ideals while apprehending society and portraying the rich diversity which he found in human life. It was to a form of comedy that he returned when, at the end of his career, he wished to present his matured and comprehensive judgement on man in relationship with men, and on man under the Heavens.

CHAPTER IX

The Life of the Last Comedies

There is no lack of interpretative criticism of Shakespeare's last comedies; rather it is the rule. Perhaps someone has yet to 'read a philosophy into Shakespeare' in any rigorous way, but during the last thirty or so years many have found in these plays, *Pericles*, *Cymbeline*, *The Winter's Tale* and *The Tempest*, a pattern of thought that is simple and constant. By outlining their plots, critics have shown that each involves birth, separation, tempest, remorse, penitence or patience, reconciliation and peace. By noting the juxtaposition of some scenes and recurrent phrases and ideas, they have argued that in all but *Pericles* civilization or art is contrasted with natural life or nature. Most persuasively, they have abstracted certain speeches which are straightforward in stating issues of life and death, and have drawn attention to their mutual echoes:

> *I am great with woe, and shall* deliver *weeping.*
>   . . . *O, come hither,*
> *Thou that beget'st him that did thee beget;*
> *Thou that wast* born at sea, buried *at Tarsus,*
> *And* found *at sea again!*
>   (*Pericles*, V. i. 107-99)
>   . . . *did you not name a* tempest,
> *A* birth, *and* death?
>   (*Ibid.*, V. iii. 33-4)

> *O, what, am I*
> *A mother to the* birth *of three? Ne'er mother*
> *Rejoiced* deliverance *more . . .*
> *Thou hast* lost *by this* a kingdom.
> > *No, my lord;*
> *I have got two* worlds *by't.*
> > > (*Cymbeline*, V. v. 368-74)

> *. . . thou mettest with things* dying, *I with things*
> new-born. . . .
> > (*Winter's Tale*, III. iii. 116-8)
> > Welcome hither,
> *As is the* spring *to the earth.* . . .
> > > (*Ibid.*, V. i. 151-2)
> *. . . they looked as they had heard of a* world ransomed, *or*
> *one* destroyed. . . . (*Ibid.*, V. ii. 16-7)

> *O, wonder!*
> *How many goodly creatures are there here!*
> *. . . O brave* new world!
> > (*Tempest*, V. i. 181-3)
> > *In one* voyage
> *. . . Ferdinand . . .* found *a wife*
> *Where he himself was* lost, *Prospero his* dukedom
> *In a poor isle and all of us ourselves*
> *When no man was his own.*
> > (*Ibid.*, V. i. 208-13)

More than anything else, these recurrent phrases have led
critics to believe that they can pluck, with ease, the 'meaning', ideas or themes from the last comedies. They write with
an assurance that fails them when discussing earlier plays:
a serious, hortatory tone is heard contending that the 'Final
Plays of Shakespeare *must* be read as myths of immortality',[1]
or that the 'characters in these late romances are *less im-*

[1] G. W. Knight, *The Crown of Life* (1947), p. 30 (*italics mine*).

portant as persons than as symbols and what they are is *much less important* than what they say'.[1] In a recent book Mr Derek Traversi described the very insemination of these last plays in Shakespeare's mind and proceeded to define their meaning:

> At the heart of each . . . lies the conception of an organic relationship between breakdown and reconciliation, between the divisions created in the most intimate human bonds . . . by the action of time and passion and the final healing of these divisions.

He discerned a 'harmonizing theme' which 'produces a conception of drama completely removed from realism and properly definable in symbolic terms.'[2]

Yet, remembering the subtle interrelations of the other comedies, we may be suspicious. These critics sound both too simple and too vague. Traversi's phrase, 'the conception of an organic relationship between breakdown and reconciliation', is neither clear nor agile enough to seem appropriate to the mind that shaped the earlier plays and had these qualities among others. Professor Wilson Knight's 'must' seems too restrictive for the dramatist who finished *Twelfth Night* with Feste's riddling song and made the characters of *Much Ado* capable of several different interpretations. Such pronouncements as these have led Professor Clifford Leech to complain that 'all the romances seem generally to inhibit thought in their readers'.[3] And a few dissentient voices strengthen our doubts. Dr D. G. James, in his *Scepticism and Poetry* (1937), discussed the symbolic meanings of these plays but added that they do not explain everything:

> the symbols are there; but they rarely liberate compulsive significancies. We hover between apprehension of

[1] S. L. Bethell, *The Winter's Tale: a study* (1947), p. 23 (*italics mine*).

[2] *Shakespeare: the Last Phase* (1954), p. 2.

[3] *Shakespeare's Tragedies and other Studies* (1950), p. 142.

momentous significancies, of a luxurious imagination, and of absurdities.[1]

Professor Kermode, while claiming that in *The Tempest* 'Shakespeare offers an exposition of the themes of Fall and Redemption by means of analogous narrative', expressed a fear that his criticism had not done justice to the 'complex' in which the 'elements of the pattern of ideas . . . occur'; 'they derive from each other meanings', he declared, 'which are beyond the last analysis of criticism'.[2] If this play is viewed against the wide pastoral tradition, as Professor Kermode has helped us to do, it suggests precise subtleties which do not accord with the statement of a simple theme. And *The Tempest* has yet another aspect, for many playgoers might feel some agreement with Professor Parrott roundly declaring that it was 'primarily meant to be a good show; it would be absurd to call it great drama'.[3]

Each of the last comedies offers a simple 'meaning' to the critics, who seize upon it and seldom wait to look a second time at the whole play. Yet even some of those key passages which are resonant with great issues, when they are scrutinized afresh, may reveal qualities which a 'symbolic' reading does not explain or appreciate:

> *did you not name a tempest,*
> *A birth, and death?*

has a movement—a hesitation and, perhaps, a final ease —which portrays embarrassment, courage and renewed confidence; and clearly this effect does not depend on symbols but on the imitation of the pulse of actual human speech. Or, again, the interplay of syntactical and metrical units in:

> *. . . found a wife*
> *Where he himself was lost, Prospero his dukedom*

[1] *Op. cit.*, p. 210.

[2] *The Tempest*, Arden Edition (1954), pp. lxxxiii and lxxxviii.

[3] T. M. Parrott, *Shakespearean Comedy* (1949), p. 394.

THE LIFE OF THE LAST COMEDIES

In a poor isle and all of us ourselves
When no man was his own

suggests a tension and, perhaps, a delicacy in the mind of the speaker which is at odds with its reception as a choric comment voicing a clear, central truth. We should beware of judging too hastily: such individualized qualities may not be impertinent to an imaginative acceptance of the dramatic life of these plays.

Because of our doubts and those of some earlier interpretative critics, our task is to recognize the patterns, statements and meanings which are obvious enough once they are looked for, and then proceed to detailed re-examination. So we may discover the same 'meanings' in other particulars, or further 'meanings' developed contrapuntally, or a judgement that is implicit in the whole but never developed towards a clear statement. Against immediate appearances, these comedies may be as difficult to interpret as the earlier ones.

*   *   *

Since the last comedies present narratives of personal relationships, we may approach them by using the terminology developed for the other comedies. *The Winter's Tale* is the most consistently concerned with love and friendship and will therefore be discussed in greatest detail. It was written in 1610, the third in order of composition but the first which is widely considered to be a complete artistic success.

The opening is talk between two courtiers. Giving information about Leontes King of Sicilia and Polixenes King of Bohemia, its obvious purpose is exposition. And interpretative critics have drawn attention to words like 'separation', a 'vast' or 'opposed winds', and claimed that these serve to herald symbolic action. But this is only one of several possible readings: after a study of the earlier comedies we shall hear other matters. Camillo's reply to praise of Sicilian hospitality—'You *pay* a *great deal* too *dear* for what's *given freely*' (I. i. 18-9)[1]—is a reminder of love's wealth, of mutual, unprompted giving in friendship. Or, again,

> *We will give you sleepy drinks, that your senses, unintelligent of our* insufficience, *may, though they cannot praise us, as little accuse us.* (ll. 14-7)

speaks of a friend's response to free granting ('And for that riches where is my deserving?'[2]), and shows an awareness of different degrees of truth. This second theme is again echoed in 'Sicilia cannot *show* himself over-kind to Bohemia' (ll. 23-4) and 'Wherein our entertainment shall shame us we will be justified in our loves' (ll. 8-9). The description of the two friends:

> *they have seemed to be together, though absent, shook hands, as over a vast, and embraced, as it were, from the ends of opposed winds.* (ll. 31-4)

speaks of more than tempests; it is also a reminder that love has its own order and that 'true' hearts never know complete separation. (So Claudio, in *Much Ado*, had rediscovered Hero in 'his study of imagination'[3] or Valentine, in *The Two Gentlemen*, had found that Silvia 'inhabited in his breast' (V. iv. 7) when he was banished by her tyrant father to a 'shadowy desert' and 'unfrequented woods'.) In the opening scene of *The Winter's Tale* all these ideas crowd upon each other: the imagination and judgement that had informed the earlier comedies were at work in writing this complex duologue about personal relations.

But the presentation is arrestingly different. The perspective is new: before the main characters have appeared, their actions have been described by two accomplished talkers. And the scale is new: in a little over thirty lines Shakespeare has outlined an emotional and intellectual world previously

[1] See above, p. 68, for the quibble on 'dear', and pp. 48-9 for 'freely'.

[2] *Sonn.*, lxxxvii; and see above, p. 72.

[3] IV. i. 227; see also V. i. 259-60 and above, pp. 117 and 120.

portrayed in whole plays. And there is a new sophistication, a continual attempt by the speakers to overreach each other in knowledge, compliment and promise. We may detect a kind of relish, or, to misquote Troilus, a too-potent subtlety, in the minds through which we are shown the affairs of Leontes and Polixenes: action does not follow immediately, but is fancifully planned for the future and entails a disguise of truth between professed friends rather than an unmasking. Such an introduction is not reassuring: again remembering the early comedies we may wonder if

> *manhood is melted into courtesies, valour into compliment, and men are only turned into tongue, and trim ones too.*[1]

Any unease will be heightened when the scene concludes with a recognition that joy may turn to loss, words that may sound like foreboding:

> *—The heavens continue their loves!*
> *—I think there is not in the world either malice or matter to alter it.* (ll. 34ff.)

These characters seem to sense that love is precarious, even when it seems unassailable. Having asserted that the kings' friendship is safe, Archidamus immediately assures Camillo that there is a remedy for ills; he continues:

> *You have an unspeakable comfort of your young prince Mamillius. . . .*
> *— . . . they that went on crutches ere he was born desire yet their life to see him a man.*
> *—Would they else be content to die? . . . If the king had no son, they would desire to live on crutches till he had one.*

Lightly, within the complimental talk, an 'unspeakable' loss is considered. And it introduces another element which is both old and new: sonnett xiii had welcomed an heir to perpetuate beauty and here he is said to 'make old hearts fresh' (l. 43). Perhaps this development indicates that

---

[1] *Ado,* IV. i. 321ff.

Shakespeare was now concerned with 'myths of immortality', but we should also notice that the praise of Mamillius arises from the other interests of this duologue. The whole of the first scene of *The Winter's Tale* shows that the vision and concerns of the early comedies have not been supplanted. They have been presented in a wider context, in a new perspective which is more acute and more subtly uneasy.

When the principals enter, they speak like their introducers. Polixenes starts by evoking the ideal of love's wealth:

> ... *time as long again*
> *Would be fill'd up, my brother, with our thanks;*
> *And yet we should, for perpetuity,*
> *Go hence in* debt. ...

(I. ii. 3-6)

'Cipher', 'rich place', 'multiply' continue the talk of friendship in commercial terms. And here again is a sophisticated attempt to express more than words are able, at once hinting at an unspoken truth and increasing any uneasiness we may feel about the persistent hyperbole and compliment. Remembering Shakespeare's earlier use of a varying dramatic 'truth', according to the imagination which sustains each performance,[1] we may assume that we are meant to view the stage critically, to feel insecure in accepting 'shadow' for 'substance', outward appearance for inward reality. This reading is probably correct, for immediately several devices are introduced to increase our curiosity. Leontes is the central figure and initiates the attempt to persuade Polixenes to prolong his visit, but Shakespeare has given him less to say than his wife, Hermione, or the friend who is his guest. Hermione is in an advanced stage of pregnancy but no reference is made to this obvious visual fact; while this is normal behaviour off-stage, it is peculiar as dramatic exposition, a reminder that words do not express all thoughts and feelings. With intensified attention we may become aware of strange or, perhaps, unbelievable features in the

[1] See above, pp. 91-102, and 109-23.

'performances': how briefly yet pungently Leontes speaks;
how Polixenes does *not* argue that he must go home to see
his son although Hermione says that that excuse would
have greatest strength; how in gracious and friendly talk
she is ready to make Polixenes her 'prisoner' (l. 52), to use
force ' 'gainst the nature of love'.[1] There is something
incomplete or constrained in the image of life shown upon
the stage.

  ⁻ When the playful threat of imprisonment makes Polixenes agree to stay, Hermione directs the conversation
towards the time when the two kings had been boys together.
And now the dramatic illusion is steadier: sophistication
yields to a calm memory of childhood and of an ideal friendship. Consciousness had been timeless; there had been give
and take, equality of spirit:

> Polixenes.   *We were, fair queen,*
>   *Two lads that thought there was no more behind*
>   *But such a day to-morrow as to-day,*
>   *And to be boy eternal.*
> Hermione.   *Was not my lord*
>   *The verier wag o' the two?*
> Polixenes. *We were as twinn'd lambs that did frisk i' the sun,*
>   *And bleat the one at the other: what we changed*
>   *Was innocence for innocence....*

(ll. 62ff.)

Ideal love is remembered briefly and then Polixenes suggests
that with adult passions—the flowing of 'stronger blood'
(l. 73) and the knowledge of what Shakespeare had called
'the manner of a man'[2]—that perfection had been destroyed.
His implication that they had 'tripp'd since' cannot be lost,
for Hermione draws attention to it (ll. 75-6) and it is this
that leads the talk back to compliments which now carry
outspoken allusions to possible disorder through the
'blood'. It is in this context, after a notable silence, that

[1] *Gent.*, V. iv. 58.

[2] *LLL.*, I. i. 211-2; see above, pp. 130-1.

Leontes, the central figure, speaks again. His speeches are still terse and there are disquieting allusions to love as possession so that the 'reality' of the drama is probably more unsteady than before. Shakespeare has presented the main characters to an alert and uncertain view; they inhabit the ideological world of the early comedies, for the same perfection is recognized, but the audience will sense tensions beneath the expert courtesy and so be led to observe all three characters intently in their personal relationships. They are married men and women rather than youthful lovers, but the echoes of earlier comedies are manifold and continuous; and the dangers and suggested resolutions are the same. The essential difference between this play and those is found in its perplexing presentation; Shakespeare is now concerned with ideals of love in a society whose members are involved subtly with each other, who hide and pretend, are familiar with ideals and imperfections, who feel momentary regrets for a lost innocence or take momentary comfort in a new generation. Here he has presented a more comprehensive image of the 'knowing' and intelligent aspects of society—aspects of which we are particularly conscious today.

The next movement of the play shows Leontes more completely. His question, 'Is he won yet?' (l. 86) starts an inquiry which draws forth his 'true' concern. He compares potencies in love, his own, his wife's, his friend's; in Shakespeare's earlier phrases, we may say that he requires an 'acceptable audit', or 'as much as he deserves'.[1] Then, in his first extended and sensitive description, he remembers the possibility of waste, death and disorder in love:

> *Why, that was when*
> *Three crabbed months had sour'd themselves to death,*
> *Ere I could make thee open thy white hand*
> *And clap thyself my love: then didst thou utter*
> *'I am yours for ever.'*

(ll. 86ff.)

[1] *Sonn.*, iv. 12 and *Mer. V.*, II. vii. 7, etc.

He quotes the last five simple words simply, as a pledge, or bond, of possession. (Schooled in earlier plays we may remember Shylock standing 'on his bond' or Adriana demanding her 'rights', and we may notice that he does not recognize that property is 'appalled' when 'either is the other's mine'.[1]) Because of the questioning view encouraged by the complimental talk and Leontes' earlier silences, we may wonder if he thinks that Hermione had used these words as 'mere words, no matter from the heart'.[2] This suspicion becomes a certainty when he speaks in a long aside which soon has the freedom and force of released passion.

> *Too hot, too hot!*
> *To mingle friendship far is mingling bloods.*
> *I have tremor cordis on me: my heart dances;*
> *But not for joy; not joy. This entertainment*
> *May a* free face *put on, derive a* liberty
> *From* heartiness, *from* bounty, *fertile bosom,*
> *And well become the agent; . . .*
>
> (ll. 108ff.)

All Shakespeare's ideals are denied: Leontes doubts the 'truth' of Hermione's words and actions, his passion is 'disordered'; he cannot watch the manifestation of love's 'wealth', its 'free face', 'liberty', 'bounty'. So he calls for Mamillius, the 'unspeakable comfort'; but his presence brings no release. Leontes sees only what his imagination can see—affection controlling judgement makes 'possible things not so held, Communicates with dreams' (ll. 139-40): if his son is indeed like him he carries a dagger which may 'bite his master' (ll. 156-7). His heart's reality has to find expression in irony until he is alone with Mamillius, and then it has no hindrance. So, from a savage reversal of a pun which Shakespeare had used several times to accentuate the wealth of love—'Let what is *dear* in Sicily be *cheap*' (l. 175)

---

[1] *The Phoenix and the Turtle*, ll. 37 and 36.
[2] *Troil.*, V. iii. 108-9.

—the king's possessive love at last speaks clearly, tortured
by fear of dispossession; the world of pledges is disordered:

> . . . *many a man there is, even at this present,*
> *Now while I speak this, holds his wife by the arm,*
> *That little thinks she has been sluiced in's absence*
> *And his pond fish'd by his next neighbour, by*
> *Sir Smile, his neighbour. . . .*
> *No barricado for a belly. . . .*
>
> (ll. 192ff.)

This general denunciation is an evasion of intensity, but
Camillo's disbelief brings him back to the feeling that 'stabs
the centre' (l. 138): 'My wife is slippery. . . . My wife's a
hobby-horse . . .' He swears 'as he had seen' what he
describes (ll. 414-6), for his heart's imagination or 'truth'
displaces all other reality:

> . . . *is this nothing?*
> *Why, then the world and all that's in't is nothing. . . .*
>
> (ll. 292ff.)

(We may remember Troilus' cry: 'If there be rule in unity
itself, This is not she.'[1]) The clearest statement is of
dispossession: Polixenes 'wears her like her medal, hanging
About his neck' (ll. 307-8). It is from this point that
murder is planned, the death of Polixenes not of Hermione.
Leontes does not seek to maintain the 'honour' of his wife
by death, as Othello did, but to kill his rival, whom he had
once loved as a friend in all bounty, and to 'take again his
queen' (l. 336). As Orsino's jealous savagery towards
Cesario, and not Olivia, in the last scene of *Twelfth Night*
had betrayed the true bias of his love,[2] so Leontes' anger
against Polixenes whom he had loved in liberty shows that
he had loved Hermione only in so far as he had needed to
hear and believe her pledge, 'I am yours for ever'.

From a wide, uncertain view of the main relationships,

[1] *Troil.*, V. ii. 141-2; and see above, p. 199.

[2] See above, p. 180.

the inward truth of Leontes is thrust upon the audience's attention. His sudden and early domination of the stage with sustained utterance has no parallel in earlier comedies. But as the sophisticated expository technique was a development of earlier manifestations of implicit judgements, so the 'truth' of Leontes' outburst depends on earlier theatrical and poetic devices. However important symbols of Fall and Redemption, death and rebirth, were to Shakespeare in writing this scene, he was as concerned as he had been in the past to create a precisely judged picture of personal relationships. He has written no explicit statement of a comprehensive theme—the slight sense of foreboding in the expository duologue was too vague to announce the main issue. But this is the technique of the early comedies. As in those plays, he has provided an implicit judgement revealed in a choice of words and images that can, unconsciously rather than consciously, animate in the minds of the audience the same detailed attitude to love and friendship based on ideals of 'wealth', 'truth' and 'order'. And again he has used varying levels of dramatic illusion to make the audience recognize contrasts between performances and reality, between 'mere words' and 'matter from the heart'. Here the essential difference from the early comedies is that the group of characters is smaller and centred compellingly on one who has found love an inescapable and isolating danger, one whose 'heart' is 'disordered' by fear of 'loss'. In this play Shakespeare has extended the world of the comedies so that it holds the mirror up to a wider range of life, and for this he has developed from proved techniques an appropriate mode of presentation.

Thus far Shakespeare has not emphasized the old interests which sustained this new play. An audience or reader will be chiefly impressed by the uneasy sophistication and then the outburst of Leontes' jealousy. In general, the immediate impression is uncertain and then strong, rather than subtly considered, so that the comprehensive involvement with ideals of love can be adequately defined only after informed analysis of detail. But this does not mean that this aspect of the play is unimportant. We should expect it to be un-emphasized, as in the early comedies it was implicit in an apparently capricious and light-hearted entertainment. There the judgement became effective because it was con-sistent and because of the handling of multiple plots. It is the presence of the same techniques in *The Winter's Tale* which assures us that the 'hidden' judgements deriving from Shakespeare's ideals of love are essential to its dramatic life. The minute consistency will become apparent as we read further, but the structural similarities must be shown by more specific consideration.

From the beginning of his career Shakespeare had experi-mented to develop a form for comedy which could present several characters or groups of characters in relation or contrast with each other and which would conclude by bringing these various elements into a stable relationship. So he learnt to depend on multiple plots and, as we have seen, the implicit judgements of the comedies can often be judged by the contrasts and relationships suggested by the interweaving of different narrative strands. For *The Winter's Tale* he chose a single plot, but he developed various characters, especially Paulina, the shepherds and Autolycus, far beyond the strict demands of his story; in this way they serve much the same structural function as sub-plots. For example, the penultimate scene of the play presents none of the main characters, but three courtiers, Autolycus and the shepherds, and in the final scene Paulina is given a large part in the conclusion of the main story. Such devices are clearly related to the form of earlier comedies. And there is further indebtedness in the use of music, dancing, a feast and a formal trial to give still points of visual clarification at important crises.[1] To study these devices is to observe the enforcement and importance of the play's implicit judge-ments.

[1] See above, pp. 136-41.

Hermione falsely condemned is in simple contrast with Leontes. She also manifests the truth of her 'heart', but in doing so she speaks with new directness and in continued relationship with her husband: even when shocked by his accusation, she thinks of his point of view, concerned for 'How will this grieve *you*' (II. i. 96). And *she* can wait; like Viola,[1] she recognizes the necessity of being 'patient' (l. 106) and committing much to time. Paulina is then introduced to mark these contrasts and elaborate them. Her first words show that she is certain of the queen's inward truth and prepared to identify herself with her cause.[2] But not caring for Leontes as Hermione does, she speaks out clearly of his 'unsafe lunes' (II. ii. 30) and immediately resolves on action. Shakespeare probably wished a further contrast, of head and heart, in giving her a husband, Antigonus, who is the most fluently politic of Leontes' courtiers. Compared with her, the men are sycophants who 'creep like shadows' in the king's presence and 'sigh At each his needless heavings' (II. iii. 33-5). She has intelligence as well, but trusts her 'wit' because it flows 'as boldness from her *bosom*' (II. ii. 53). Carrying Hermione's new-born daughter, she forces her way before Leontes and the effective range of the contrasts increases. Leontes cannot argue with her, for his unreasonableness, like her certainty, comes from the heart. Instead he tries to reduce her claims to the exaggerations of marital comedy: he calls her 'dame Partlet' (II. iii. 75) and gives Antigonus the role of helpless husband who lets his wife 'run' when 'she will take the rein' (l. 51). Yet in a bizarre way there is a parallel between the two husbands, and Shakespeare has drawn attention to it several times, as in:

Leontes (to Antigonus). *What, canst not rule her?*
Paulina. *From all dishonesty he can:* in this,
    Unless he take the course that you have done,

[1] *Tw.N.*, II. iv. 113-8, and II. ii. 41-2 and I. ii. 60; see above, pp. 177-8.
[2] See II. ii. 1-6.

> Commit me for committing honour, *trust it,*
> *He shall not rule me.*

(ll. 46-50)

To Leontes' charge that Antigonus 'dreads his wife', Paulina answers immediately, 'I would *you* did' (ll. 79-80). Because he cannot judge aright, Leontes has put himself into a position that is potentially ridiculous as well as painful: yet he sees with his disordered imagination and tries to laugh at the world, not at himself. Paulina, Hermione and Leontes all speak with a certainty that depends on the 'truth' of their hearts, but in different ways. These are subtle distinctions to be made in the presentation of a 'strong' and exciting narrative: it is the developed character of Paulina which, by the old device of contrast, helps most in defining the precise ways in which these characters arrive at certainty, and the precise way in which the king is assuredly 'mad' (l. 71).

Leontes, separated from the others on stage by disordered feelings, isolates himself more clearly by sending Paulina away and commanding Antigonus to take his daughter, whom when words had failed Paulina had left to plead by the 'silence . . . of pure innocence' (II. ii. 41), and to leave her in 'some remote and desert place' out of his knowledge (II. iii. 176). He then summons a 'just and open trial' of Hermione (l. 205). Words and silence, order and disorder, are thus contrasted as so often in the earlier comedies, and the same devices are then used to accentuate the issues. First, a contrast is introduced by a brief scene showing another kind of order (as the action moved from Venice to Belmont or from Duke Frederick's court to his brother's in Arden). So Cleomenes and Dion, returning from Apollo's oracle, speak of a delicate 'climate', 'reverence' and a sacrifice that was 'ceremonious, solemn and unearthly' (III. i. 1-22); the very quality of the verse is unusually composed in statement and rhythm. Then the trial of Hermione follows with its own 'due course' (III. ii. 6). This displays Leontes'

ordering: he enters with his court and officers and there is a
call for silence, the prisoner's entry and a reading of the
indictment. The separation of husband and wife is now
presented emphatically by visual elaboration and a halt in
narrative development as they take their places—a device
analogous to formal feasts or the taking up of positions for a
dance or procession. But the 'order' of the scene is soon
broken: Hermione protests her innocence before she is
called to make a statement and Leontes is stung to sudden
personal controversy, denial and expression of pain. Proper
procedure is abandoned: the king is accuser as well as sole
judge; there is no counsel, no evidence is brought forward;
the 'normal course of criminal justice is reversed, and
Hermione is guilty until she can prove herself innocent'.[1]
Only when she refers to the oracle is public ceremony
restored. As oaths are taken and the scroll with Apollo's
judgement opened and read, the earlier scene with the
messengers may be remembered and its evocation of ceremonious awe. But this is not for long: although Hermione's
innocence is vindicated, Leontes is isolated again and more
completely, by crying:

> There is *no* truth *at all i' the oracle!*
> *The sessions shall proceed: this is mere falsehood.*
>
> (ll. 141-2)

But his 'order' is the false one, and the ceremony expressing
it cannot proceed. When a servant enters wildly to announce
the death of Mamillius, Leontes at once is awe-struck: the
course of the trial is forcefully suspended as he accepts the
god's order by proclaiming his own guilt:

> *Apollo's angry; and the heavens themselves*
> *Do strike at my injustice.*
>
> (ll. 147-8)

He has lost the son whom he had thought a 'copy' of himself (I. ii. 122), his last and 'dearest' possession (I. ii. 137);

[1] G. W. Keeton, *Shakespeare and his Legal Problems* (1930), p. 151.

he has no other resource in his loneliness. He asks for aid to be given Hermione who has swooned and acknowledges that he has 'too much believed' his own suspicion (ll. 150-4). But after a brief prayer to Apollo it is clear that this loss cannot awaken love. Leontes is now chiefly concerned to vindicate Camillo who had saved Polixenes' life at the cost of exile, who, in contrast to himself, had trusted 'the hazard of all incertainties' for honour's sake (ll. 169-70). In fastening on Camillo's truth, Leontes is making a personal valuation and showing that he had been concerned for himself not for Hermione. A commercial reference links his present words to the talk of love's wealth in the first Act: Camillo is:

> *No* richer *than his honour: how he* glisters
> *Thorough my* rust.
>
> (ll. 171-2)

When Paulina returns to announce the death of Hermione, Leontes is silent until he again acknowledges his own guilt:

> *Go on, go on:*
> *Thou canst not speak too much; I have deserved*
> *All tongues to talk their bitterest.*
>
> (ll. 215-7)

Now he needs to be told the truth: his possessive love is destroyed and he will accept words that speak his responsibility as he could not accept Hermione's words of trust. His 'shame' (l. 239) must be proclaimed daily, and upon the tomb of his son and queen his crime recorded. When Claudio in *Much Ado* was forced to believe he had caused Hero's death, her truth and beauty came at once to his mind accentuating his grief, and he wrote verses to speak her 'praise' when he himself should die;[1] but no love is reawakened when Leontes is forced to recognize Hermione's truth. Paulina speaks of the 'sweet'st, dear'st creature'

---

[1] *Ado*, V. i. 259-60 and V. iii. 10.

(l. 202), but Leontes does not. In his isolation, with terrifying rapidity, he has turned from accusation to grief and guilt: fearing dispossession he had neither given in love nor received its bounty; now his physical isolation mirrors that of his heart. The scene ends as he commands that he should be led to 'sorrows' (ll. 243-4). By staging his attempted order—

> ... *the matter*
> *The* loss, *the* gain, *the* ordering *on't, is all*
> *Properly ours*

(II. i. 168-70)

—and then his subsequent isolation, Shakespeare adapted a formal device from earlier comedies and showed that in settling his accounts Leontes had lost all that he had counted as dear possessions, even the thought of them.

After the trial there are many structural changes. Leontes is absent from the stage for more than eleven hundred lines and the course of the narrative, which had been largely controlled by his actions, now seems more the result of chance or fate, particularly the events which lead to the meeting of Florizel, son of Polixenes, with Perdita, Leontes' daughter. At the same time new characters are introduced, all requiring less penetrating attention: a sailor, a hungry bear, shepherds, Time (who appears as Chorus announcing the passage of sixteen years), and Autolycus. There is a new range and quicker alterations of mood: a storm suddenly arises, Antigonus is chased off-stage by the bear, Polixenes and Camillo rapidly decide to disguise themselves. And there is the relaxation of laughter, even in such pathetic matters as the discovery of the infant Perdita and accounts of the loss of a ship at sea and the death of Antigonus. Under such conditions the audience's view of the stage is wider and less intimately concerned: in short, Shakespeare has created abundant scope for contrasts. This is exploited to the full, and we shall see by further analysis how the implicit judgements on the main personal relationships, in accordance with the ideals of love's order, truth and wealth, are in this way pointed more clearly.

The 'order' associated with Apollo's oracle is not re-enacted, except by references to its prophecy at the end of the play. Time, the Chorus, is given some authority, but this is specifically independent of any fixed state:

> *The same I am ere ancient'st order was*
> *Or what is now received.*
>
> (IV. i. 10-1)

But the theme of order continues to shape the play. First, in Antigonus' account of his dream, there is a reminisence of the ceremonial order of the oracle as he says Hermione appeared in 'pure white robes, Like very sanctity' and bowed three times (III. iii. 22-4). But he also says that in directing her daughter to be left alone in Bohemia and be called Perdita she had gasped and wept, and had vanished 'with shrieks' (l. 36). Here a personal order is contrasted with personal disorder. Then there is a representation of the 'savage clamour' (l. 56) of a storm and Antigonus is chased by the wild animal. This gives a rapid sketch of a disordered nature: and it is accompanied with the entrance of the shepherd who, by a stroke characteristic of many earlier comedies, relates the natural disorder to disordered man: his first words are:

> *I would there were no age between sixteen and three-and-twenty, or that youth would sleep out the rest; for there is nothing in between but getting wenches with child, wronging the ancientry, stealing, fighting—Hark you now! Would any but these boiled brains of nineteen and two-and-twenty hunt this weather? . . .* (ll. 59ff.)

The pursuing bear had itself been pursued by wild hunters. And finding the abandoned Perdita, the shepherd immediately assumes that she is illegitimate and further evidence of 'hot blood': 'they were warmer that got this than the poor thing is here' (ll. 77-8). Having presented personal disorders, Shakespeare has used the new freedom of his narrative to widen this theme's relevance to include the general condition of man.

As the play proceeds to show events sixteen years later, new 'orders' are attempted. There is a sheep-shearing feast with Perdita the mistress of it: believing herself a shepherdess, she is uncertain in her new authority, but to Florizel she is like Flora, the feast 'as a meeting of the pretty gods' and she the 'queen on't' (IV. iv. 1-5). He is content to be a 'poor humble swain' in her service, and knows that unlike the masquerades of gods who took the shape of beasts to enjoy their loves, his transformation involves a strict order:

> my desires
> Run not before mine honour, nor my lusts
> Burn hotter than my faith.

> (ll. 25-35)

The ordering of Florizel's desires is the order of true love and is in contrast with the shepherd's view of the 'boiled brains' of youth. A further contrast is also offered in the easy acceptance of Autolycus, the 'out of *service*' rogue who has just been introduced singing merrily of the '*reign*' of 'red blood' and of 'tumbling in the hay' (IV. iii. 1-14). As the feast proceeds two dances, in Shakespeare's earlier manner, give visual form to these contrasted acceptances of the 'blood'. Florizel and Perdita join in the first, paired as turtles 'that never mean to part' (ll. 154-5), and for this the clown with Mopsa and Dorcas have to 'stand upon their manners' (l. 164): it is a ceremonious dance which, as we saw in connection with earlier plays, is an imitation of 'the pristine *order* of all created things', or of 'matrimony'.[1] The second dance is quite different, being performed by twelve satyrs or men covered with hair, a 'rough' piece of 'foolery' for which the shepherd feels called upon to apologize. It is this display which is followed by the disguised

[1] See above, p. 139.

Polixenes fearing that the young lovers have 'too far gone' (l. 354) and confronting Florizel and revealing himself. This dance is a meaningful contrast, an anti-masque, to the first, being full of great 'jumps' and representing the antics of men without 'order', without control over their 'blood'. (In Shakespeare's day the lustful bestiality of these 'wild' men would be easily recognized, for they were figures frequently found in allegorical 'shows' and romances.[1]) It is the possibility of such disorder that alarms Polixenes and over against which Florizel and Perdita assert the mutual order, the formal dance or concord, of their love. They do not reject the power of 'blood': Florizel feels the compulsion of his love to be greater than the power of 'monarchs' or his father's remonstrances (ll. 382-8 and 486-91), and Perdita speaks boldly of her love to Florizel, feeling a changed 'disposition' as if she were participating in 'Whitsun patorals' (ll. 130-5) or rites of spring. Their mutual order is founded on 'service' and 'honour' of each other, a concord which accepts and gives true, ordered freedom to the 'blood' as to every other element of their beings.

At the very end of the play various characters are shown finding their places in the order of society, according to their various natures: Autolycus is a knave still—'Now, had I not the dash of my former life in me, would preferment drop on my head' (V. ii. 125-6)—and the shepherd and the clown, despite their rich clothes and brave talk of being 'good masters' (l. 189), are still at the mercy of the knave, meaning well rather than doing well. Then, for the last scene there are more 'blossoms of fortune' and more men and women acting according to their natures. The tone is set by Leontes' first words calling Paulina 'grave and good', and then, as the gathered company encircle Hermione standing as a statue, there is solemn music: it is to this harmonious image of 'union' and 'mutual ordering' that Hermione moves from

[1] See, for example, *Faerie Queene*, IV. vii. For their ancestry, see R. Bernheimer's *Wild Men in the Middle Ages* (1952); their sexual disorder and aggressiveness was contrasted with the control of courtly love.

the pedestal to be reunited with her husband.[1] His first response, 'O, she's warm', echoes the many earlier allusions in the play to the 'blood' which has to be part of man's ordering: Polixenes had blamed 'stronger *blood*' for the loss of innocence; Leontes had declared his jealousy with 'Too *hot*, too *hot*! To mingle friendship far is mingling *bloods*'; the shepherd had preferred sleep to 'boiled brains' and seen 'warm' work in the begetting of Perdita; Autolycus had welcomed and made profit from the reign of 'red blood'; Camillo had watched Florizel and Perdita as:

> *He tells her something*
> *That makes her* blood *look out.*
> (IV. iv. 159-60)

And now, there is 'warmth' in silent concord:

Leontes. *O, she's warm!*
 If this be magic, let it be an art
 Lawful as eating.
Polixenes. *She embraces him.*
Camillo. *She hangs about his neck:* . . .
 (V. iii. 109-12)

The pairing together of Camillo and Paulina as man and wife is often held to be a faulty patching up of the end of the play: but it can be accepted as another manifestation of order and concord. Camillo takes Paulina 'by the hand' (l. 144), as Florizel had taken Perdita when they wished to express their mutual love in a dance. And, with the same weight of meaning, Hermione 'looks upon' Polixenes (l. 147), as an expression of love towards Leontes' 'brother'. Such actions, or visual images, have now become eloquent of the acceptance of love's full order, and the quiet, rapt atmosphere of the scene encourages the audience to view them with appropriate intensity. Shakespeare has slowly and steadily developed his implicit judgements on the personal relationships of this play so that his characters now express them with

[1] *Sonn.*, viii. 5-12; and see above, pp. 136-41.

economy and force, with a simple richness which we more readily accede to poetry than to the lively, individualized representations of drama.

The judgements associated with the ideal of love's wealth are also progressively manifested. In the shepherd scenes Shakespeare has introduced the familiar contrast with the wealth of commerce. As Shylock's usury had been offset by the 'usury' of Belmont,[1] and the misunderstandings of love in *The Comedy of Errors* by misunderstandings about the possession of servants, a gold chain and a bag of ducats, so the shepherd's secret hoarding of the gold found with Perdita and Autolycus' easy dealings and stealings are used to offset the wealth of love. While Florizel calls Perdita a goddess, Autolycus sings his wares 'as they were gods or goddesses' (IV. iv. 210-1). Further contrasts are defined as Mopsa reminds the clown that he had 'promised' her 'certain ribbons and gloves' (ll. 233-43), and so seeks her 'rights' against the nature of the love that 'gives and hazards'. Polixenes in disguise asks Florizel why he does not buy Perdita 'knacks' from the pedlar, and this gives occasion for Florizel to explain that the 'bounty' (l. 364) of their love does not depend on tangible wealth or bonds:

> *She* prizes *not such* trifles *as these are:*
> *The* gifts *she looks from me are pack'd and lock'd*
> *Up in my heart; which I have* given *already,*
> *But not deliver'd.*

> (ll. 367-70)

For himself, he '*prizes*' nothing 'without her love' (ll. 385-6) and that entails the 'giving' of himself, as he had sworn to Perdita:

> *I cannot be*
> *Mine own, nor any thing to any, if*
> *I be not thine.*

> (ll. 43-5)

[1] See above, pp. 64-7.

(There is a backward glance here, for, as Leontes had remembered Hermione's words 'I am *yours* for ever', in contrast Florizel emphasizes 'I am *thine*'.) When Polixenes
discloses himself the comparison with Autolycus' wares
develops yet further. Not seeing with the lovers' eyes, he
will not accept what the shepherd calls the 'bargain' of their
marriage vows (l. 393): for him, Perdita is but 'this knack'
(l. 438), a word he had used of the 'trumpery' and 'counterfeit stones' (ll. 605-8) sold to the credulous shepherds.

At the beginning of the fifth Act, Leontes is presented
with the same commercial imagery. He no longer fears the
loss of Hermione, for she exists to him only in his mind, and
so he can now appreciate the riches he has lost:

> *I might have look'd upon my queen's full eyes,*
> *Have taken* treasure *from her lips.*
>
> (V. i. 53-4)

But he is still learning what this could mean, for Paulina
has to interject a reminder of love's endless bounty:

> *And left them*
> *More* rich *for what they yielded.*
>
> (ll. 54-5)

(We may remember Juliet's 'The more I *give* to thee, *The
more I have*'.[1]) Leontes replies 'Thou speak'st truth', for he
is ready to acknowledge love's wealth. This is fully shown
when he is confronted with Florizel and Perdita and knows
that Polixenes is seeking to prevent their marriage: then he
responds to the seeming shepherdess in a way that affirms
love's values:

> Florizel. *Step forth mine advocate: at your request*
> *My father will grant* precious things *as* trifles.·
> Leontes. *Would he do so, I'ld* beg *your* precious *mistress,*
> *Which he counts but a* trifle.
>
> (ll. 221-4)

---

[1] *Rom.*, II. ii. 134-5; see above, pp. 51-2.

(The word 'trifle' echoes Florizel's dispute with his father which we have observed before.) Paulina remonstrates that Leontes' eye 'hath too much youth in't' and he gives the puzzled answer that he thought of Hermione 'Even in these looks I made' (ll. 227-8): so Shakespeare has ensured that the audience which knows Perdita to be his daughter may understand that he 'hazards' for the wealth of love in this way because he can now recognize, despite the unlikeliness of ever finding one, an image of his wife. He thus ventures more because he is now more involved than the confident Paulina.

In the next scene the shepherds innocently enjoy new riches and then the last shows Leontes' reception of *his* new wealth. He presents his 'hand' to Hermione (V. iii. 107) and his earlier possessive cry, that Polixenes 'wore her like her medal hanging About his neck', is answered as she silently 'embraces him': having been prepared to 'hazard' he can now accept. Earlier commercial imagery is again echoed as Paulina calls the united families and united lovers 'you *precious winners* all' (l. 131).

The implicit judgements according to the ideal of love's truth are also made effective by contrasts. On one hand, the shepherds are easily persuaded of the truth of Autolycus' ballads and can grow 'in love' with a song of two maids wooing one man (IV. iv. 618-9); as the knave knows:

What a fool Honesty is! and Trust, his sworn brother, a very simple gentleman! (ll. 605-7)

On the other hand, Florizel and Perdita also seem foolish. 'Be advised' counsels Camillo, and Florizel replies:

> *I am, and by my fancy: if my reason*
> *Will thereto be obedient, I have reason:*
> *If not, my senses, better pleased with* madness,
> *Do bid it welcome.*
>
> (ll. 491-6)

But the contrast lies in the fact that his folly is dependent on love's truth; moreover he is willing to face peril and the loss of every other good. Florizel had seen Perdita, whom Polixenes took for a 'knack', at her true worth, and Perdita had likewise learnt to trust Florizel, though as a shepherdess she knew:

> *With wisdom I might fear, my Doricles,*
> *You woo'd me the false way.*
>
> (ll. 150-1)

She trusts him and their mutual love in spite of perplexity. Instinctively she would rather lose the 'fairest flowers' of summer than marry a 'gentler scion to the wildest stock' (ll. 79-100): she believes herself to be such 'stock' to her prince, and although this must *seem* to deny her love she links her distrust of the flowers called 'nature's bastards' to her desire for truth in love:

> *I'll not put*
> *The dibble in earth to set one slip of them:*
> *No more than were I painted I would wish*
> *This youth should say 'twere well and only therefore*
> *Desire to breed by me.*
>
> (ll. 99-103)

Together the two thoughts must trouble her, yet she dares to express both. Her trust is neither 'simple' nor fearful: when Camillo argues to Florizel that prosperity is the 'very bond of love', she can answer for him:

> *I think affliction may subdue the cheek,*
> *But not take in the mind.*
>
> (ll. 583-7)

With such inward confidence the lovers can risk accepting the 'fair' speaking of Camillo (ll. 635-6), and can disguise themselves and sail from Bohemia, 'the slaves of chance, and flies Of every wind that blows' (IV. iv. 550-1).

All this is related to Leontes. He had mistrusted Hermione's words and actions, but now he has come to trust
'her virtues' (V. i. 7) and is able to respond in love to her
likeness in his daughter, even though he cannot understand
why or how this should be. With the disclosure of Perdita's
identity, events quickly turn prosperous beyond all hope:
we are shown the courtiers' excited and amazed response to
the 'wonder...that ballad-makers cannot be able to
express' (V. ii. 28)—which will in turn remind us of the
'simple' shepherds believing Autolycus' ballads—and we
are assured that Leontes knows extremities of grief and joy.
This is not enacted on the stage, but reported: he now accepts
a truth that 'lames report...and undoes description'
(ll. 64-5). In this way Shakespeare has reserved our closest
attention for the reunion with Hermione and at the same
time prepared us to realize the depth of the lover's 'faith'
that is then 'awakened' in Leontes (l. 95). It is grounded on
a knowledge of Hermione's true nature which is keenly
recollected again on seeing the apparent statue:

> Chide me, dear stone, that I may say indeed
> Thou art Hermione; or rather, thou art she
> In thy not chiding, for she was as tender
> As infancy and grace.

(ll. 24-7)

He now believes what he sees although it seems 'folly':

Paulina. *My lord's almost so far transported that*
  He'll think anon it lives.
Leontes.   *O sweet Paulina,*
  Make me to think so twenty years together!
  No settled senses of the world can match
  The pleasure of that madness.

(ll. 69-73)

(The word 'madness' again echoes Florizel in his affirmation
of love's 'reason' or truth.) When, to the harmony of music,
Hermione moves towards him and embraces him with her

warm body, he is silent. He does not need to hear the pledge, 'I am yours for ever': now he is secure in love's truth, the knowledge of her heart; that was the 'faith' that was 'required'.

*　　　　*　　　　*

Words like 'chapel', 'faith', 'marvel', 'Dear life', 'redeems', 'holy', 'blessing', 'gods', 'sacred vials', 'graces', in this last scene of *The Winter's Tale*, have encouraged critics to see it as a play about remorse, penitence, forgiveness and reconciliation. And the earlier references to 'innocence' and the part Perdita plays in effecting the reunion make them describe it as a presentation of the changes of time and the renewal of new generations. Professor Wilson Knight believes that the drama:

> throws up . . . a vague, numinous, sense of mighty powers, working through both the natural order and man's religious consciousness, that preserve, in spite of all appearance, the good.[1]

Mr Hoeniger has averred that Leontes':

> paradise at the end of the play is not, like Perdita's, that of a garden, but of a city and a temple, corresponding to that Heavenly City in the New Testament, the Temple of God. There he remarries Hermione, just as Dante meets Beatrice again, and Faust the eternal form of Gretchen.[2]

This comedy is, indeed, different from the early ones in being able to sustain such interpretations, but we may wonder if they relate to its full effect in performance. The last scene is quiet and impressive, but it is also uneasy. The fact that Hermione is alive is a surprise to the audience as to everyone on stage except Paulina—a sensational theatre-trick unparalleled in Shakespeare's works. Both Paulina and Leontes approach the revelation with marked discretion

[1] *The Crown of Life* (1947), p. 128.
[2] F. D. Hoeniger, *The University of Toronto Quarterly*, xx (1950), 26.

and afterwards they hurry to take leave of the scene and its mood: 'Let's from this place. . . . Lead us from hence . . . hastily lead away' (ll. 146-55). It also has to serve as the culmination of a play with various and abundant digressions from these moods—competitive and secretive sophistication, intense expression of private passions and fears, judicial propriety and impropriety, casual enjoyment, disguises and counter-disguises, garrulous excitement. All this and more was sustained by the creative energy behind the writing of this play and must be summed up in its last scene.

It is in explaining such discrepancies that the means developed for a study of its predecessors—the close analysis of contrasts and relationships, of stage techniques and recurrent imagery—prove useful in giving fresh understanding. The rapid transitions, the varied styles and digressions are all seen as part of a general purpose, and the precarious, dream-like nature of the last scene as an appropriately modest conclusion when, relieved and awe-struck, men and women take up their positions according to ideals of love like others at the end of a comedy, but after all the petty deceits and confidences of a sophisticated society and after the ordeals of the 'wide gap of time' represented since they were 'dissever'd' (ll. 154-5). In this view the ending is comparable to that of the earlier comedies in requiring our acceptance of the strange and private 'truth' of those who enact the play of love.[1]

As in Shakespeare's other comedies, the judgements dependent on his ideals of love, which we have analysed under three heads, inform dialogue, action, contrasts and relationships and are important unifying elements between different points in the narrative development and between scenes of very different moods and contents. This late comedy presents a story of separation and reconciliation, of two generations and the effects of time, and in this it is different from the celebration of love's ideals in the early

---

[1] See above, pp. 90 and 123.

comedies; and different again from the disquieting presentation of imperfect responses in the 'dark' comedies. Shakespeare has now created a picture of a man who learns by dispossession and begins to respond in true love after he has given up all hope and fear, of young people who have to risk everything for their 'affections' (IV. iv. 490-1), and of sophisticated and simple societies seen in relation to individual men and women and to the holy and just gods. The range of human responses is vast; the time represented is necessarily long, and the places and people various. But the most astonishing fact is the subtlety of the audience's involvement: the audience responds to a widely and minutely considered dramatic world, and, because nothing is circumscribed by explicit statement or judgement, responds with ease, concern and delight. The theatrical life of *The Winter's Tale*, like that of earlier comedies, derives unity, subtlety, and force from a comprehensive attitude to personal relationships and society which is never stated yet always formative.

*   *   *

The same alert mind wrote the other three late comedies, *Pericles* and *Cymbeline* immediately before, and *The Tempest* immediately after.

The first, *Pericles*, has survived only in a bad text and may not be wholly Shakespeare's, and it is not consistently concerned with love and friendship and therefore not particularly amenable to the critical approaches developed for the other comedies. But we should notice here that the single plot is presented in an episodic manner that permits many contrasts and relationships: Gower, the Chorus, at the close of the play can speak of Antiochus, Helicanus, Cerimon, Cleon, and Dionyza, as well as Pericles, Thaisa and Marina. There are signs, too, of familiar judgements. In the wooing of Antiochus' daughter and of Thaisa, the ideal of love's truth is implicit; the first lady is a 'glorious casket stored with ill' (I. i. 77)—a phrase reminiscent of the wooing of Portia in *The Merchant of Venice*—and the other sees the 'inward man' of Pericles although he looks like a mean knight in his rusty armour and 'outward habit' (II. ii. 56-7). There is a feast at the court of King Simonides where both he and Thaisa, his daughter, can take part in the formal 'order' only by centring their thoughts upon their unknown guest. As in Florizel's wooing, there is danger here, for customary status and procedure are upset, and all three 'dissemble' (II. v. 23) before they can speak simply. When Cleon and Dionyza try to murder Marina, Pericles' daughter, questions of 'wealth' are raised insistently: nothing could yield the murderer 'so much *profit*' (IV. i. 4); Marina's grief for the loss of her friend and nurse seems '*unprofitable* woe' to others (l. 26); yet she herself cannot understand how her death can yield Dionyza 'any *profit*' (l. 81); and finally, she is hailed as a '*prize*' (l. 94) when she is carried off by pirates. When Lysimachus, the disguised governor of Mytilene, finds Marina in the brothel, the ideals of 'truth' are clearly suggested and there is an obvious contrast between the ideal 'wealth' and the purchasing of prostituted pleasure. The condition of the text forbids any great reliance on verbal analysis: it must suffice to say that the choice and presentation of the story accord well with the maintenance of implicit judgements by repetitions and contrasts, and by disguises, feasts, music, and dances, and that the handling of many situations evoke Shakespeare's ideals of love.

In its more general effects this comedy is also like *The Winter's Tale*. The 'ordering' of individuals is again contrasted with a heaven-centred order, social disorder and the 'savage clamour' of disordered nature, here represented chiefly by storms at sea. And the principal characters are again seen in situations where they believe they are without hope or help, or where they seem 'mad' or 'senseless' to others. The scene which has survived with greatest power is the reunion of father and daughter; and here, especially, Pericles is shown bearing a 'tempest, which his mortal vessel tears' (IV. iv. 29-30), 'pushing' away the daughter who reminds him of his wife (V. i. 127-8), expecting the 'world to laugh' at him (l. 145), and choosing an apparent 'dream' before what is known to be reasonable (ll. 163-4). In all this there is a recognition of the power of love, after separation by time and fortune, and also a mingling of joy and sorrow as at the close of *The Winter's Tale*. Finally the peace which Pericles learns to accept in reunion with Marina leads him to hear the 'music of the spheres' (l. 231) and to see a vision of Diana. He has faith in this ordering which none but he can know and so the last scene is a ceremonial approach to the temple of the goddess and the consequent reunion with his wife an 'order' related to that centre. In so far as he shaped this fabulous narrative, Shakespeare was not celebrating ideals of love, as in the early comedies, but showing responses to those ideals in characters who experience separation, deceit, pain, fear and the passage of time, and who come at last to understand something of the will of the gods.

In *Cymbeline* he attempted an even greater scope. The action ranges from Britain to Italy and Rome, and back again, and towards the end the heavens 'open' to introduce Jove himself on an eagle's back. Its affairs are political, nationalistic, heroic, pastoral, connubial, religious, and amatory; dangers and disguises multiply freely. The characters know separation, deceit, love, hate, hopelessness, pain and death; they hope beyond reason and beyond true report. Cunning and perseverance direct many ventures, while 'Fortune brings in some boats that are not steer'd' (IV. iii. 46). No long passage of time is represented, but events of more than twenty years earlier have their consequences.

To sustain this variety—and, we may think, to present an overall judgement as in the earlier comedies—Shakespeare chose a primitive dramatic idiom. Several scenes are entirely soliloquy, while many end with soliloquy and most have comments spoken aside. Numerous characters hold the audience's attention in strong and directly presented situations, but they usually do so one at a time and intermittently; Posthumus, Iachimo, Cloten, Cymbeline, his queen and even Imogen dominate the stage severally only to relinquish the central position to another. Contrasts are incessant and sometimes violent. A casual reader might dismiss the play as a sensational toy: but it is complex as well as primitive, and these two qualities are interdependent. The dramatic idiom is entirely suitable for establishing a wide view of the stage and for exploiting contrasts and relationships. After a study of the other comedies we shall notice particularly the treatment of love and friendship, and in the contrasts observe a subtle and insistent manifestation of Shakespeare's ideals. Sweet-tongued romance and elaborate, hot-headed fantasy are yoked together and both are controlled, with astonishing care, by Shakespeare's judgement.

The ideal of personal order is invoked in the very first lines:

> *You do not meet a man but frowns: our* bloods
> *No more* obey *the heavens than our courtiers*
> *Still seem as does the king.*

And at the conclusion there is an ordered and general procession off-stage, to a formal ratification of peace in 'the temple of great Jupiter' and the celebration of feasts. As in *The Winter's Tale* this theme is represented in many different actions, from wild, isolated outbreaks of anger to the calm 'circle' (V. iv. 29, S.D.) formed by the ghosts of the Leonati as they kneel in silence for the appearance of Jupiter (l. 92, S.D.). Love's truth is also invoked in the opening duologue:

> *... not a courtier,*
> *Although they* wear *their* faces *to the bent*
> *Of the king's looks, hath a* heart *that is not*
> *Glad at the thing they scowl at.*

> (ll. 12-5)

And at once these men are compared with Posthumus who is said to be alone in having 'so fair an outward and such stuff within' (l. 23). The theme is obviously important. It recurs many times as Iachimo's 'simular proof' (V. v. 200) causes Posthumus and Imogen, and others, to question the truth of their 'hearts'. The queen's false professions of love are antithetical to Cymbeline's trust, while Cloten's disguise in Posthumus' clothes gives occasion to show how Guiderius, a prince who looks like a savage outlaw, discounts words and appearance, and how Imogen, in lonely grief can accept the foolish Cloten's body for that of Posthumus (which she believes to be godlike). Less openly, but with equal persistence, the ideal of love's wealth informs the play. As Caroline Spurgeon noticed in her pioneering analysis of the imagery, almost every character speaks of 'buying and selling, value and exchange, . . . payment, debts, bills and wages'. She believed that the 'awkward' way in which these affairs were sometimes introduced as metaphors showed that commerce was much in Shakespeare's mind while writing this play because of some event in his personal life, now of course unknown to us.[1] Mr Nosworthy, a recent editor of the play, believed these images were 'an overflow from the tragedies'.[2] But we can accept them as a continuation of interests and techniques from earlier comedies, a way of defining and contrasting the behaviour of friends and lovers. It is no surprise to find Posthumus introduced as 'poor but worthy' (I. i. 7) or a ring and bracelet interchanged between the lovers with a realization that they cannot 'sum up' the 'bounty' of their love:[3]

> *And, sweetest, fairest,*
> *As I my poor self did exchange for you,*

[1] Caroline F. R. Spurgeon, *Shakespeare's Imagery and what it tells us* (1935), p. 296.

[2] Arden Edition (1955), p. lxxii.

[3] *Rom.*, II. vi. 34 and II. ii. 133; see above, pp. 51-2.

To your so infinite loss, *so in our* trifles
I still win *of you*

(I. i. 118-21)

and again:

. . . *he is*

A man worth *any woman*, overbuys *me*
Almost the sum *he* pays.

(ll. 145-7)

Such images are also found in the hyperbole of a sophisticated society,[1] as in *The Winter's Tale*, and, with an exten-
sion of the normal range of comedy, in the gaoler's talk of
the 'payment' due to death (V. iv. 159ff.). The commercial
imagery associated with the ideal of love's wealth illuminates
the diverse parts of the play and helps to give meaning and
unity to the whole.

As in *The Winter's Tale*, Shakespeare accentuated the
dangers and conflicts of love. Ignorance and separation make
severe demands of the most faithful, and these are expressed
with sharp antitheses made forceful by reference to the
great range of judgements informing the whole play. So
when Pisanio is caught between loyalty to Imogen's 'truth'
and his master's 'words', he cries 'Wherein I am false I am
honest; not true, to be true' (IV. iii. 42), and Posthumus,
when he is led against all evidence to call Imogen 'noble'
once more, cries: 'my life Is every breath a death' (V. i.
26-7). The response of Guiderius and Arviragus to the page
Fidele, who is in fact their sister Imogen, has to withstand
all reason and moral propriety:

Guiderius.   *I love thee; I have spoke it:*
    How much the quantity, the weight as much,
    As I do love my father.
Belarius.   *What! how! how!*

---

[1] See, for example, I. iv. 38-41 and II. iv. 9-10.

240

Arviragus. *If it be sin to say so, sir, I yoke me*
In my good brother's fault: I know not why
I love this youth; and I have heard you say,
Love's reason's without reason: *the bier at door,*
And a demand who is't shall die, I'ld say
'My father, not this youth.'

(IV. ii. 16-24)

Imogen's continuing love for Posthumus when she can no
longer believe him to be true is a contradiction unresolved
until the end of the play and presented with rapid transitions
of mood suggesting a basic instability: so, for example, the
despairing 'My dear lord! Thou art one o' the false ones'
yields instantaneously to peace and courage with 'Now I
think on thee, My hunger's gone' (III. vi. 14-6); her
heart's faith, 'love's reason' that is 'without reason', has
opposed reason and proved the stronger.

Leontes and his torturing, because imperfect, love
dominated the first half of *The Winter's Tale*, and in *Cymbeline* there is a small group of characters, the destructive
agents in the story, who are presented with similar force.
The queen is the most single-minded, the only sign that she
responds to an ideal being the 'shameless-desperate' madness
with which she is said to die (V. v. 31 and 58). But Iachimo
is keenly aware of what he tries to destroy:

All of her that is out of door *most* rich!
If she be furnish'd with a mind *so rare,*
She is alone the Arabian bird, and I
Have lost the wager.

(I. vi. 15-8)

He also speaks with forceful antithesis as he knows he does
not need words to record Imogen's beauty which is 'riveted'
and 'screw'd' to his memory (II. ii. 43-4): like a lover he
becomes deeply conscious in her presence:

I lodge in fear;
Though this a heavenly angel, hell is here.

(ll. 49-50)

Back in Rome he can talk freely of love's wealth—

> *Her pretty action did* outsell *her gift,*
> *And yet* enrich'd *it too*—
>
> (II. iv. 102-3)

but he has that 'within his bosom' (V. ii. 1) that will grow until, when his life is in peril, it all but destroys him. Cloten is at first introduced as a braggart, an anti-heroic foil to Posthumus, but as a suitor to Imogen he also contrasts as a lover. When he complains 'If I could get this foolish Imogen, I should have *gold* enough' (II. iii. 9-10) the comparison seems a simple one between commerce and love, and when he argues 'You sin against *Obedience*, which you *owe* your father' (ll. 116-7) he is simply trusting another 'order' than that of love. But when Imogen tells him that she respects the 'meanest garment' of Posthumus before thousands of Cloten's (ll. 138-41) his repeated echoing of her words and violent reactions betray a stronger, divided response: now he goes alone to the forests to rape Imogen and kill Posthumus, risking danger in a wholly unexpected way. Belarius will not believe that he could do this:

> . . . *not* frenzy, *not*
> *Absolute* madness *could so far have* raved
> *To bring him here alone.*
>
> (IV. ii. 134-6)

Cloten, however, now knows something of the power of love to establish a new reason and new order, and he recognizes Imogen's wealth that 'outsells' all others' (III. v. 74). Yet he loves himself too and envies Posthumus; therefore, with the sharp antithesis associated in this play with the deepest feelings, he cries aloud: 'I love and hate her' (l. 70). In the power of these conflicting passions he 'foams at the mouth' and even 'enforces' the honest Pisanio to his purposes (V. v. 274-85). He dies asserting his own importance, but not before he has risked all for 'love and hate'.

The conclusion of this play follows the appearance of Jupiter to Posthumus in prison and shows in detail how his riddling prophecy is fulfilled; and the god is praised and honoured. But our reading does not lead us to think that the dramatic interests are primarily religious: because of the issues awakened through the whole play, the last scene is concerned with the ways in which the remaining *dramatis personae* take up their final positions in relation and contrast with each other; and, as in the earlier comedies, these last movements appear eloquent of Shakespeare's implicit judgements. The gaoler who had reminded Posthumus of the new 'reckoning' to be made in death, remains on stage for a soliloquy which, like the final soliloquies of Bottom, Launce and Parolles, prefigures the judgement of the conclusion:

> *I would we were all of one* mind, *and one mind good; O, there were desolation of gaolers and gallowses! I speak against my present* profit, *but my wish hath a* preferment *in't.*
> (V. iv. 212-6)

So many minds have been divided from each other and within themselves that the dramatic idiom has to be simple and unusually economical if it is to contain the full resolution. The succession of dénouements in short space draws attention to its own contrivance and belittles the human beings who seem impelled by the logic of a comic catastrophe: but some of the feelings expressed are strong and direct, linked to judgements implicit throughout the play; these stand large among the lesser shifts and changes of opinion and thus gain greater eloquence. Posthumus strikes the 'scornful page' who interrupts his cries of grief, but when Fidele becomes Imogen she 'hangs' upon him and he 'anchors upon Imogen' (ll. 263 and 393); their understanding is secure and almost silent among the glissading events. Some distinctions are given strength antithetically: on one count Imogen has 'lost a kingdom' by the discovery of her brothers, but in the fulfilment of 'love's reason' and 'truest' speaking she acknowledges love's wealth in this very loss as the *'gaining'* of 'two worlds' (ll. 373-8). Iachimo, having confessed, kneels to Posthumus expecting death and returns the ring and bracelet: but now Posthumus has 'power' only to 'spare' and forgive, and this leads the king to learn 'freeness' and doom 'Pardon's the word to all' (l. 412-22). Our view of the play as it is concerned with love and friendship cannot give a full reading, for many other interests have been interwoven, but we may understand enough to appreciate the nature of this conclusion as a sharpened, weighty image of men and women attempting a mutual mind and that 'one mind good'. Even the contrivance of the dénouement gathers meaning when the soothsayer assures the others that the 'fingers of the powers above do *tune* The *harmony* of this peace' (ll. 466-7). Then piety is placed in the background, as a structural line in a wider and more lively composition:

> *Laud we the gods;*
> *And let our crooked smokes climb to their nostrils*
> *From our blest altars.*
>
> (ll. 476-8)

The stage fills at the close with an orderly procession of men and women at peace with each other, a stable relationship which has been given eloquence through a persistent and minute judgement on divided minds throughout the play.

Cymbeline is often considered to be eccentric among the other last comedies, for it is hard to see it as a 'myth of immortality' or as a treatment of 'fall and redemption'. Mr Traversi, believing these to be Shakespeare's intentions, has argued that the play's 'central theme is partially obscured' and that Shakespeare's ideas were expressed 'with less than complete clarity'.[1] Dr Tillyard believed that in all the last

[1] D. Traversi, *Shakespeare: the Last Phase* (1954), p. 2.

comedies Shakespeare intended to follow 'tragic events' to their final and 'regenerative' phase: but *Cymbeline* ill suits his thesis:

> The tragic events (for which Cymbeline's original error is ultimately responsible) are curiously apt to end in insignificance, while the existence into which the tragic action issues is, as any recognizable and convincing way of life, a pallid and bloodless affair.[1]

Fastening on some newly introduced elements in these last plays, Dr Tillyard has missed the way in which Shakespeare's imagination has given meaning to theatrical worlds as wide, or wider, than those of his earlier comedies. Perhaps he would find that all these plays gain in unity and life if he responded to them as products of Shakespeare's continuous interest in comedy and in love and friendship. In this view, the concluding scene of *Cymbeline* seems to be at one with those of the other last plays: its wide view of life has the comprehensive eloquence of the earlier comedies and the reticence appropriate to a play that has shown such discords before such peace.

*   *   *

For *The Tempest*, the last of these four comedies, love and friendship only commanded a small part of Shakespeare's interest. The main action turns on the conflict between Prospero's 'virtue' and his desire for 'vengeance' (V. i. 28), and the wooing of Ferdinand and Miranda is presented as much for the illumination of this issue as for its own sake. This means that our study of Shakespeare's treatment of personal relationships in earlier comedies will not provide the terms for a central study of this play. Yet it can help us to recognize the devices whereby he controlled the various narrative strands.

At least four stories may be distinguished all involving Prospero and presented so that they lead towards the most

[1] E. M. W. Tillyard, *Shakespeare's Last Plays* (1951), pp. 27-8.

comprehensive conclusion of all, the only one from which not a single character is missing. The dramatic idiom is again deceptively simple, but Prospero's magic powers can effect the manifold comparisons characteristic of Shakespeare's comedies without recourse to the sensationalism of *Cymbeline* or the digressive amplification of the second half of *The Winter's Tale*. Easily and abundantly effected by the enchanter's spells, transitions of mood and sudden changes of situation have a dream-like completeness which encourages a relaxed and wide view of the stage. At every point the drama is reflected as in a hall of mirrors: Ferdinand carrying logs succeeds Caliban's escape from the same servitude; Caliban's rebellious curse succeeds the insurrection of Antonio and Sebastian; Sebastian's acceptance of Antonio's leadership is succeeded by Caliban's acceptance of Stephano's; Stephano and his confederates follow music as Ferdinand had done; Stephano's dressing up in stolen finery is antithetical to Prospero's assumption of ducal robes. Each individual reaction to the storm, or to the island's beauty, to authority, responsibility or affection, is contrasted in neighbouring scenes or within the same scene. Moreover the dialogue seldom has the immediacy which can draw an audience intently towards a single person: when this does occur, the effect is momentary only. For instance, when Alonso is desperate with grief and guilt, he has a short speech which is descriptive rather than exploratory, and then a rapid exit: when he returns after more than an Act has passed, his state of mind is represented by a 'frantic gesture' (V. i. 57, S.D.). The tension and excitement of this incident are not exploited; its presentation ensures before all else that Alonso's guilt should take due place in a larger picture. Even Prospero's soliloquies, which are essential to the development of the action, are written almost wholly in a considered, measured manner which progressively reveals a single state of mind. When he is angered as 'never' before (IV. i. 144-5), his inner struggle is cloaked with concern for Ferdinand and Miranda, and the audience's attention deflected or even repulsed by:

> *. . . a turn or two I'll walk,*
> *To still my beating mind.*
> (ll. 162-3)

By enchantment, by contrasts and by the handling of the dialogue, Shakespeare has ensured that the audience's view takes in a wide group of characters, and observes them over against each other and in relation to the whole action of this subtly wrought play.

The individual elements are as minutely judged as before. We may assess this by observing the wooing of Ferdinand and Miranda. Here, again, the ideals developed in the early comedies inform the action. Miranda finds a new order through love, so that she 'prattles something too wildly' by other standards and forgets her father's 'precepts' (III. i. 57-9). She knows both the abundance and embarrassment of love's wealth, acknowledging:

> *. . . mine* unworthiness *that dare not offer*
> *What I desire to* give, *and much less* take
> *What I shall die to want.*
>
> (III. i. 77-9)

Ferdinand, a 'slave' to Miranda's 'service' (ll. 64-7), vows that

> *. . . I*
> *Beyond all limit of what else i' the world*
> *Do love, prize, honour you*
>
> (ll. 71-3)

and so in fewest words responds to the ideals of wealth, truth and order. As in the other late comedies Shakespeare was concerned with the dangers of love. Miranda's ready assurance places her entirely in the power of the third man she has seen; to speak indirectly seems 'bashful cunning' (III. i. 81), so she displays her inmost desires, eagerly and defencelessly: 'I am your wife, if you will marry me' (l. 83); when Ferdinand gives his hand she gives hers, 'with my heart in't' (ll. 88-91), and then, bashful if not cunning, runs away. Later, when Prospero has removed all unnecessary restraint, Ferdinand shows himself willing to wait for all 'sanctimonious ceremonies' to bless the 'contract' of their marriage (IV. i. 12-31); then there is a still moment in the narrative as their ordered love is glorified and reflected in a masque with a 'graceful dance' between apparitions of 'fresh nymphs' and 'sunburnt sicklemen' (IV. i. 132-8).

The love of Ferdinand and Miranda is thus judged with Shakespeare's accustomed precision, and it is further defined by the direct contrast of Caliban's brute instinct to 'violate the honour' of Miranda (I. ii. 347-8). So established these characters take their places in the general design so that their responses to the main issues reflect significantly upon those of others. We have earlier noticed[1] how the dance celebrating the 'order' of their love is disturbed by Prospero's memory of the 'disorder' of the 'beast Caliban and his confederates' (IV. i. 139-40). In a similar way, Ferdinand's delight in Miranda's service, 'with heart as willing As bondage e'er of freedom' (III. i. 88-9), contrasts with the desire of Ariel and Caliban, Prospero's subjects, to escape from service. His eagerness to make an unknown girl the 'Queen of Naples' (I. ii. 448-9) contrasts with the deliberate concern of others about crowns and power. Miranda's frankness contrasts with her father's artifice and in the last scene the mutually absorbed and contented lovers at their game of chess—playing at 'playing false' and 'wrangling'—contrast with other characters who have been divided by striving and deceit. Here as in other comedies, only more extensively, Shakespeare's carefully judged presentation of love reflects upon the whole course of human life.

The concluding scene is different from those of the companion plays, but a development from them, not a departure. Instead of presenting, with due reticence, the ideal and stable relationships between the *dramatis personae*, it suggests such a resolution but presents several reactions

[1] See above, p. 140.

which are out of alignment with this pattern. The ideal conclusion is suggested by the circle into which Prospero charms his enemies and the concurrence of everybody at one time and place, and by Gonzalo's careful summing up of the deepest happiness possible (V. i. 205-13) and Alonso's plea for pardon even before he knows whether he is truly confronted by Prospero. But on the other hand, Antonio remains silent and gives no sign of penitence, and Sebastian's intended treachery, which is alluded to privately by Prospero, is never confessed. Even Ferdinand and Miranda, in this last scene, can remind the audience of imperfections and dangers: they are pretending to 'play false' (l. 172); and Miranda's judgement that this 'new world' is full of 'goodly creatures' (l. 182) stands out, to an audience which has witnessed the revelation of their inward natures, as a notably imperfect response. Stephano and Trinculo are brought into the final scene as no other clowns in these comedies, but when confronted with their own criminal foolishness they display only fuddled reactions to their sore bones. Caliban does offer willing service to his old master—'I'll be wise hereafter And seek for grace' (ll. 294-5)—but Prospero is still severe with him, suggesting that bestial instincts and resentment will need, or seem to need, continual tutelage. The play ends in a procession to Prospero's cave, an image of mutual accord and responsibility, but an audience will be aware that this 'peace' may not last long. And at the latest possible moment Prospero releases his airy spirit to enjoy freedom: Ariel, who could sing merrily of summer as Prospero's enemies were gathered together and who can hide from the owl's cry of death,[1] does not seek a place in this imperfect society.

There are references to gods in the last scene, but of a new kind. In other late comedies, Fortune or Providence play a large part in effecting the final resolution and in two of them a god appears to instruct or prophesy. In *The Tempest*, however, the resolution is contrived by Prospero,

[1] V. i. 88-94; for the owl's cry see above, p. 134, n. 1.

SHAKESPEARE AND HIS COMEDIES

working according to his knowledge of a 'most strange, bountiful Fortune' (I. ii. 178). This reflects on a major theme of the play, an old one which was, perhaps, most clearly stated in *Measure for Measure*:

> *He who the sword of heaven will bear*
> *Should be as holy as severe;*
> *Pattern in himself to know,*
> *Grace to stand, and virtue go. . . .*
> (III. ii. 275ff.)

Now, in presiding over the conclusion and tuning the 'harmony of the peace', he cannot enforce repentance or true love and service; he can only draw men to the place where such responses are possible and then act with mercy, rather than justice. This play, which is often fantastic in action and setting, is 'realistic' in its conclusion. Finally the enchanter loses his special powers and speaks the epilogue. It was customary for the chief actor to drop his characterization and step forward to ask acceptance for the play; but here the actor seems to remain as Prospero:

> *Now I want*
> *Spirits to enforce, art to enchant,*
> *And my ending is despair,*
> *Unless I be relieved by prayer,*
> *Which pierces so that it assaults*
> *Mercy itself and frees all faults.*
> *As you from crimes would pardon'd be,*
> *Let your indulgence set me free.*

The audience is invited to accept the wisest character, with the play itself, as an image of any imperfect human performance, including their own.

* * *

Shakespeare continued to experiment until the end of his writing career and we may learn much about his art by tracing the reliance of one play upon another. Critics of the

last comedies have often been content with restrictive interpretations because they have considered these plays as unique
'romances' and failed to see their affinities with other
comedies.

All the comedies, early and late, are shaped by consistent
and minute judgements; these may be missed on casual
reading because they are implicit rather than explicit, but
they can be described by analysing some of the simpler
means which Shakespeare always used to present them—
the repetition of words, images, actions and ideas. The
comedies are also at one in having multiple plots or similar
structural devices, as episodic narrative or especially
developed subsidiary characters. All have incidents which
interrupt narrative development to clarify personal relationships by visual and sometimes musical means. The chief
innovations of the last comedies are in subject matter and the
development of old techniques to meet these new demands.
There are fuller references or presentations of the gods, a
delineation of a more sophisticated society, and new emphasis
on the dangers of separation, deceit, pain, fear and the
mingling of virtues and vices. The effects of time and the
interdependence of two generations are more fully shown
and, in *The Tempest* particularly, the experiments of *As You
Like It*, *Measure for Measure* and *Troilus* are pursued further
to portray a wider range of life than can be shown through
narratives of love and friendship. The last scene of *The
Tempest* acknowledges, more clearly than ever before in
comedy, both ideals and imperfections.

Of course the customary view of the last plays as myths of
immortality or narratives of Fall and Redemption should
not be dismissed. These are interests which may most
readily hold the attention of an audience; but we must
remember that as precise and deeply considered judgements
were presented within the entertainment of the earliest
comedies, so similar judgements are presented within these
'romances' in lively and abundant detail. If we wish to
understand Shakespeare's achievement we must understand

SHAKESPEARE AND HIS COMEDIES

those judgements and not underestimate them because they are not explicit. Shakespeare used much skill and drew on a long experience of writing comedies in order to create this inner life. It is, perhaps, the unique achievement of these plays.

INDEX

to Principal References to Shakespeare's works